Hard Steam Photography's

ORCHIDS

Through Our Eyes

Compiled & Edited by:
BRUCE B. BROWN

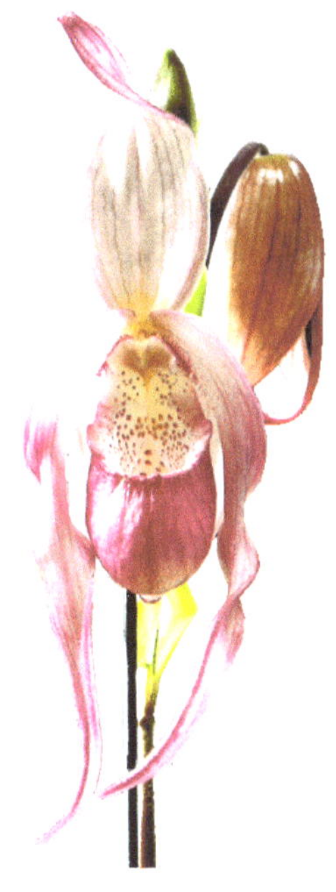

A River Valley Orchidworks - OrchidTalk Members' Publication

'FOR LOUIS'

ACKNOWLEDGEMENTS

Hard Steam Photography gratefully acknowledges the generous support of the *River Valley Orchidworks - OrchidTalk members* who have contributed to this publication. My Thanks to: Tim Balgos, Aaron Brothers, Valerie Burnes, Virginia (Gin) Carter, Jason Chang, Clint M. Dawley, Murray Gyde, Cindy R. Hicks, Dr. Hiep-Hoa T. Nguyen, and Lynda Schwemmer for their beautiful photographs given as donations to support the publication of this book. Without your support this publication would not have been possible.

SPECIAL THANKS TO: Louis Aszod and Diane Suprock for their support, encouragement, beautiful photographs and exquisite words. True friendship is hard to measure, but you allow yourselves to be my friend always. Thank you.

First Edition, January 2007
ISBN 978-0-6151-3921-0

Front Cover photograph: L purpurata (fma. carnea 'Hihimanu' x fma. semi-alba 'Carmencita')
Title page photograph: Phrag Albopurpureum 'Sir Arthur' AM/AOS
Rear Cover photograph: Blc. Rugleys Mill 'Mendenhall'

CONTENTS

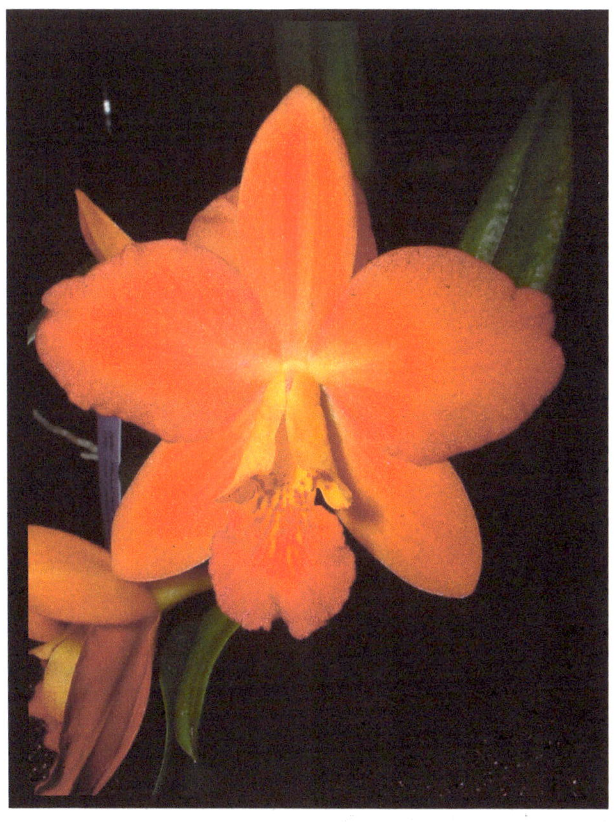

Sophrolaeliocattleya Precious Beauty

(Slc. Fire Lighter x Lc. Trick or Treat)

Preface

THE ADDICTION OF LIFE…

I remember the first time I saw an orchid—rather, the first time I actually acknowledged that the bloom I was admiring was an orchid. I am sure I had seen lots of orchids on television and in nice homes, but I had always thought of them as out of reach, since orchids were meant for the "wealthy and powerful."

That notion was shattered about 12 years ago in Charlottesville, Virginia while I was in graduate school at the University of Virginia. I was studying Theatre Design & Technology. I found inspiration in almost everything back then.

The orchid that had caught my eye was a cattleya. Sure, I had seen the blooms used as corsages, but I had never actually seen one on a plant. My best friend in the world, Louis Aszod, had this tiny little greenhouse in his back yard in Earlysville, Virginia. He had invited me out to his place, and on the 'grand tour,' I saw this little shack with a translucent roof built into the side of a hill. I asked about the building, so Lou took me to see what was inside. As he opened the glass door, I felt the heat and moisture escaping the tiny space that he called his greenhouse. I was amazed by the vivid colors of the flowers inside against the short rock wall and white benches. Then, the smell came to me. I was overwhelmed by the glorious fragrance of cattleyas in bloom. I couldn't believe something existed that produced such an amazing fragrance. I quickly asked what "that flower was," and was told that it was a 'catt'. I can remember talking for hours about where he got his 'catts' and how long he had been growing them. I found out he had worked for a local orchid nursery over the past couple of summers. He would go out and divide the cattleyas that were growing out of their pots, and in lieu of pay, the growers would let him keep the back bulbs and some divisions. The growers got a lot of dividing and repotting done, and Lou got to start his orchid collection. Of course, I had to see this orchid nursery for myself, so the very next day we drove out and I got to see hundreds of different varieties of orchids. They were all so expensive! I was so scared to buy one for fear that I would surely kill it or that my cat, Nikko, would eat it! I left that day empty-handed and a little sad. But less than a year later, I was growing my own collection - my own addiction. Like my dad always says, "I don't drink, I don't smoke, I don't really have anything to spend my money on, so why not enjoy myself when I want something?" That is exactly what I am doing. I love spending time with my orchids.

Louis and I moved to Arkansas in the summer of 1996 and built a large hobby greenhouse. And, on August 15, 2003, we launched the River Valley Orchidworks OrchidTalk Forum on the World Wide Web. We have been incredibly blessed by tremendous support from our orchid growing friends and the orchid community. Each day, hundreds of people gather on the forum from all over the world to get and give advice on how to grow and bloom their orchid plants.

This book is the culmination of those many hours spent discussing orchids and their care with people who grow them from places as far away as Vietnam, Australia, and the Philippines-- just to name a few. The photographs found within these pages were taken by our members and donated to help support the OrchidTalk forum through the publication and sale of this book. This is, then, a small representation of ***Orchids Through Our Eyes*** as photographed by members of the RVO OrchidTalk Forum.

Louis once wrote "Each orchid has a mystery about it and demands our attention in a different way. And each of them rewards us with sublime beauty when they complete their growth cycles and bloom." Well, that is my wish to you who are reading this—good growing and lots of blooms!

--Bruce B. Brown,
January - 2007

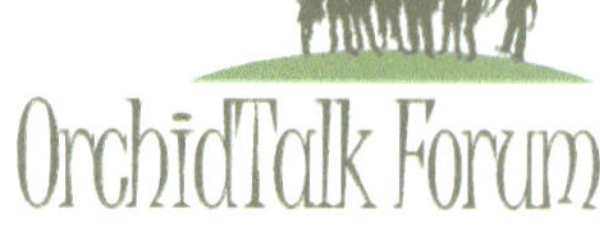

Images of the Orchids we grow and bloom

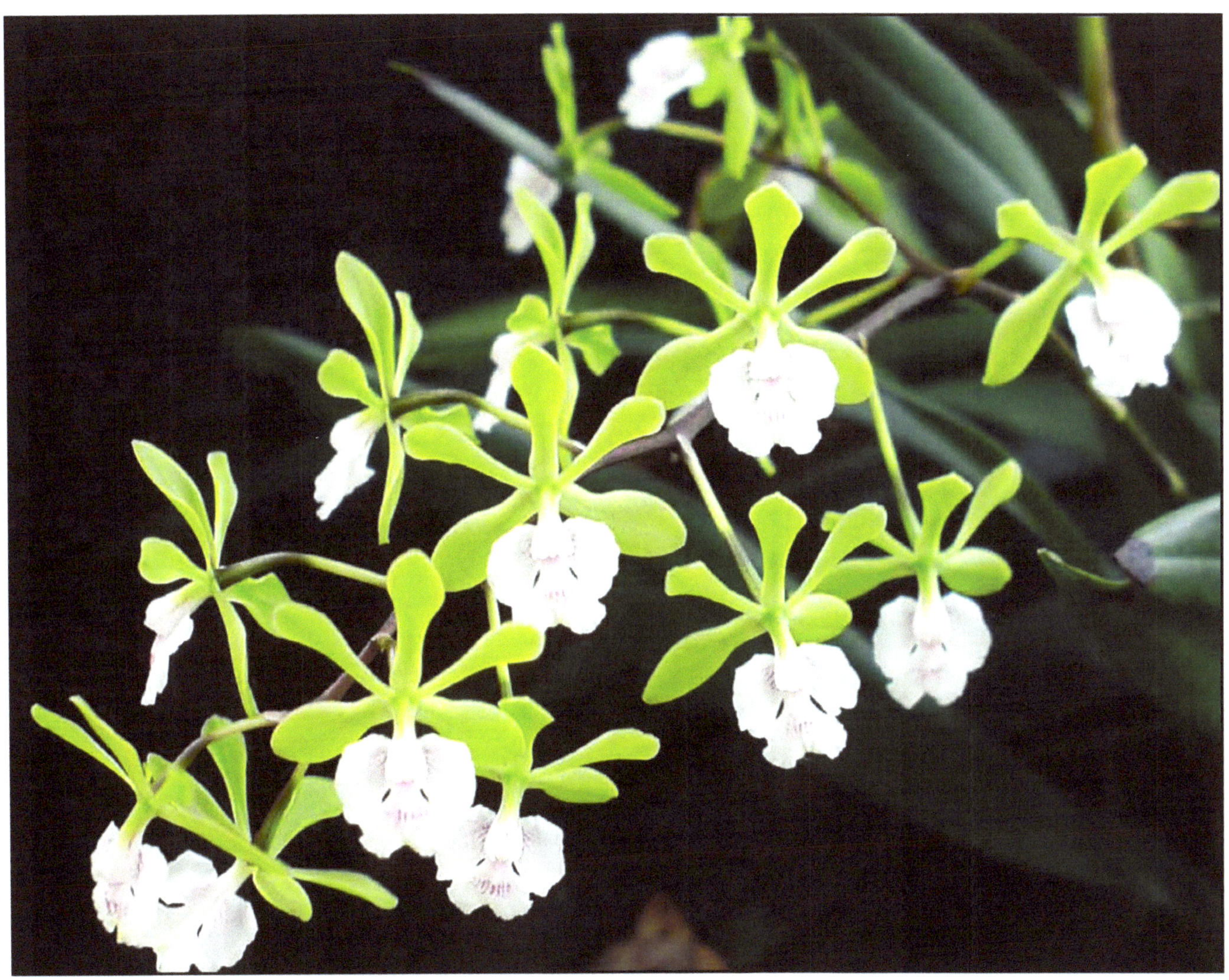

ABOVE
Epidendrum floribundum

OVERLEAF LEFT
Brassidium Fly Away 'Taida' ((Brassia. longissima x Onc. wentworthianum) X Onc. maculatum)

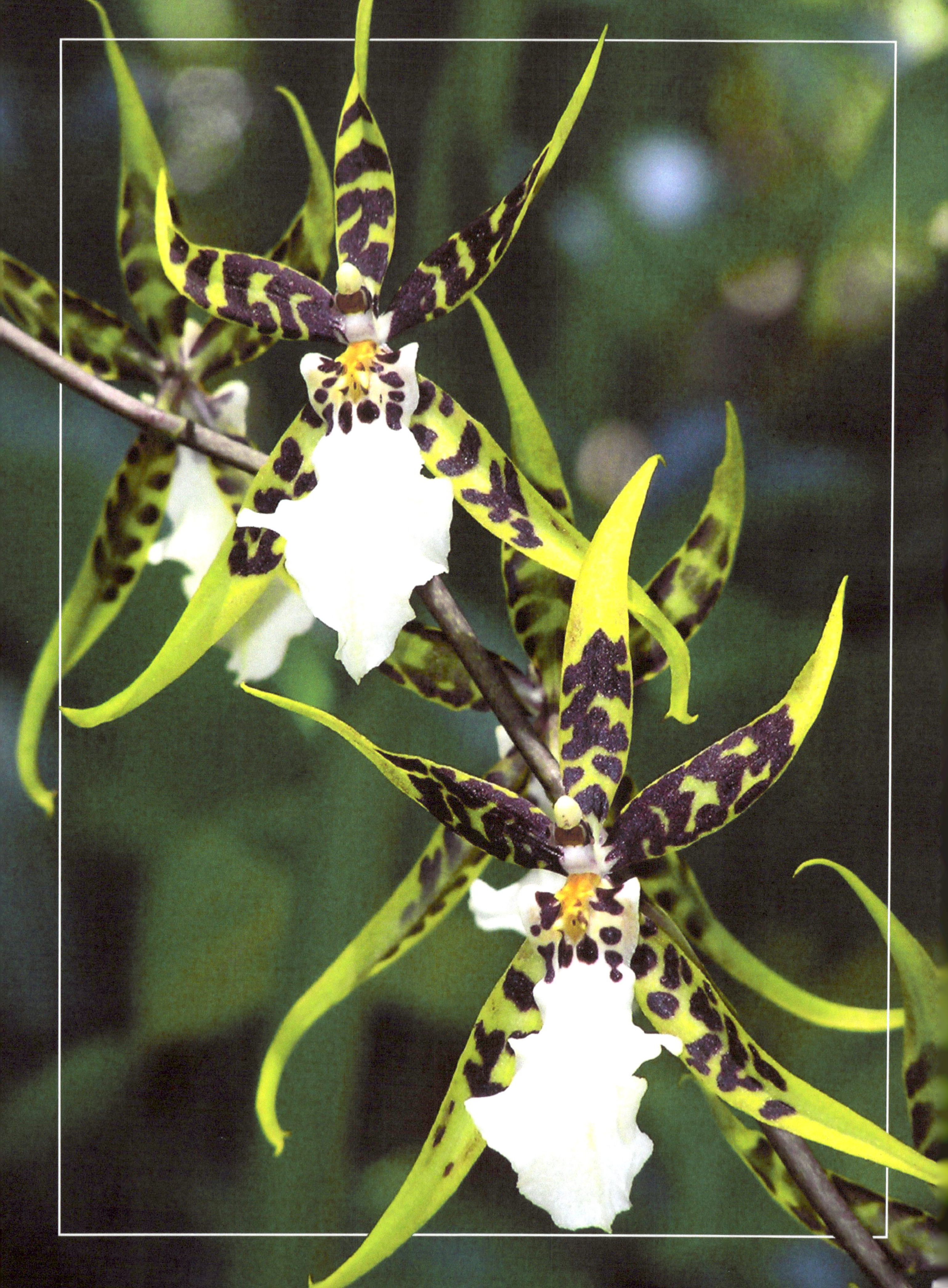

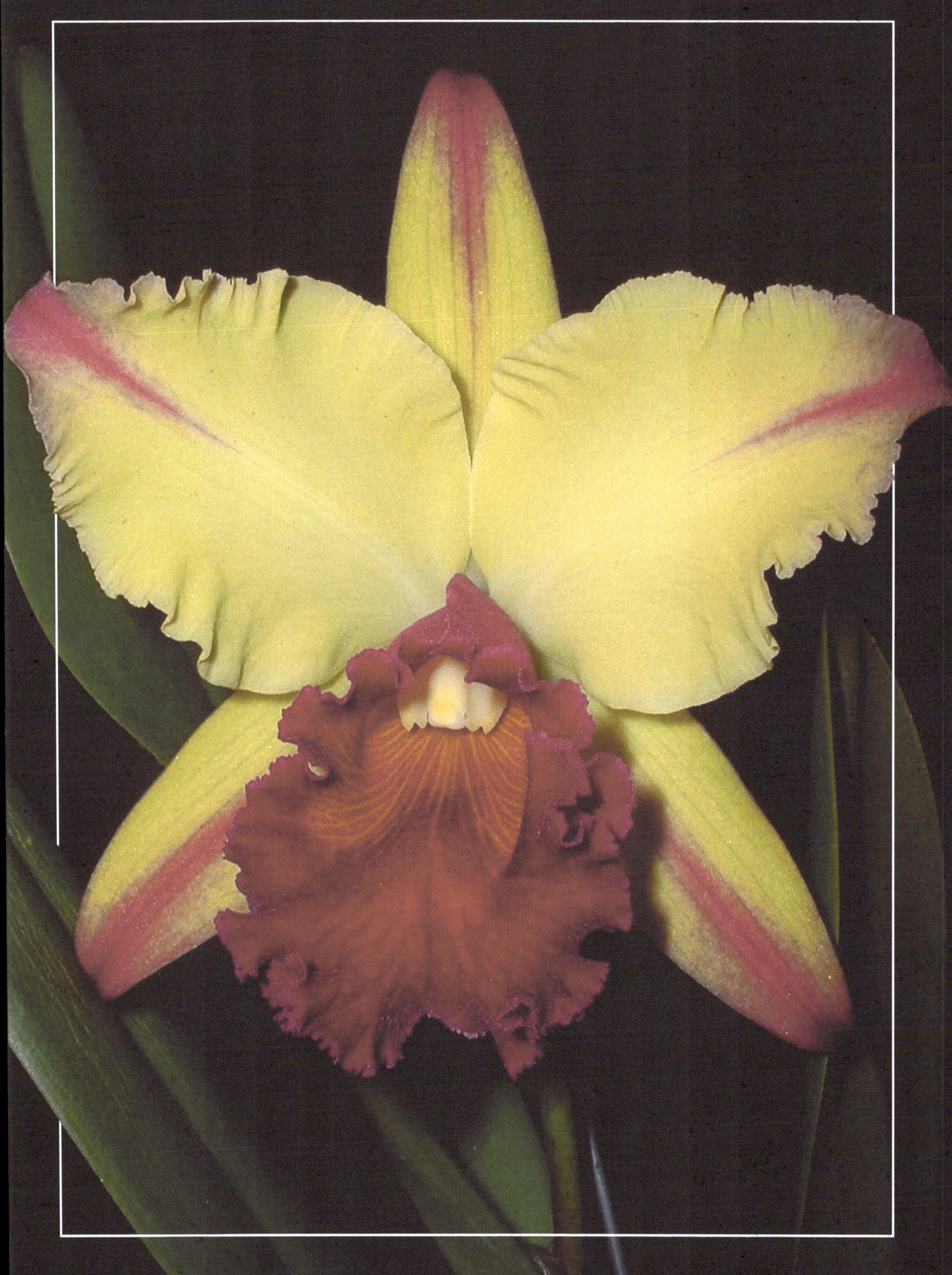

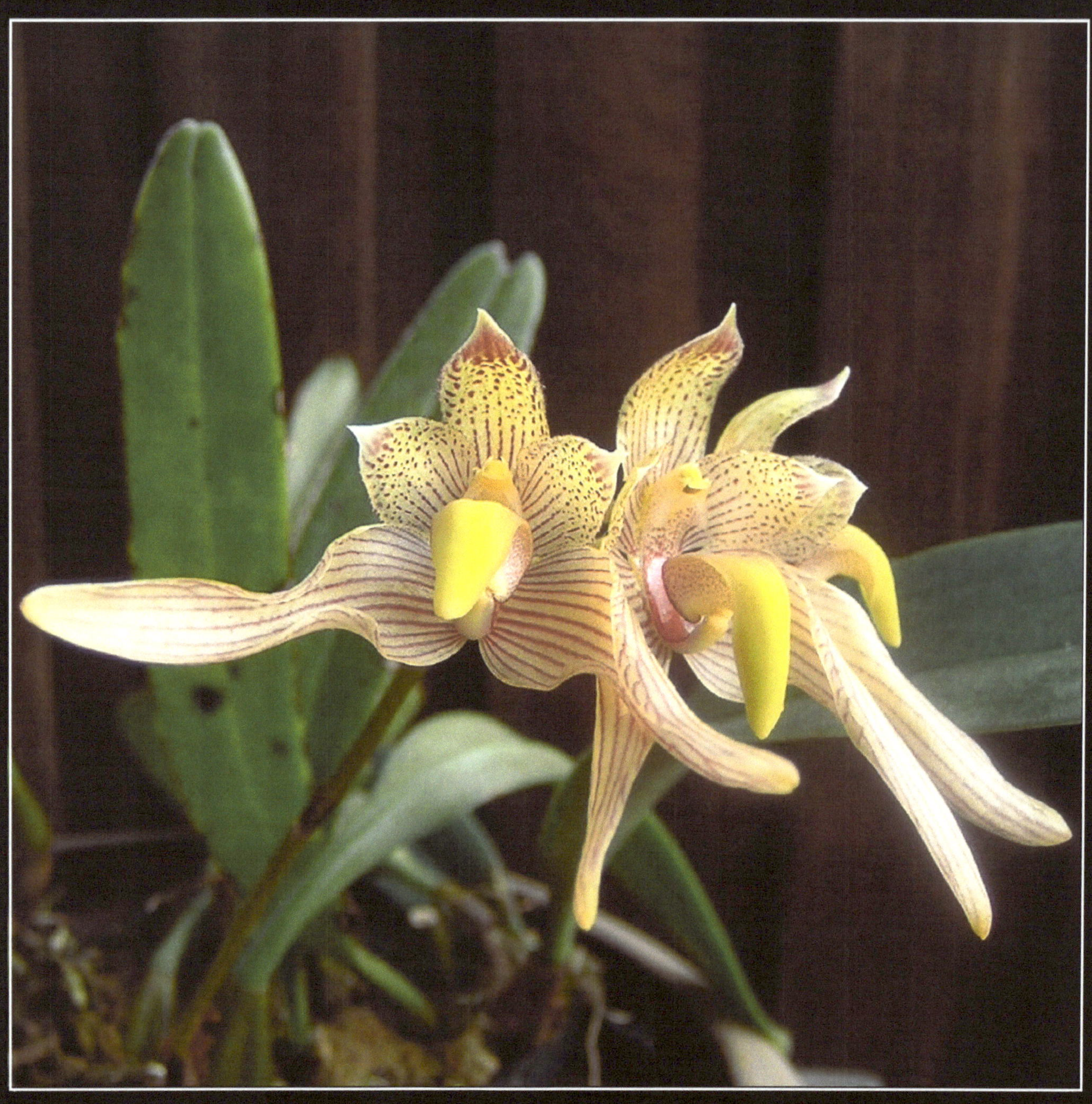

PREVIOUS OVERLEAF
Brassolaeliocattleya Dora Louise Capen'Lea'HCC/AOS
(C. Moscombe x Blc.Toshie Aoki)

ABOVE
Sunipia bicolor

RIGHT
Paphiopedilum Hsinying Fairbre
(Paph. Macabre 'Black Eagle' X Paph. fairrieanum 'Clark')

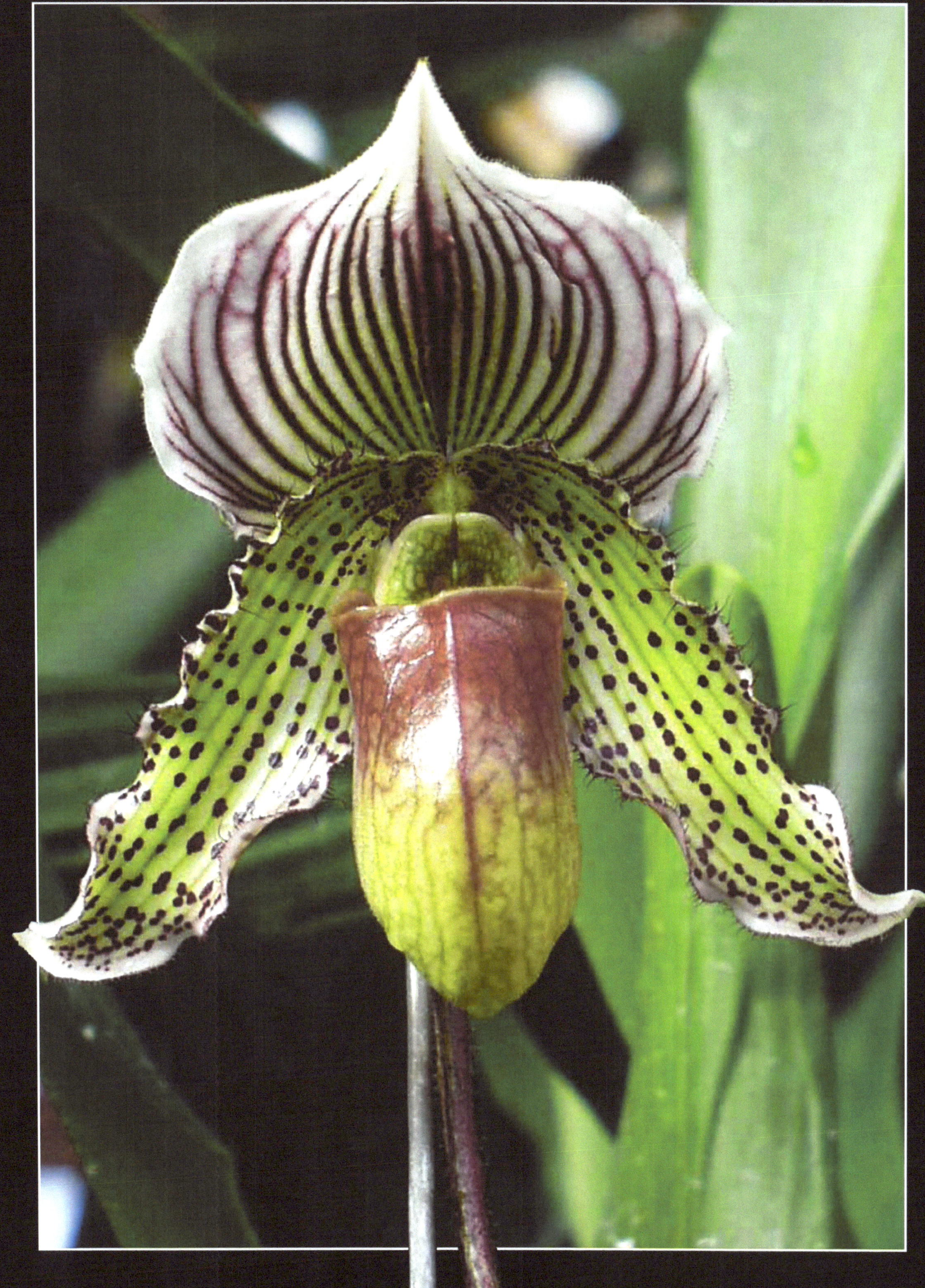

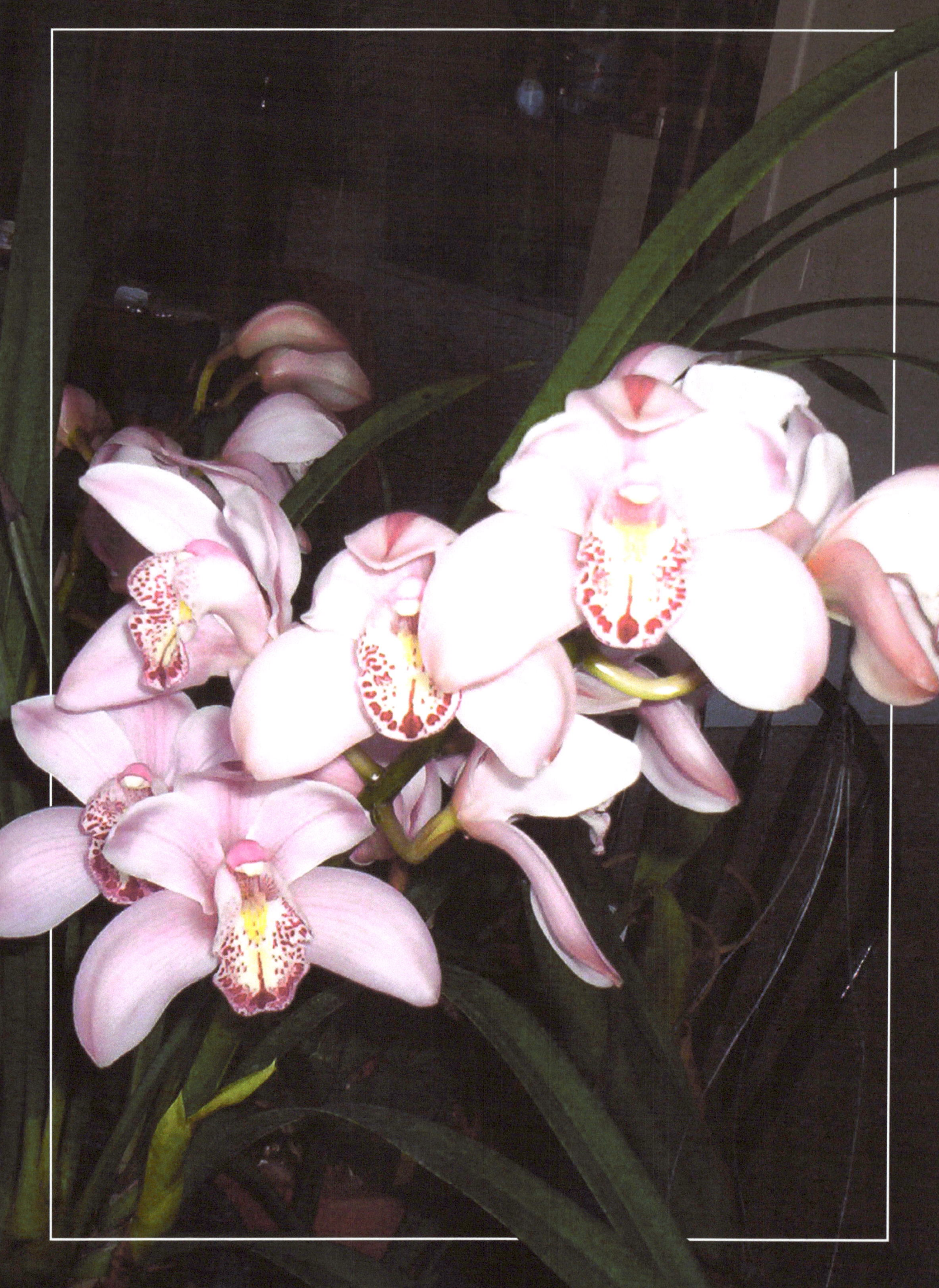

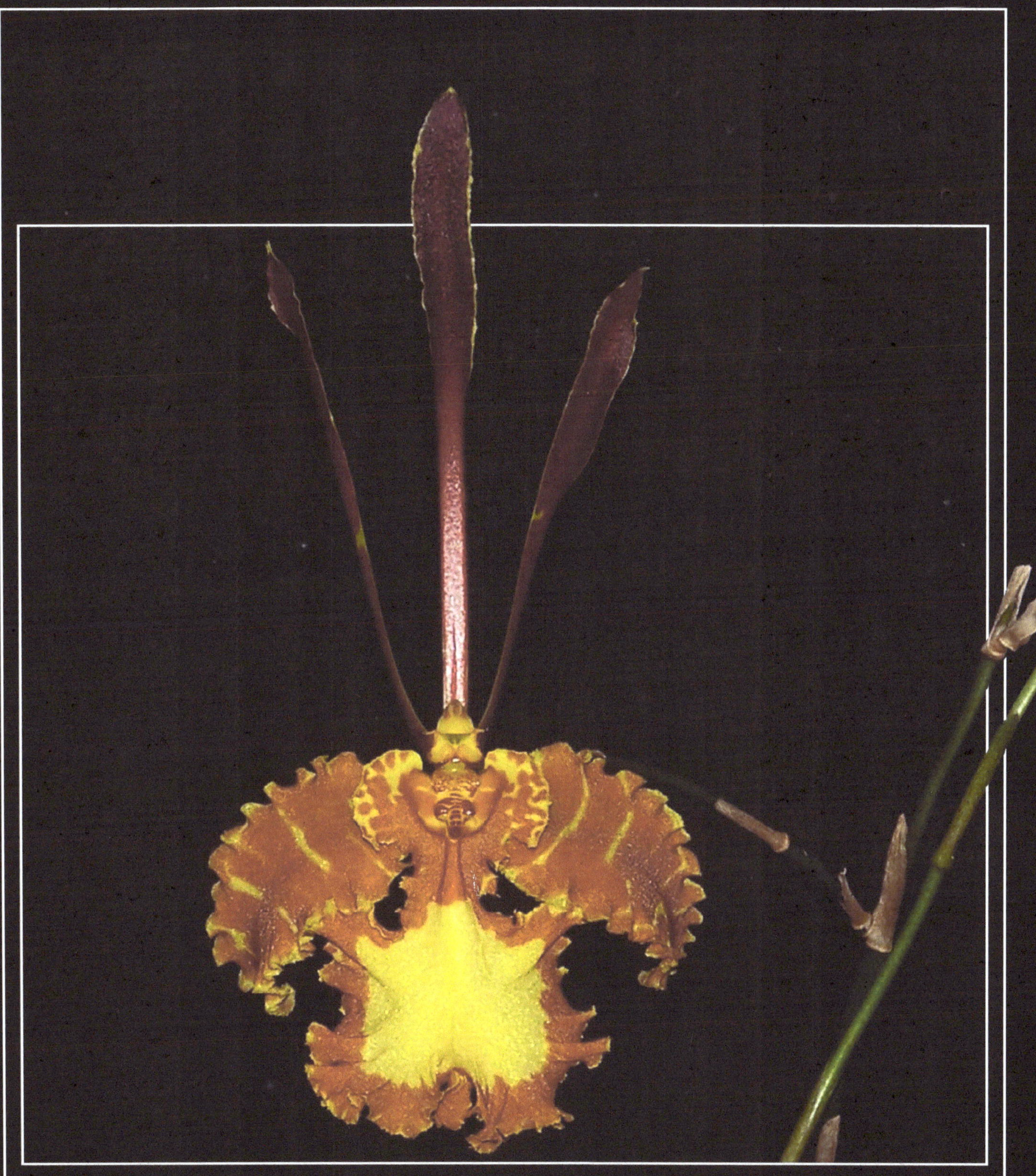

LEFT
Cymbidium Fred's Beauty

ABOVE
Psychopsis Kahili 'Big'
(kramerianum x papilia)

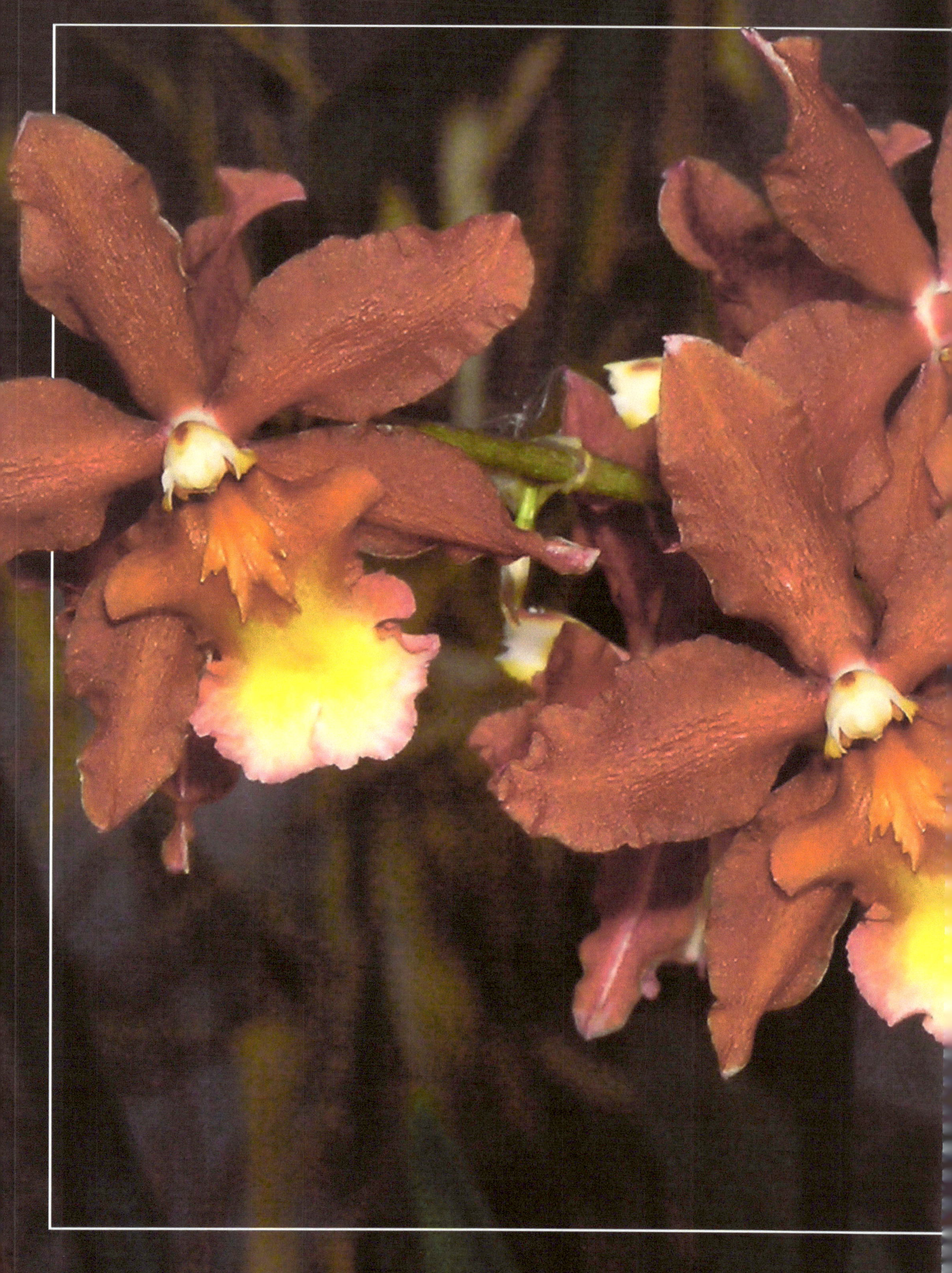

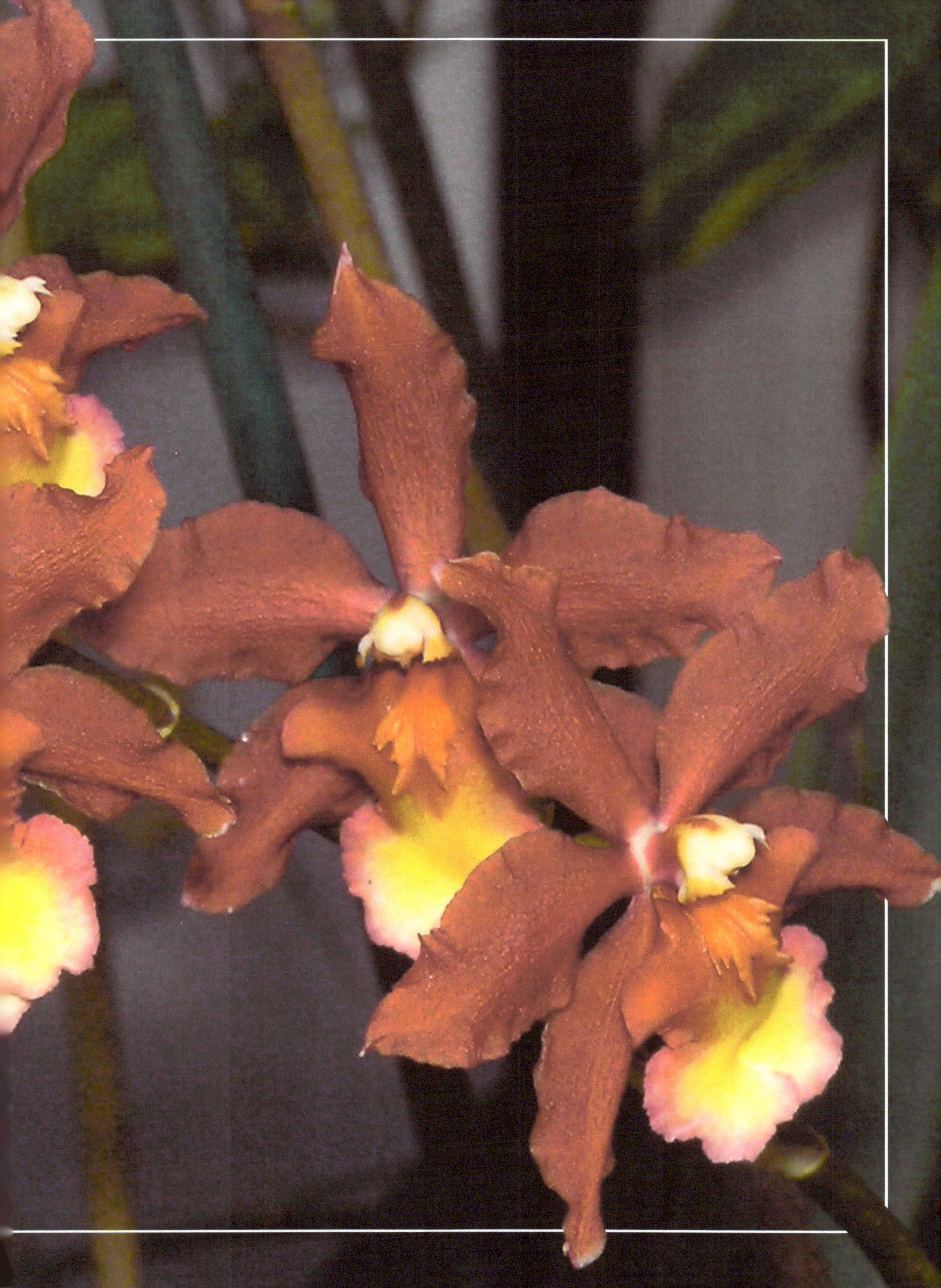

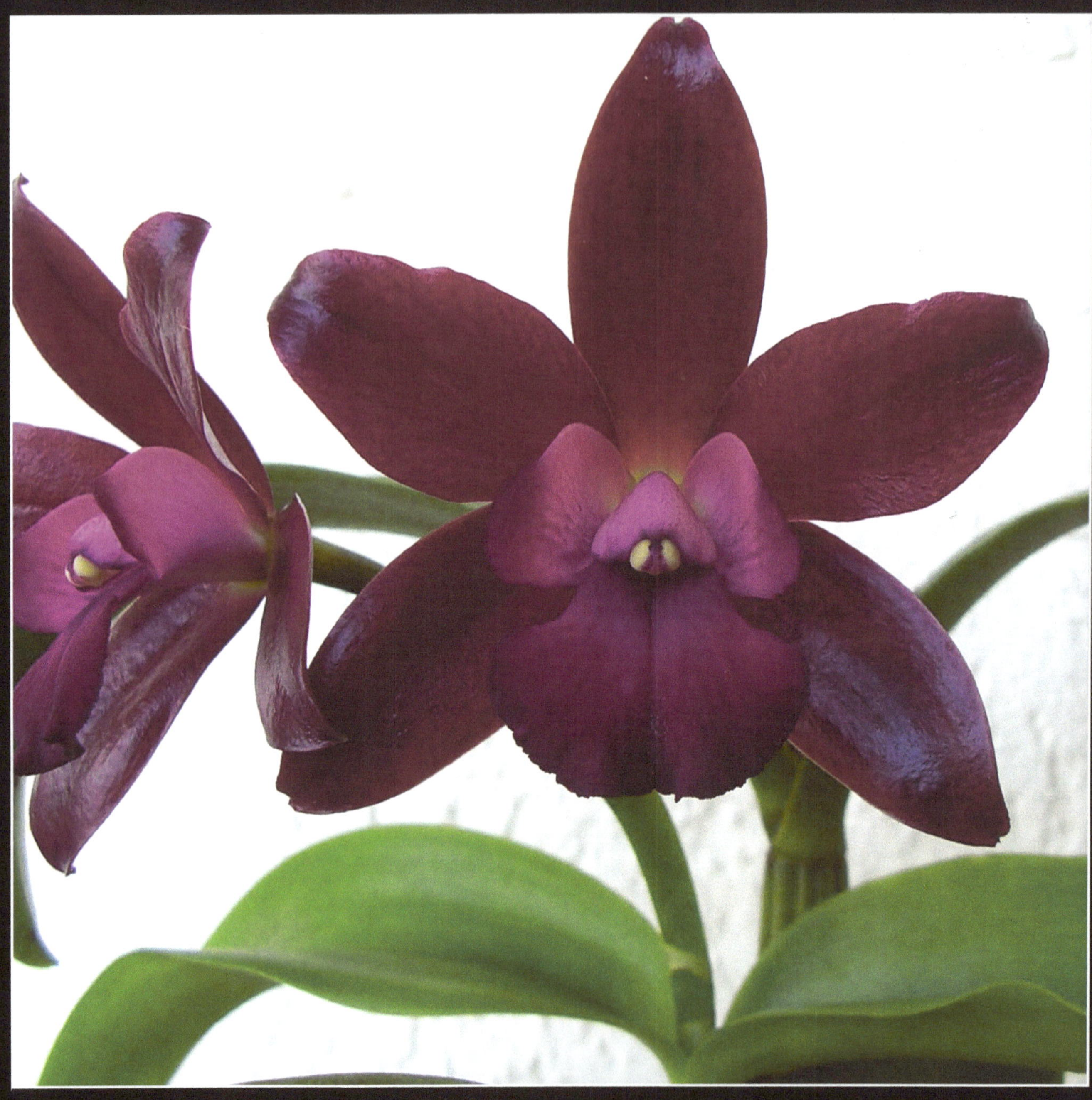

PREVIOUS OVERLEAF
Vuylstekeara Aloha Sparks'Ruby Eyes'

ABOVE
Laeliocattleya Netresiri Waxy'Jairug'

RIGHT
Phragmipedium besseae ('ChiliPepper' x 'Colossal')

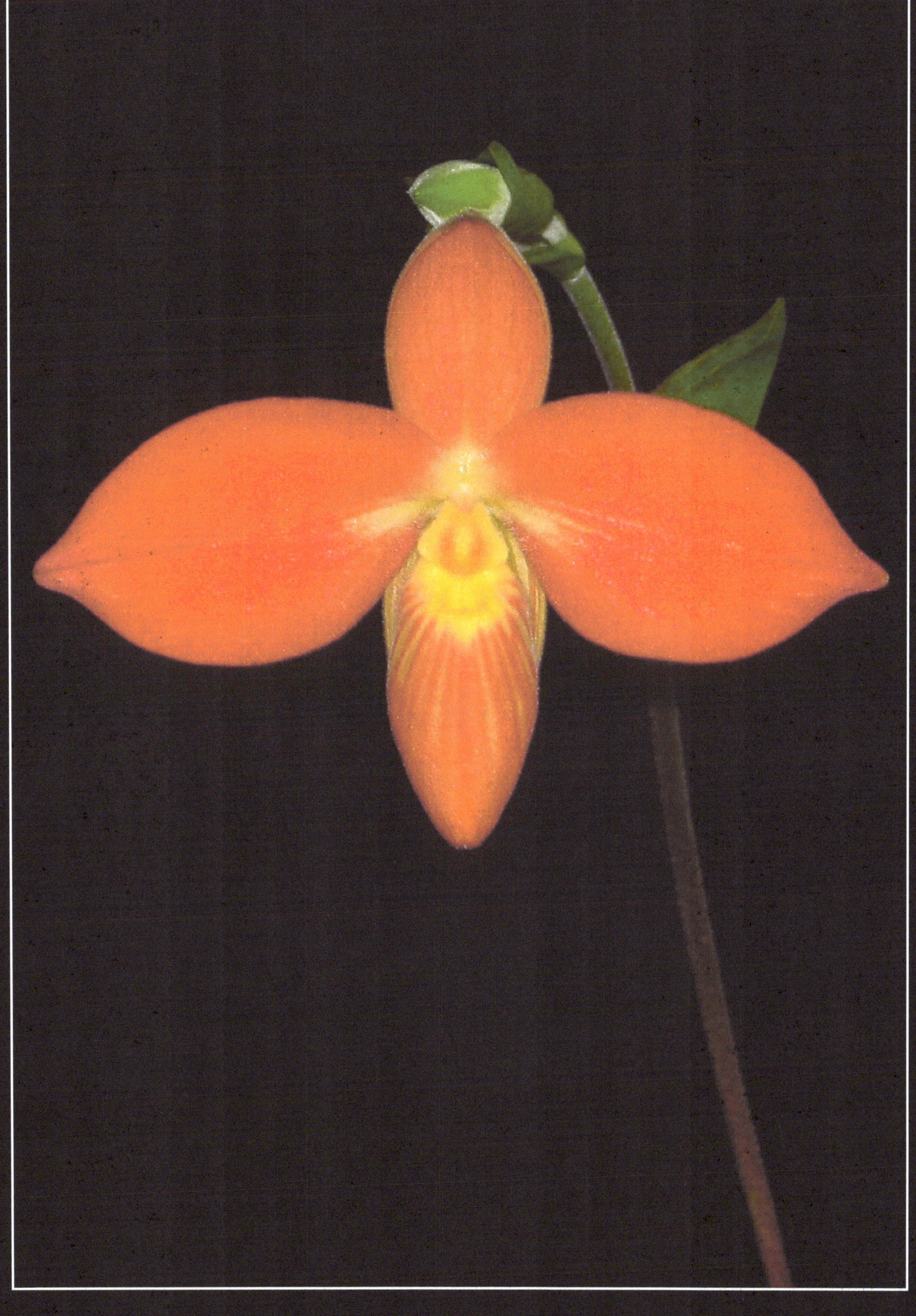

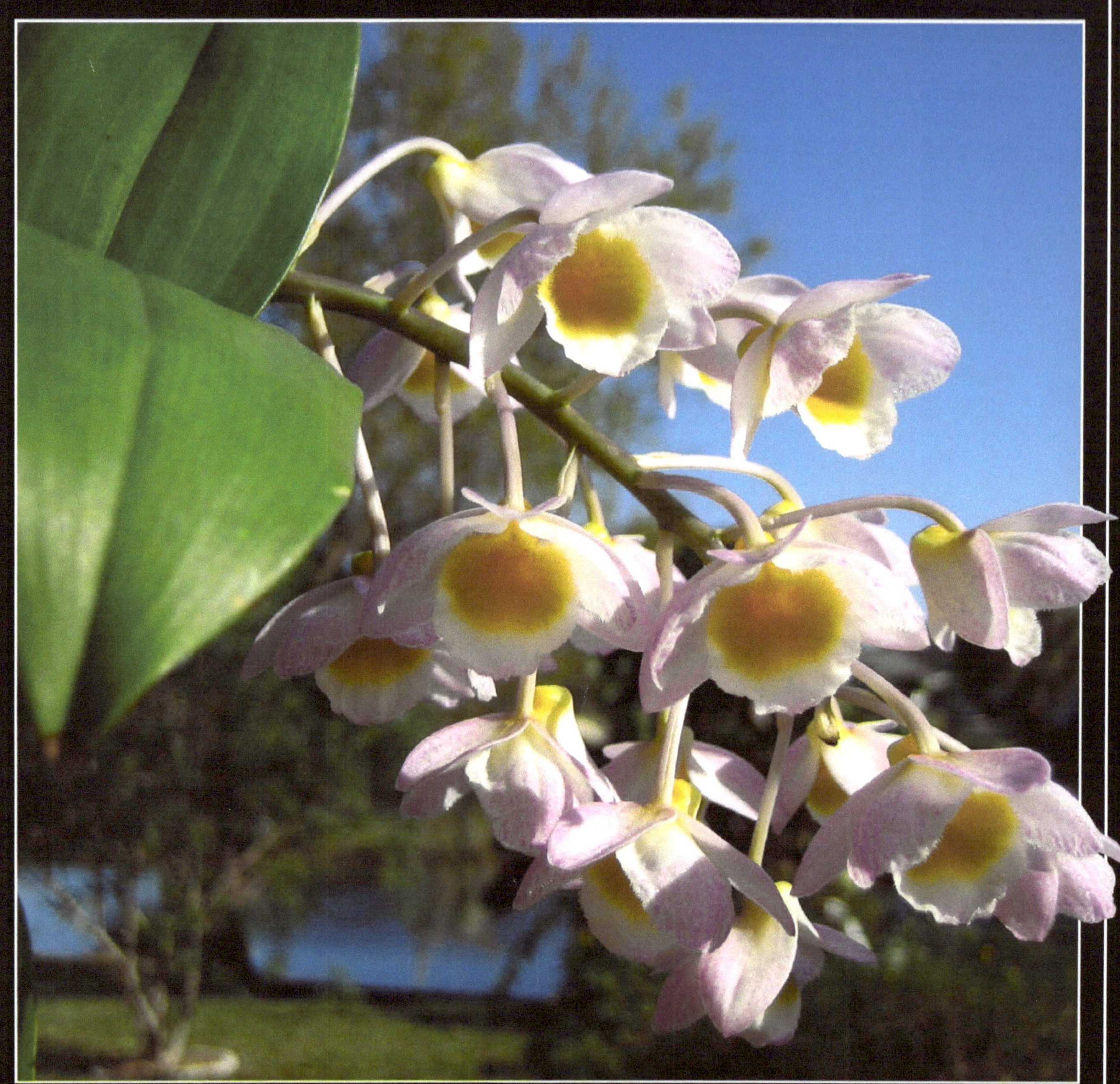

ABOVE
Dendrobium farmeri

RIGHT
Zygoneria Adelaide Meadows 'Fat Cat'

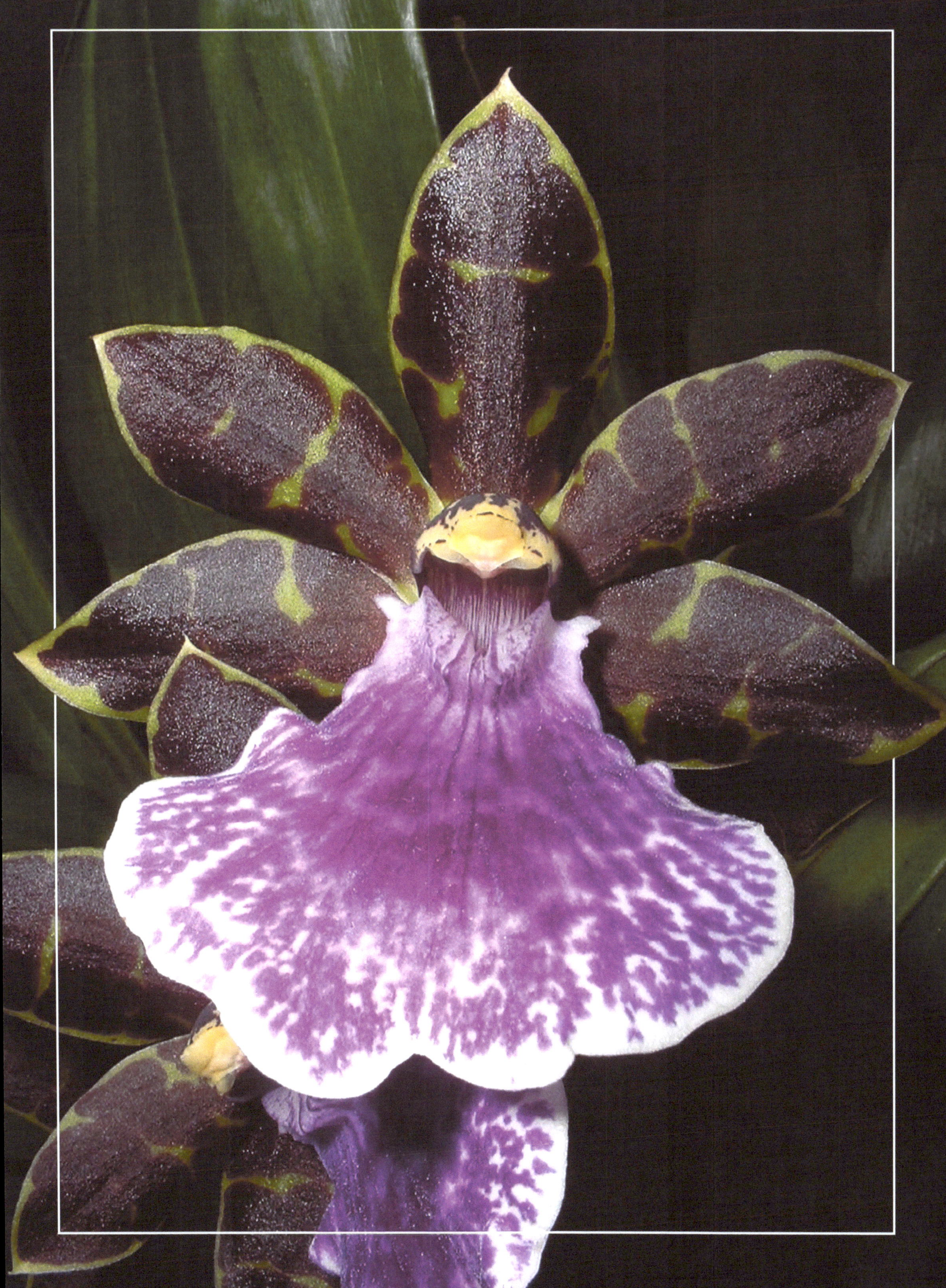

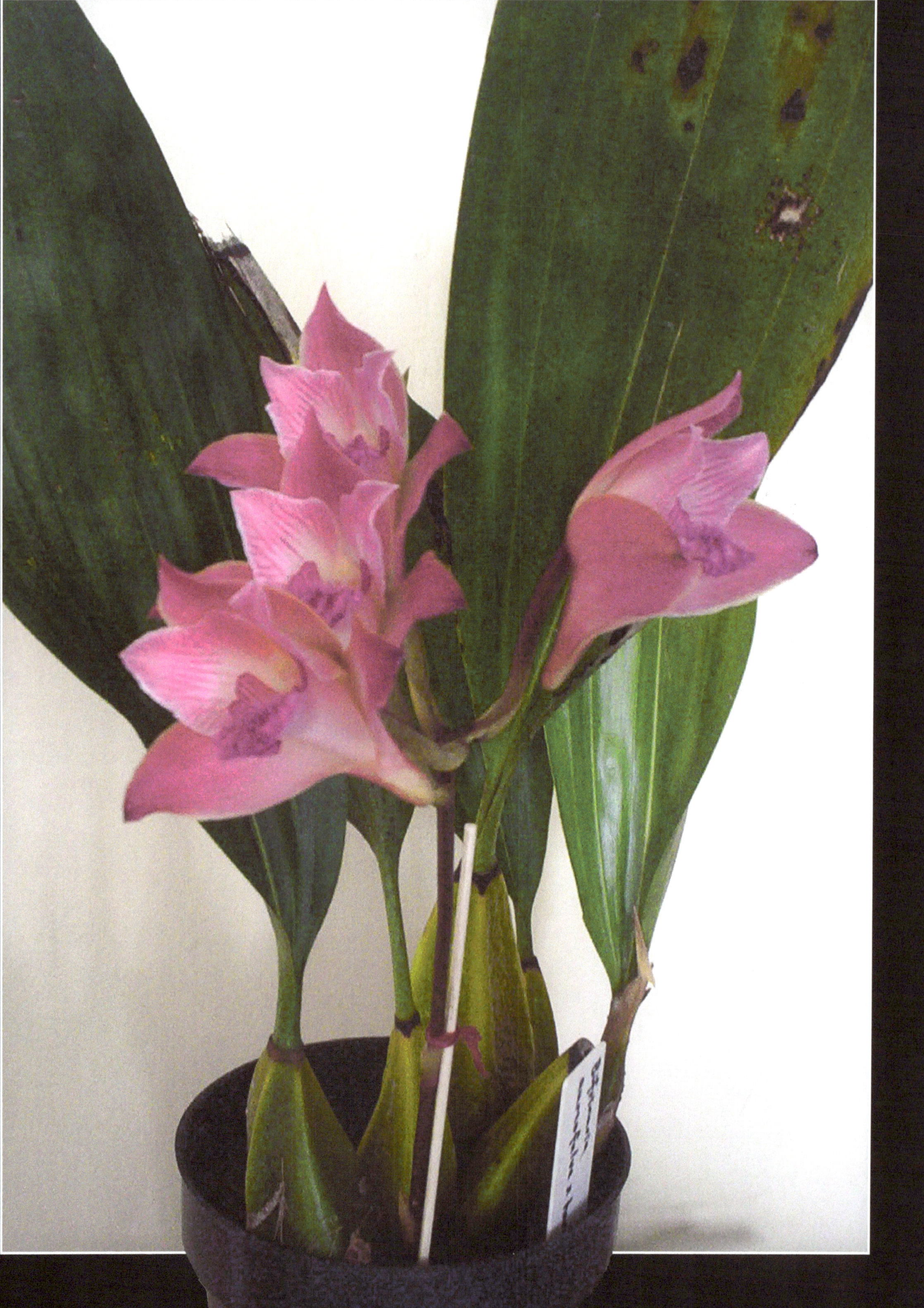

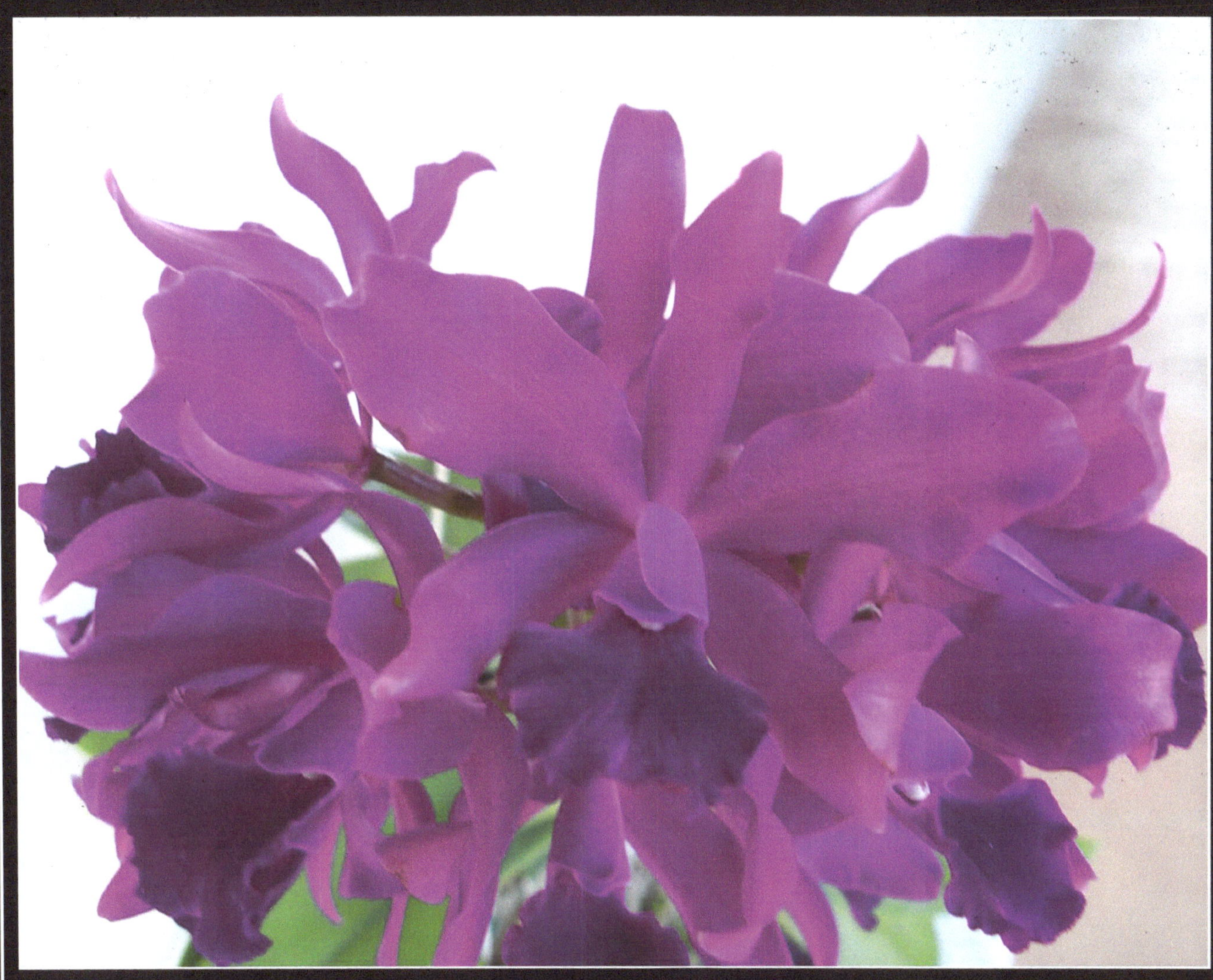

LEFT
Bifrenaria aureo-fulva
x harrisoniae

ABOVE
Cattleya Bacti 'Grape Wax'
(bowringiana x guttata)

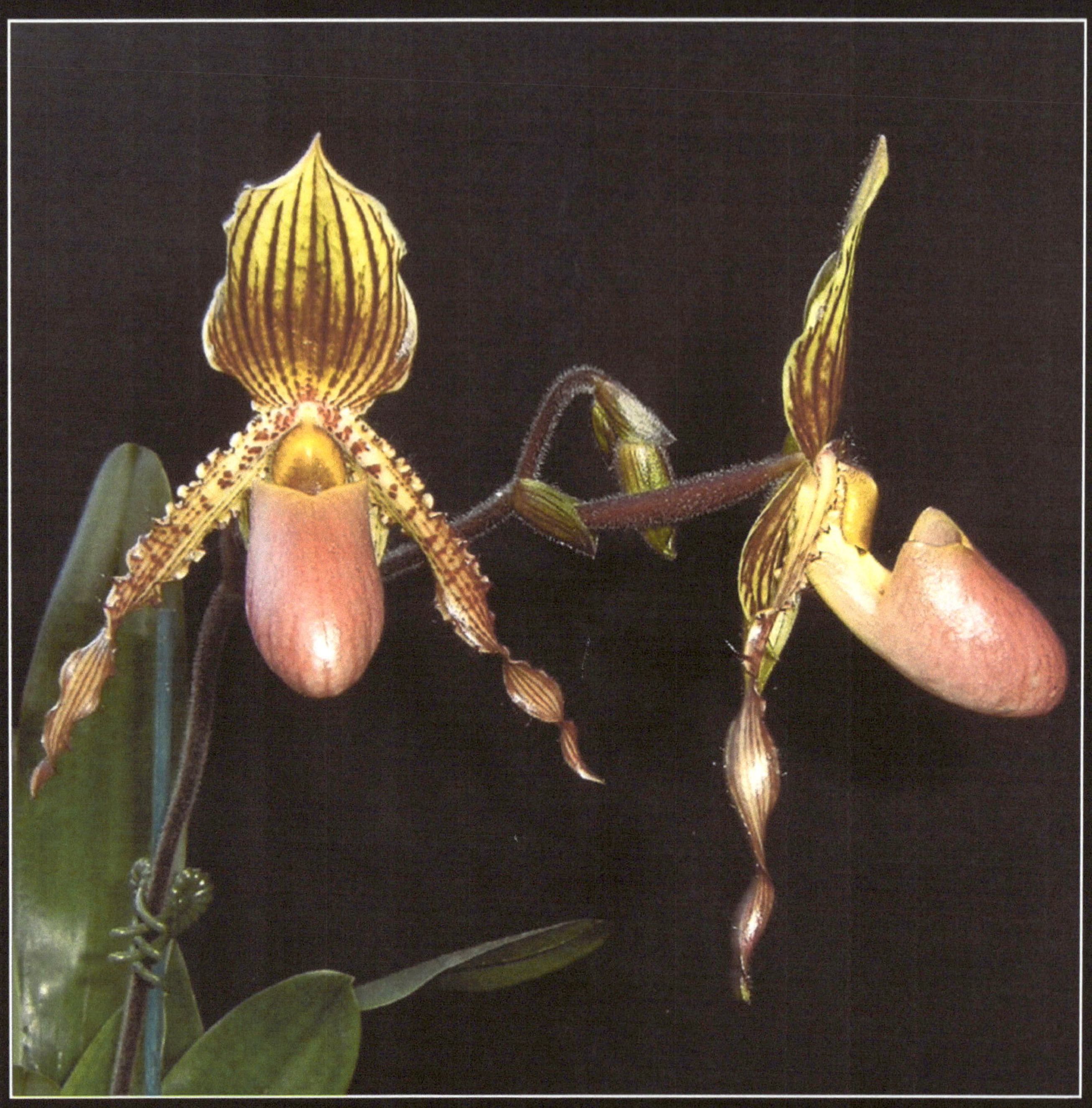

ABOVE
Paphiopedilum Coos
(Paph glanduliferum
x Paph chamberlainianum)

RIGHT
Odontonia Memoria Martin
Orenstein 'Lulu' HCC/AOS
(Odm. Aglaon x Milt. Martin
Orenstein)

OVERLEAF LEFT
Dendrobium thyrsiflorum

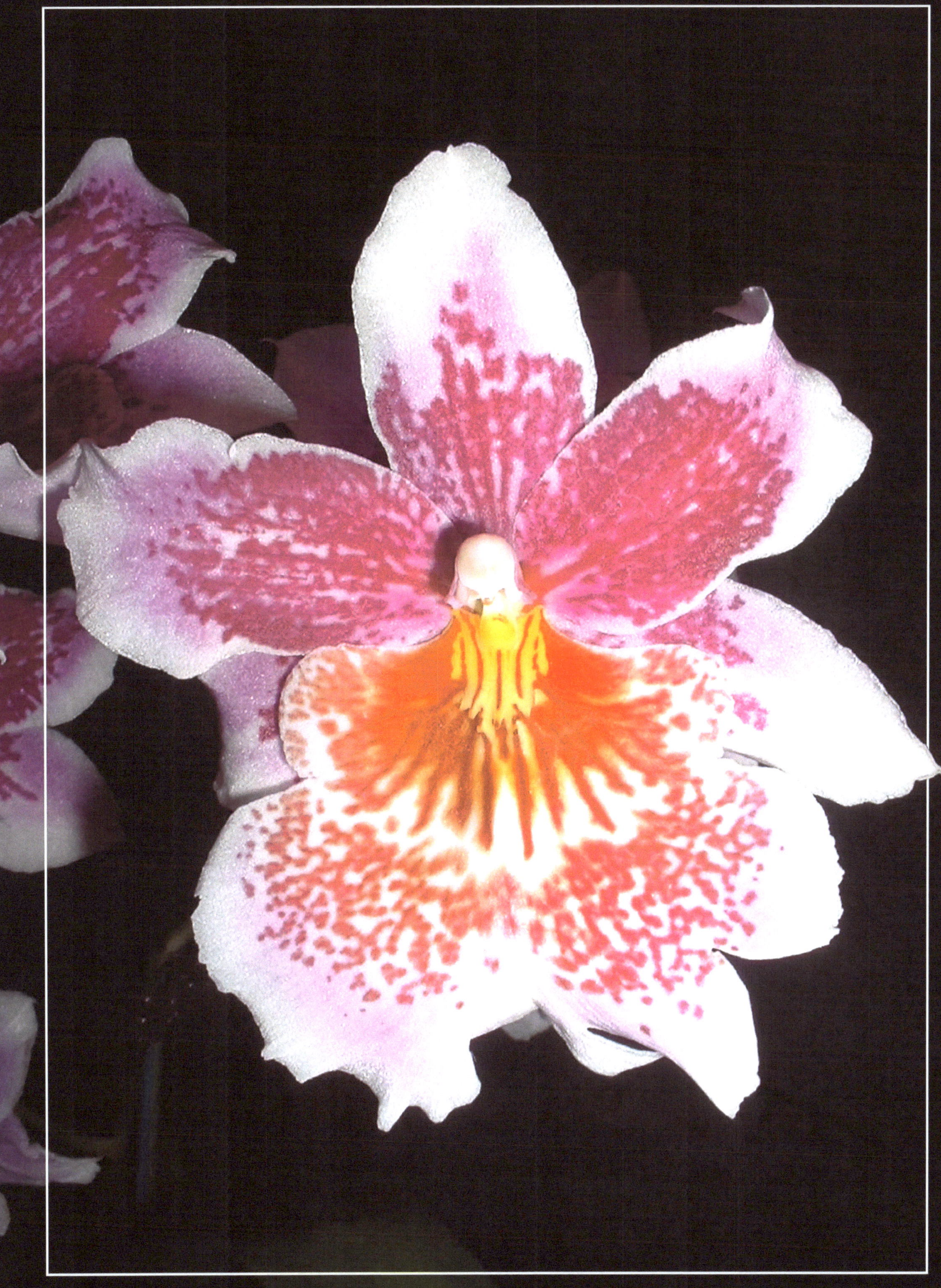

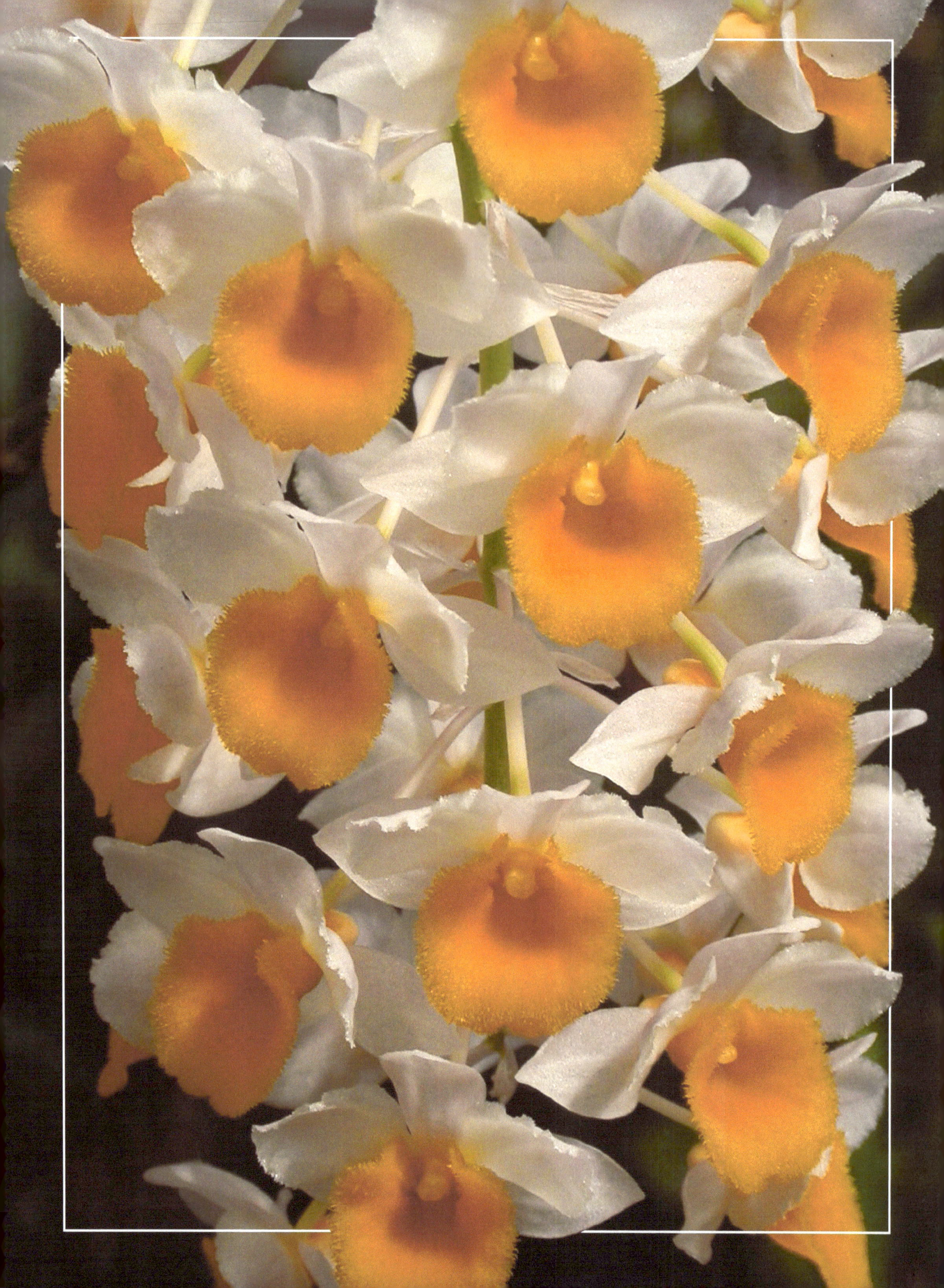

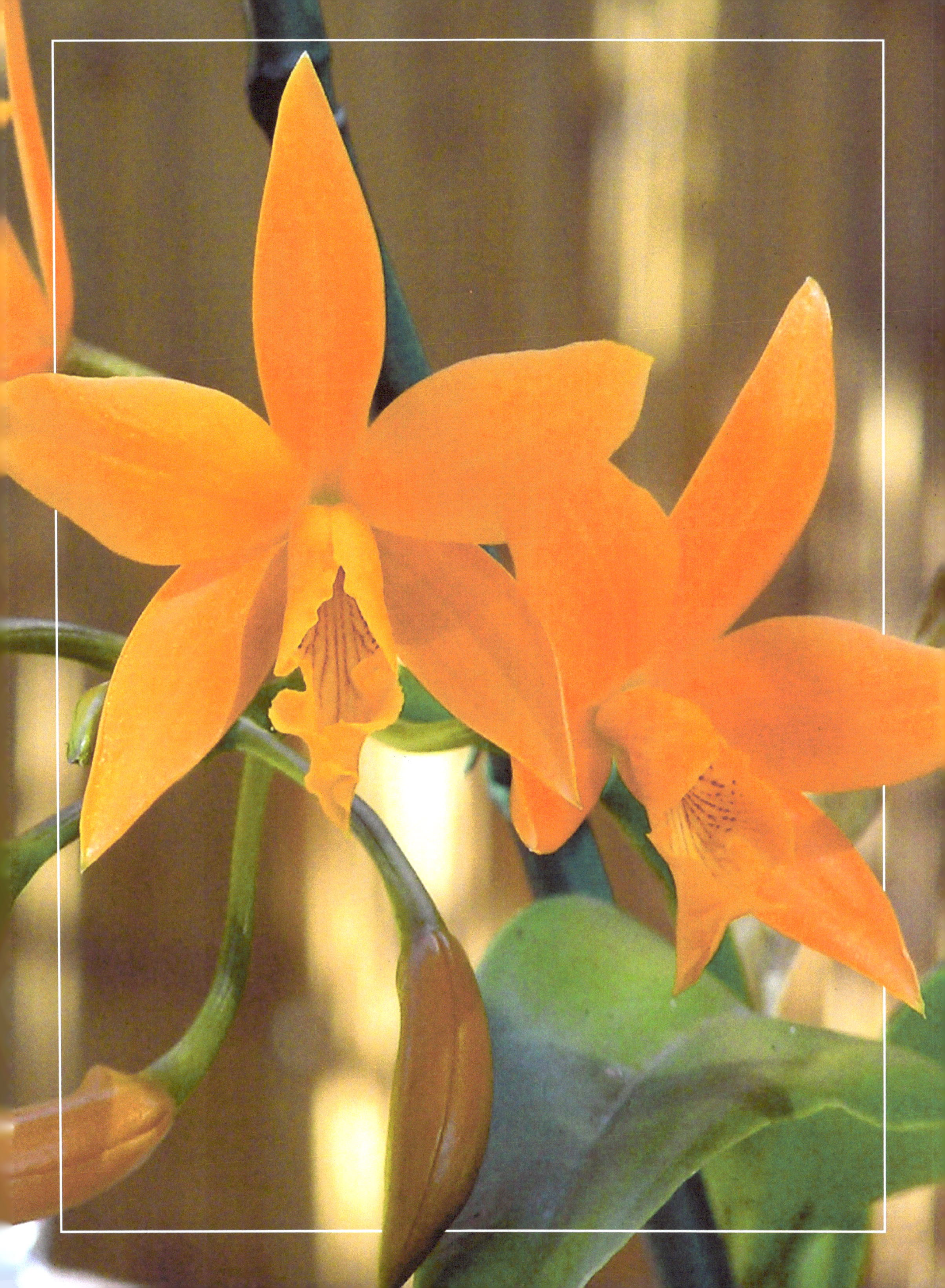

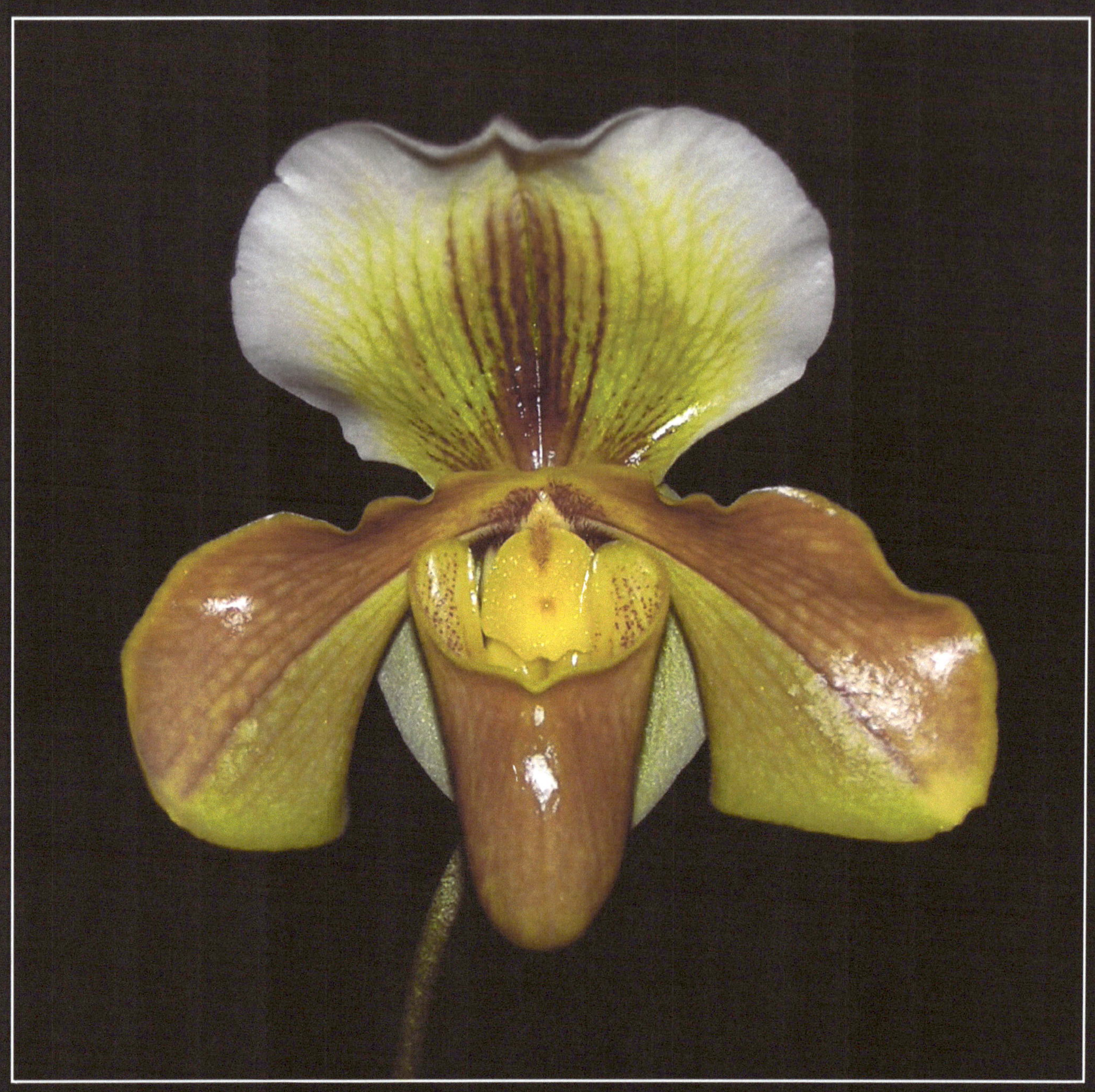

PREVIOUS OVERLEAF
Laeliocattleya Trick or Treat (Lc. Icarus X C. Chit Chat)

ABOVE
Paphiopedilum Hillsview HV-895

RIGHT
Dendrobium Super Ise Abundance x Super Star Shapely

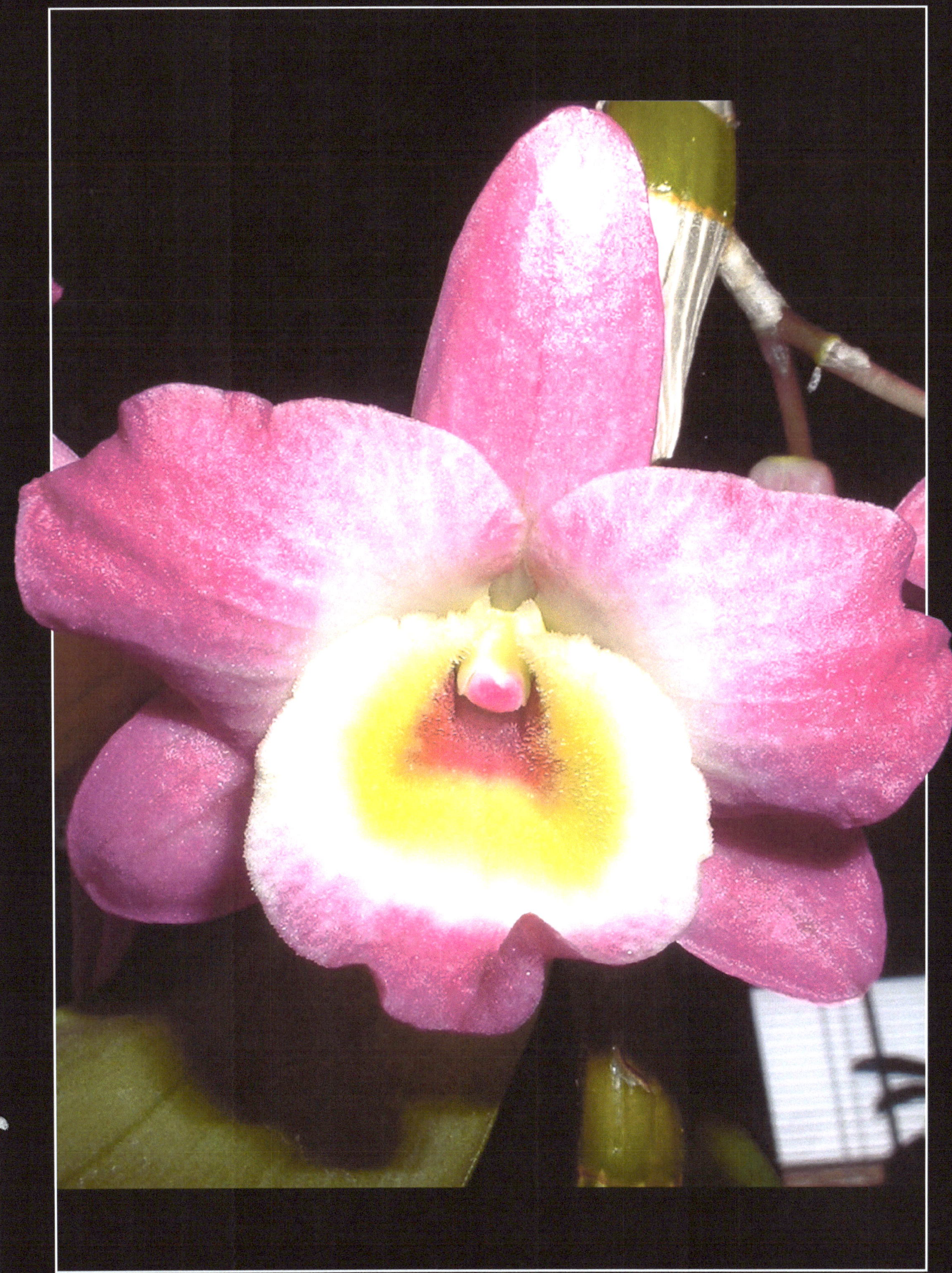

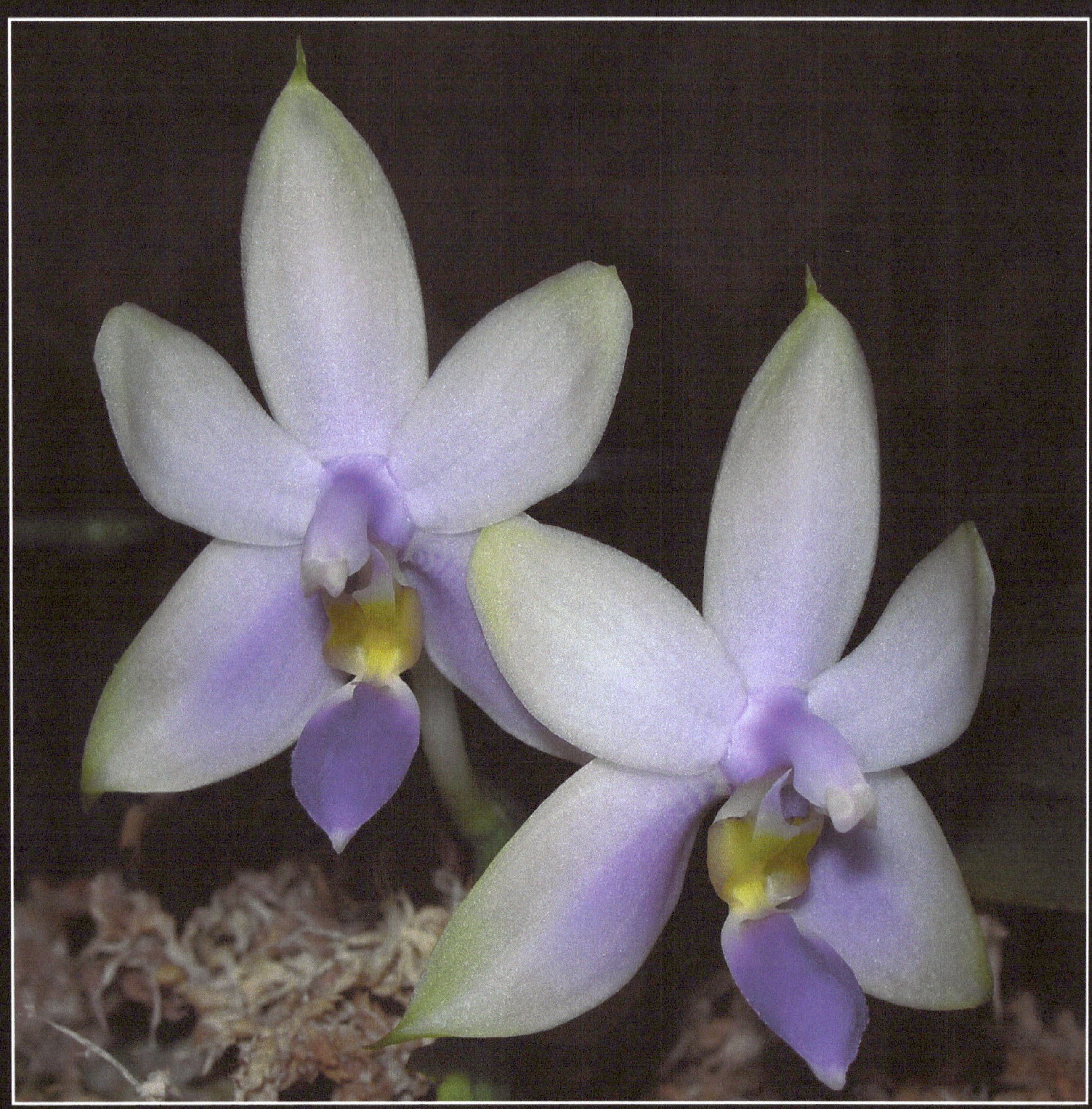

ABOVE
Phalaenopsis violacea var. coerulea

RIGHT
Vanda Sansai Blue 'Meechai'AM/AOS

OVERLEAF LEFT
Trichocentrum Nathakhun

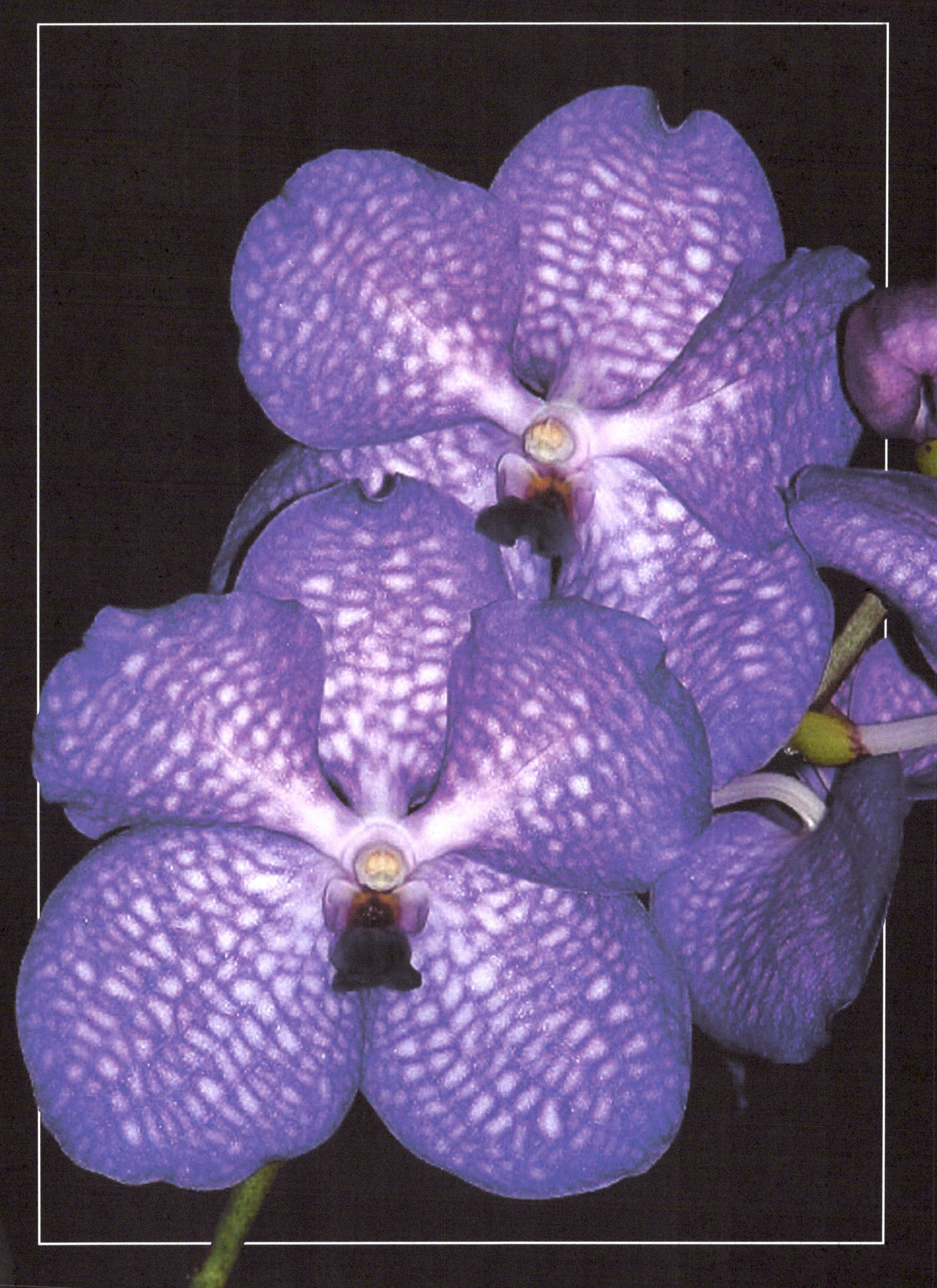

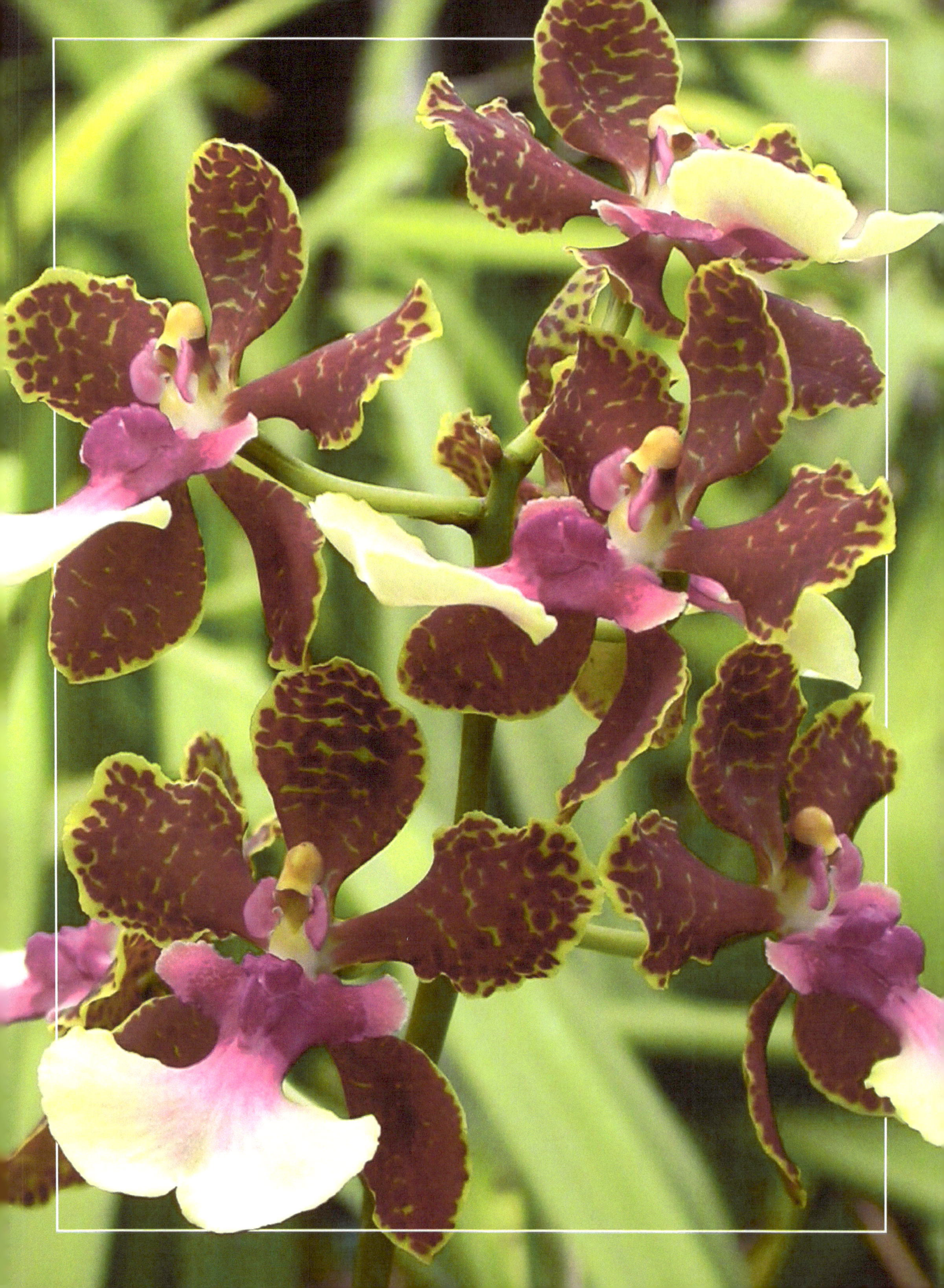

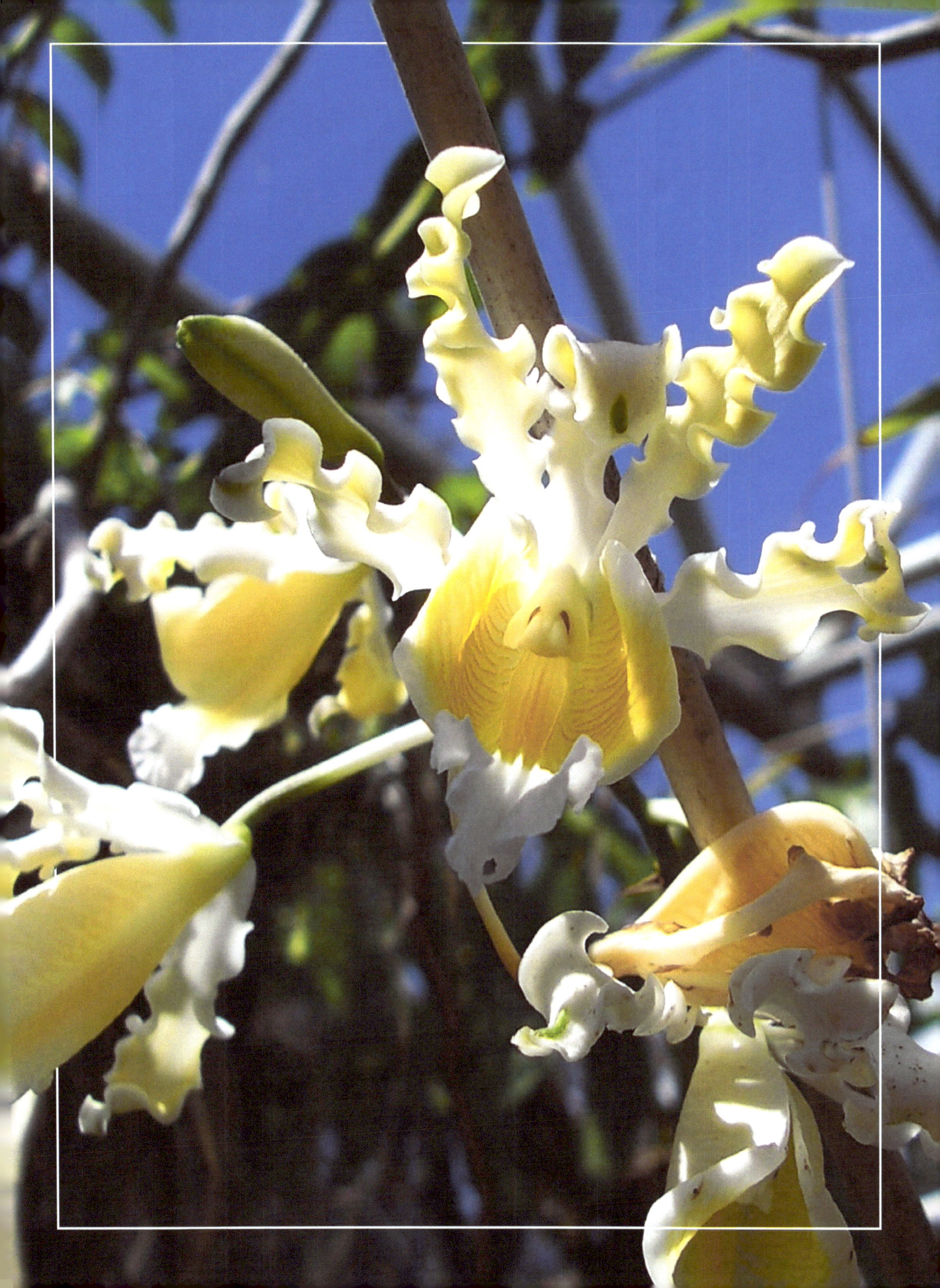

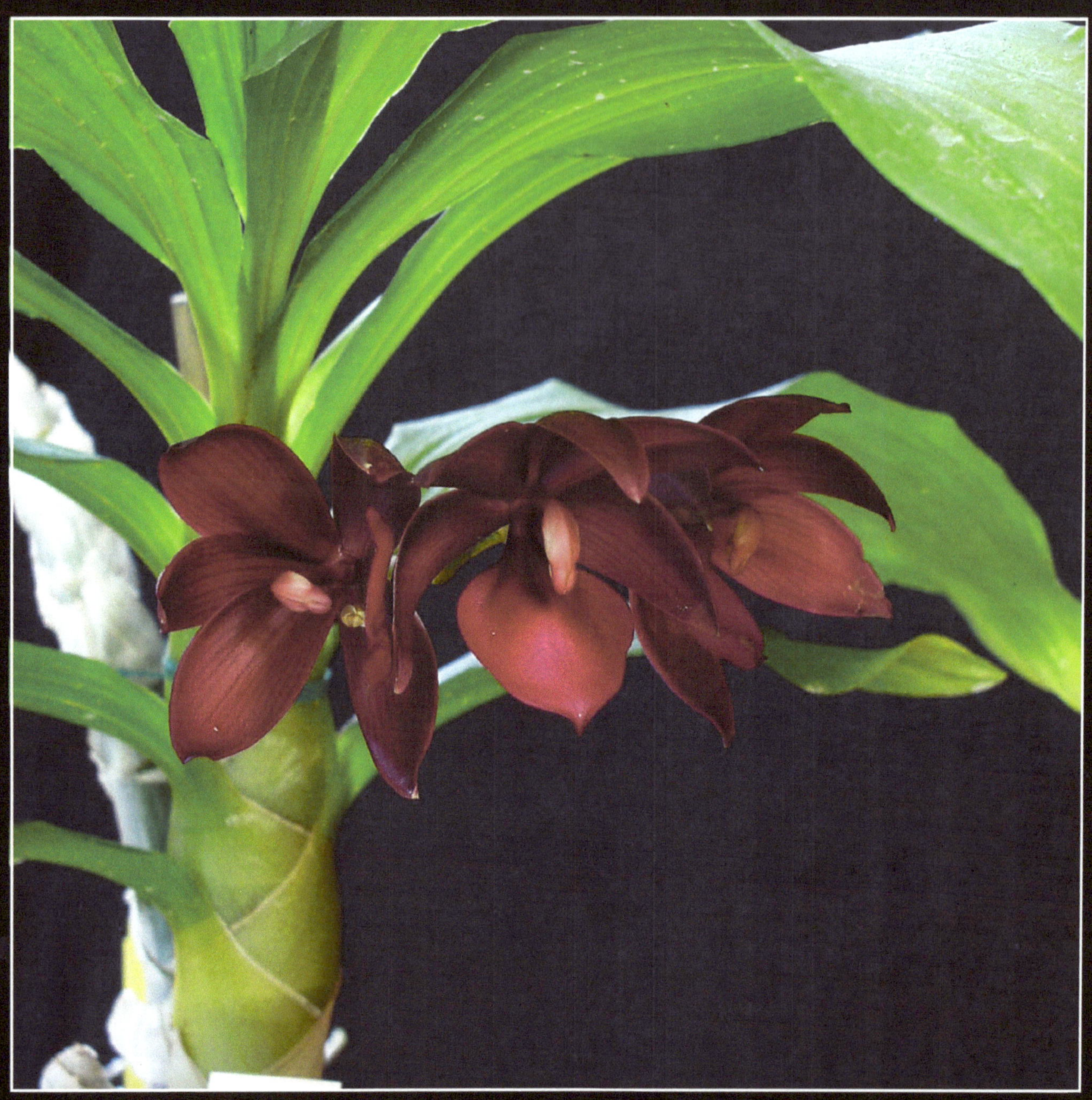

PREVIOUS OVERLEAF
Schomburgkia Brysiana 'Robert x self'

ABOVE
Cycnodes Wine Delight 'Jem' FCC/AOS

RIGHT
Maxillaria Tenuifolia

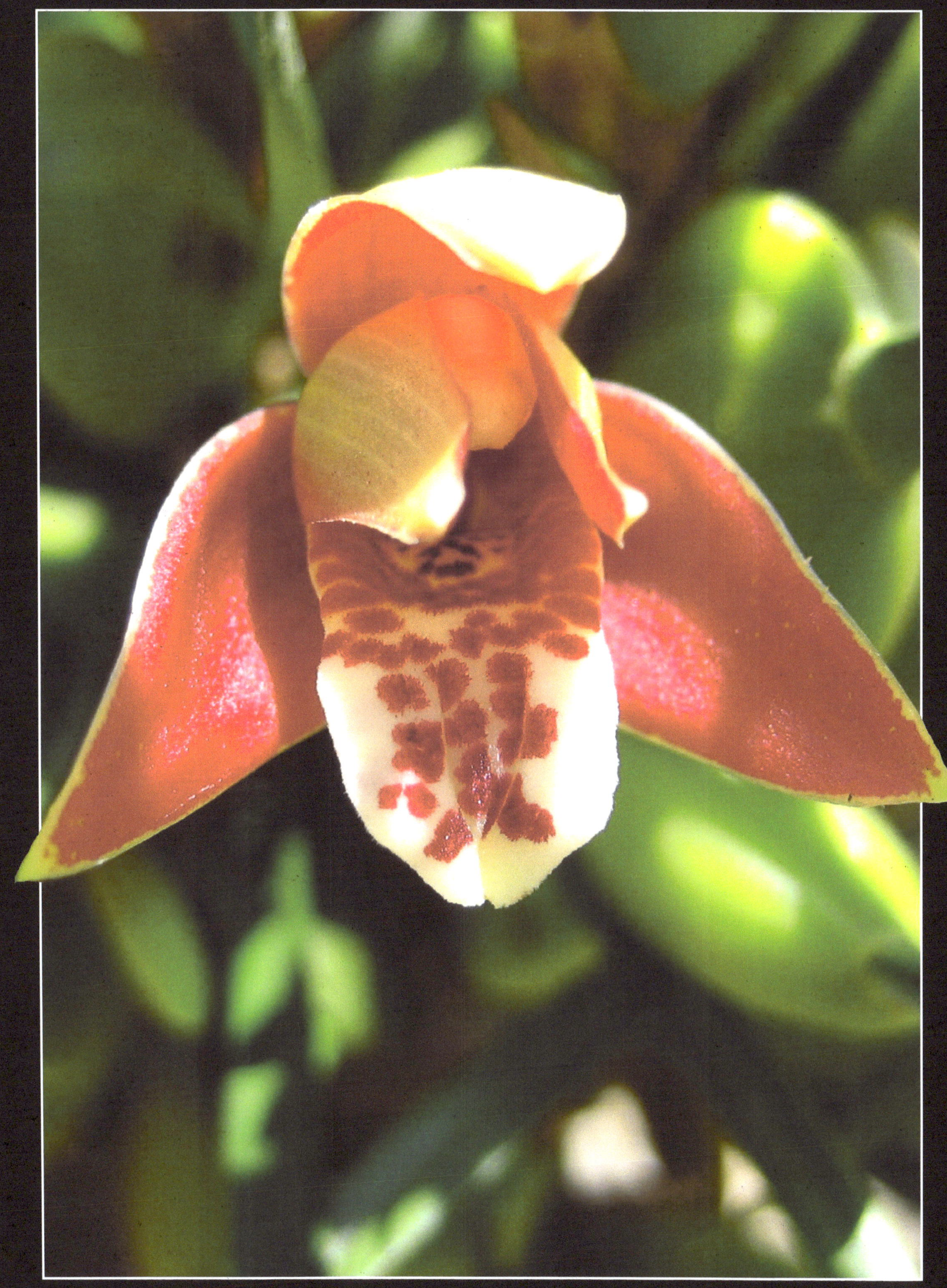

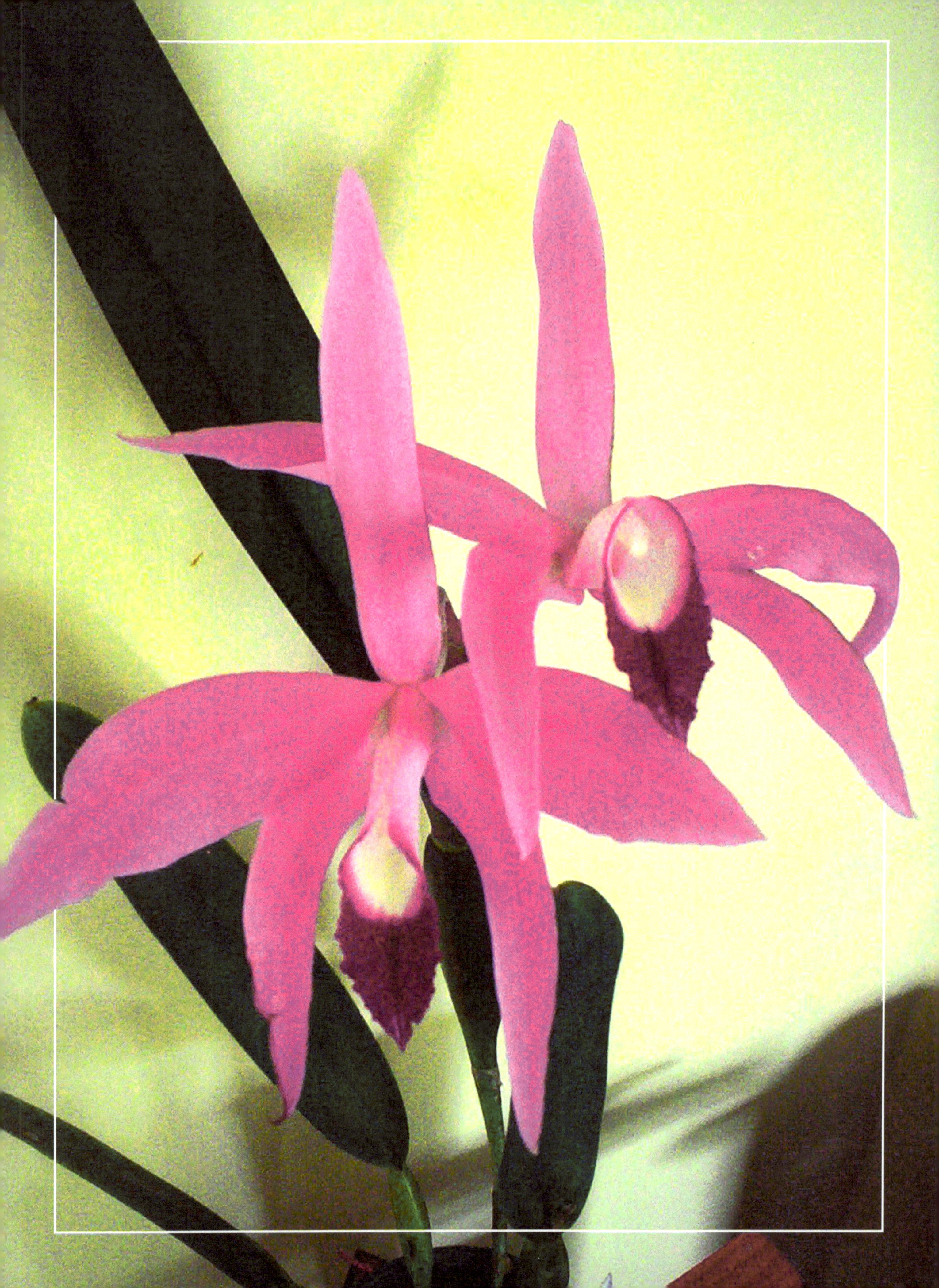

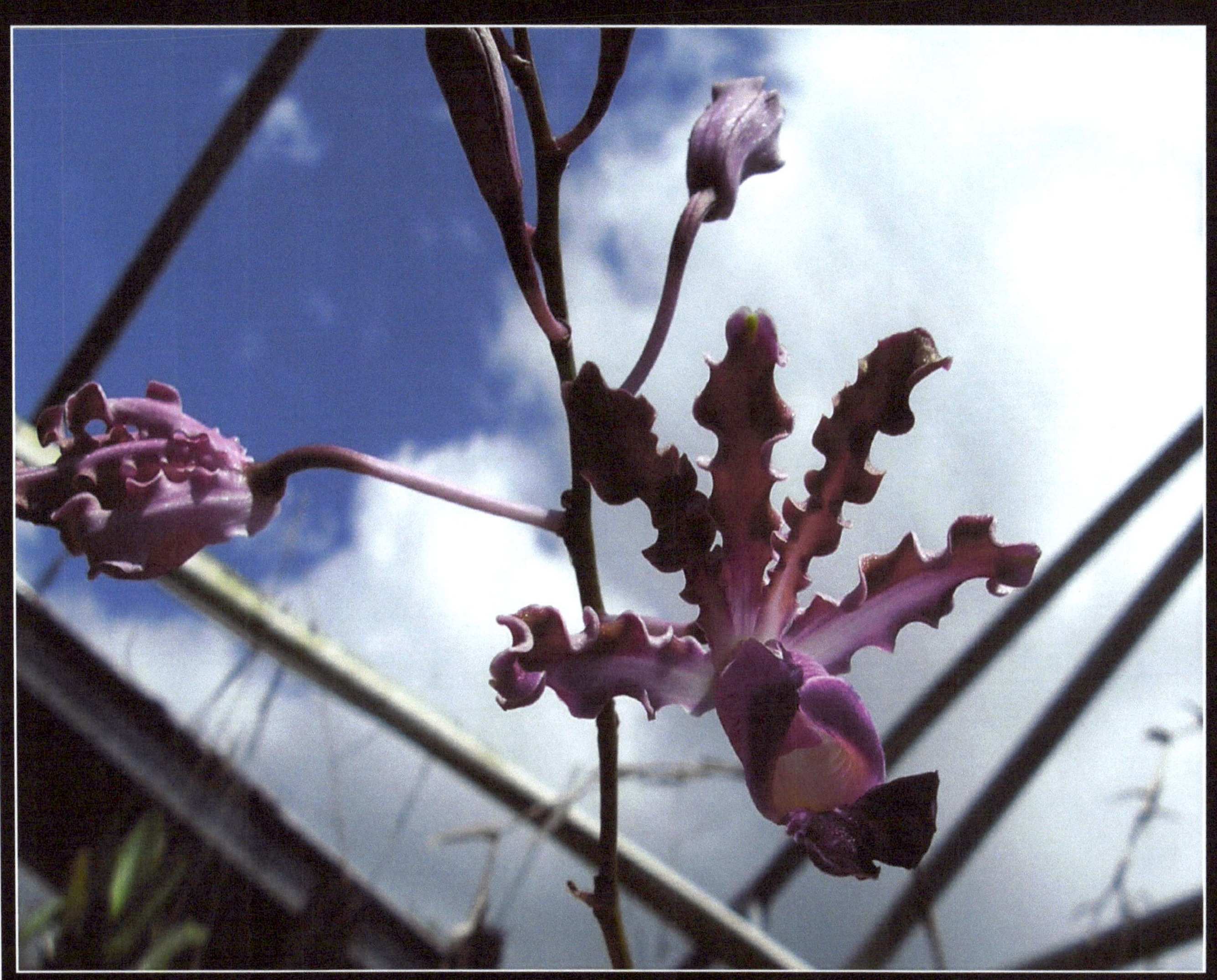

Left
Laelia perrinii

Above
Schomburgkia exaltata

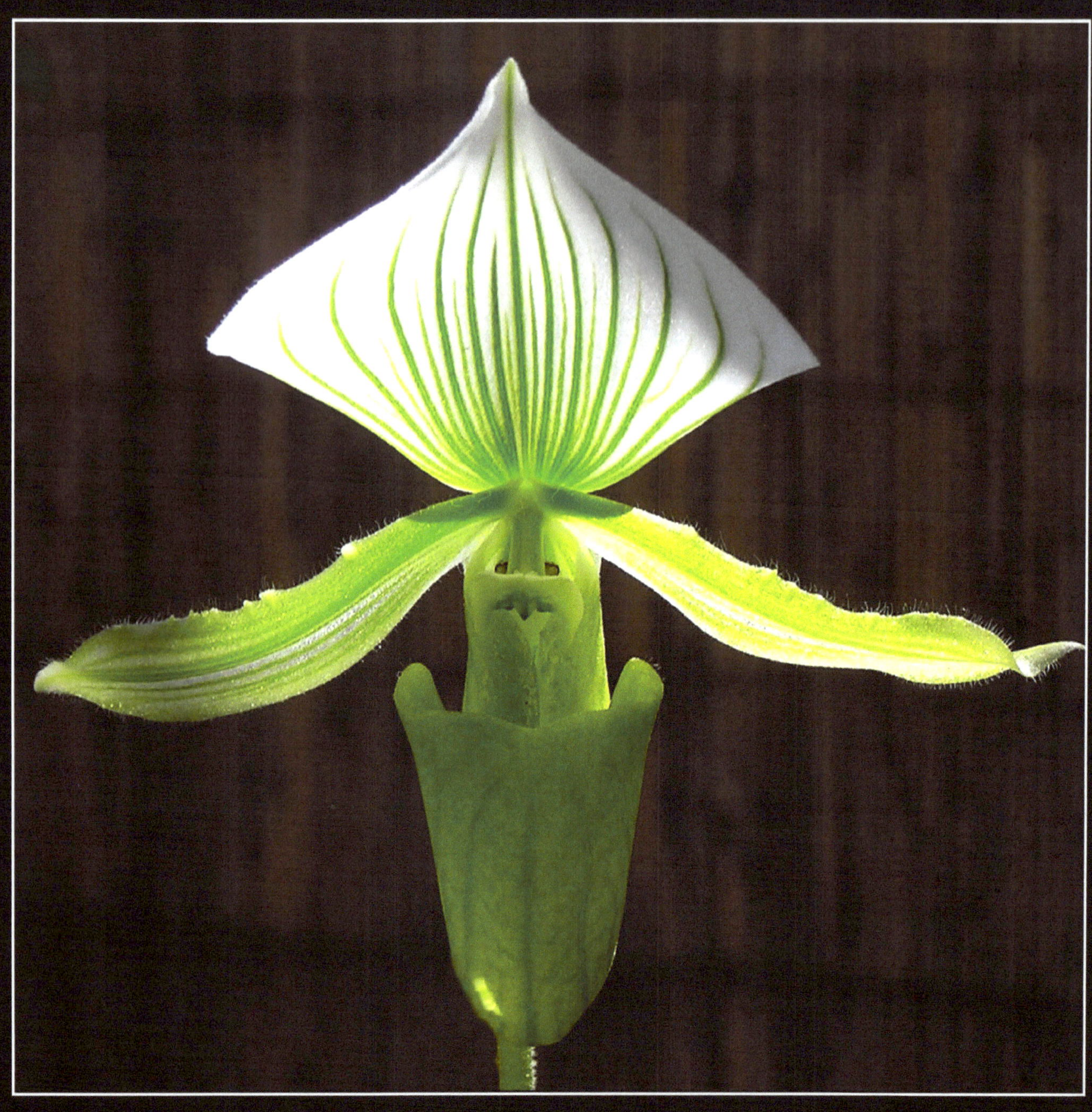

ABOVE
Paphiopedilum Maudiae Alba x Paph. Mitylene Alba

RIGHT
Odontocidium Tiger Crow 'Golden Girl' HCC/AOS (Odcdm. Tiger Hambuhren x Odcdm Crowborough)

OVERLEAF LEFT
Coryanthes alborosea

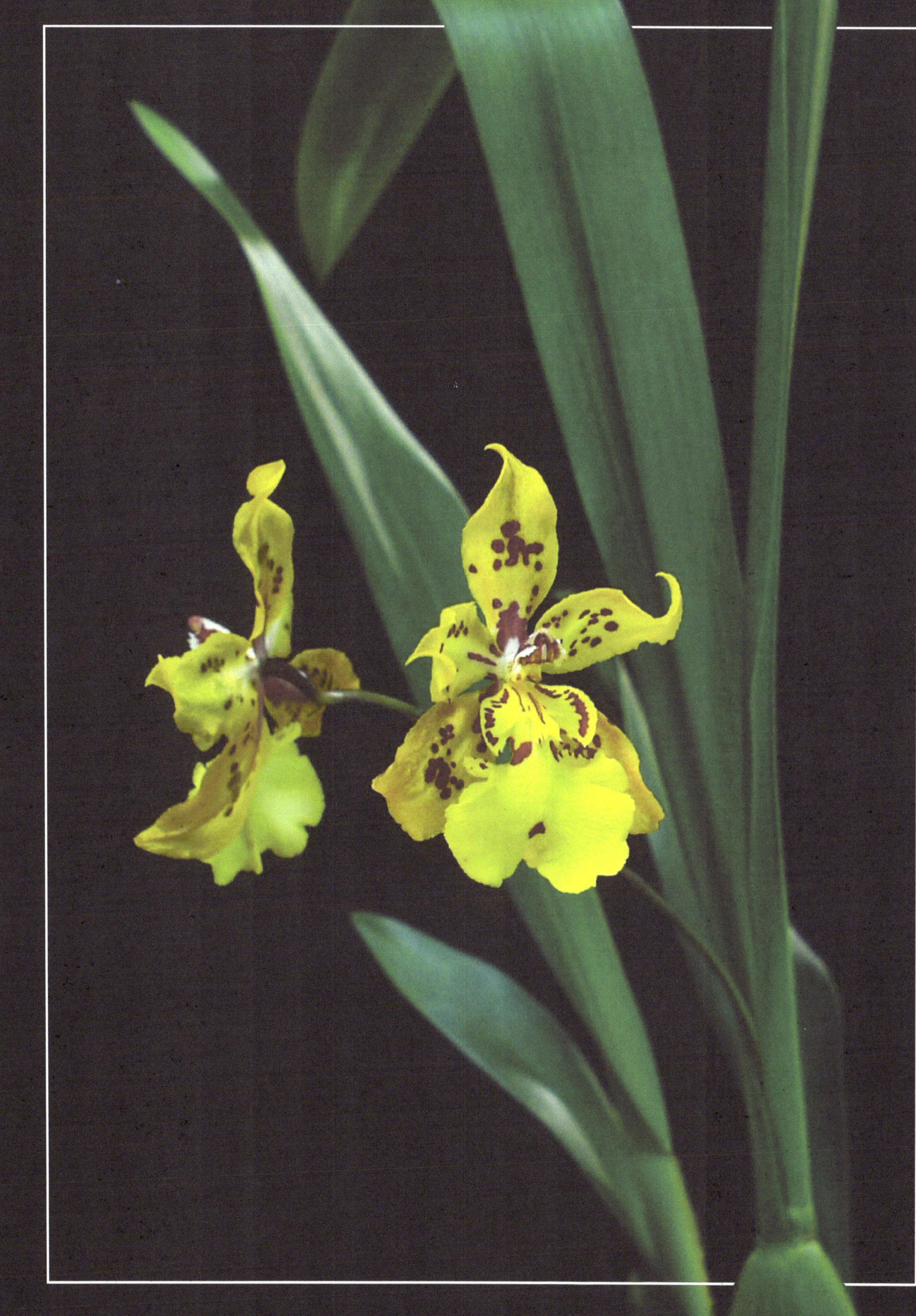

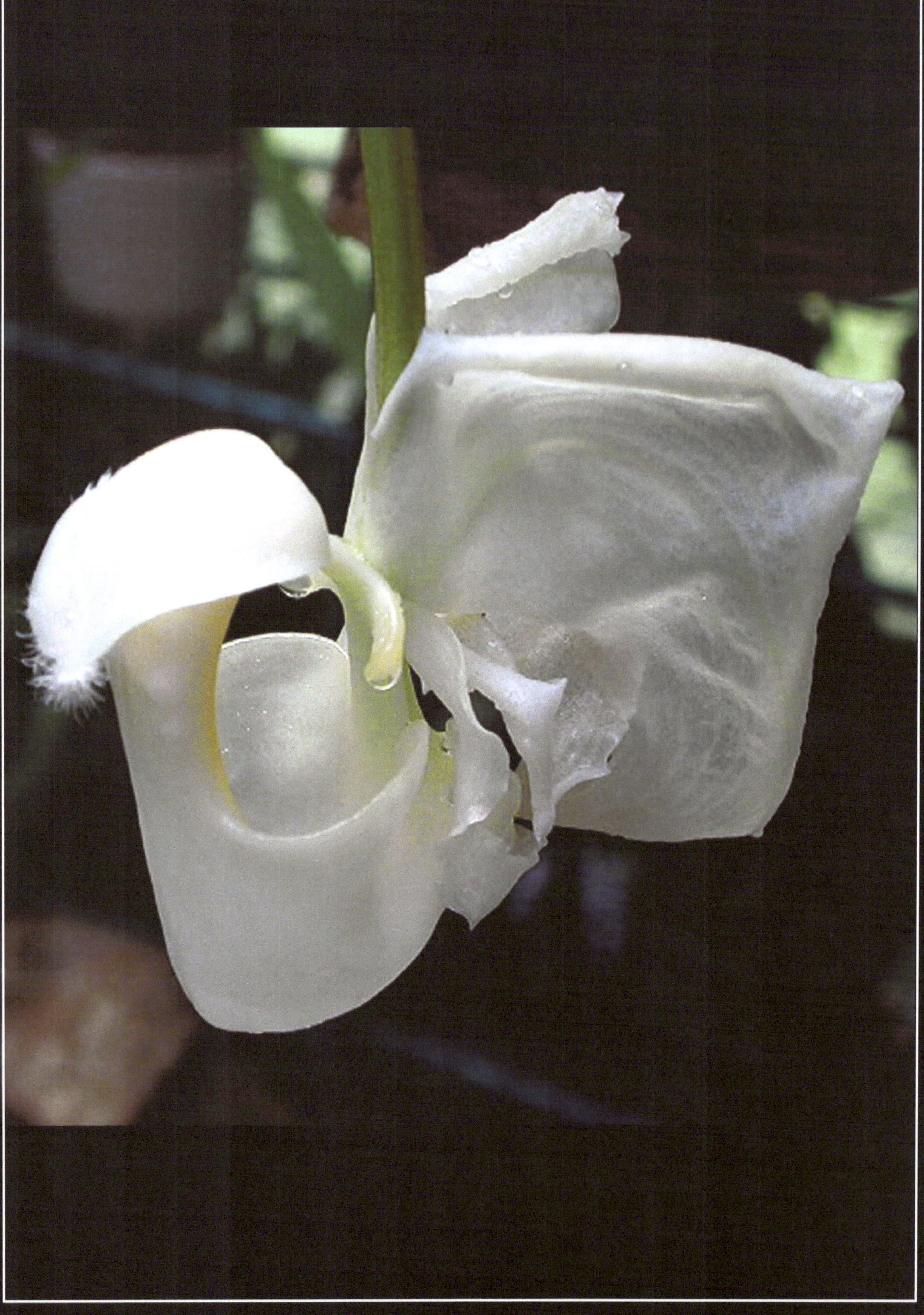

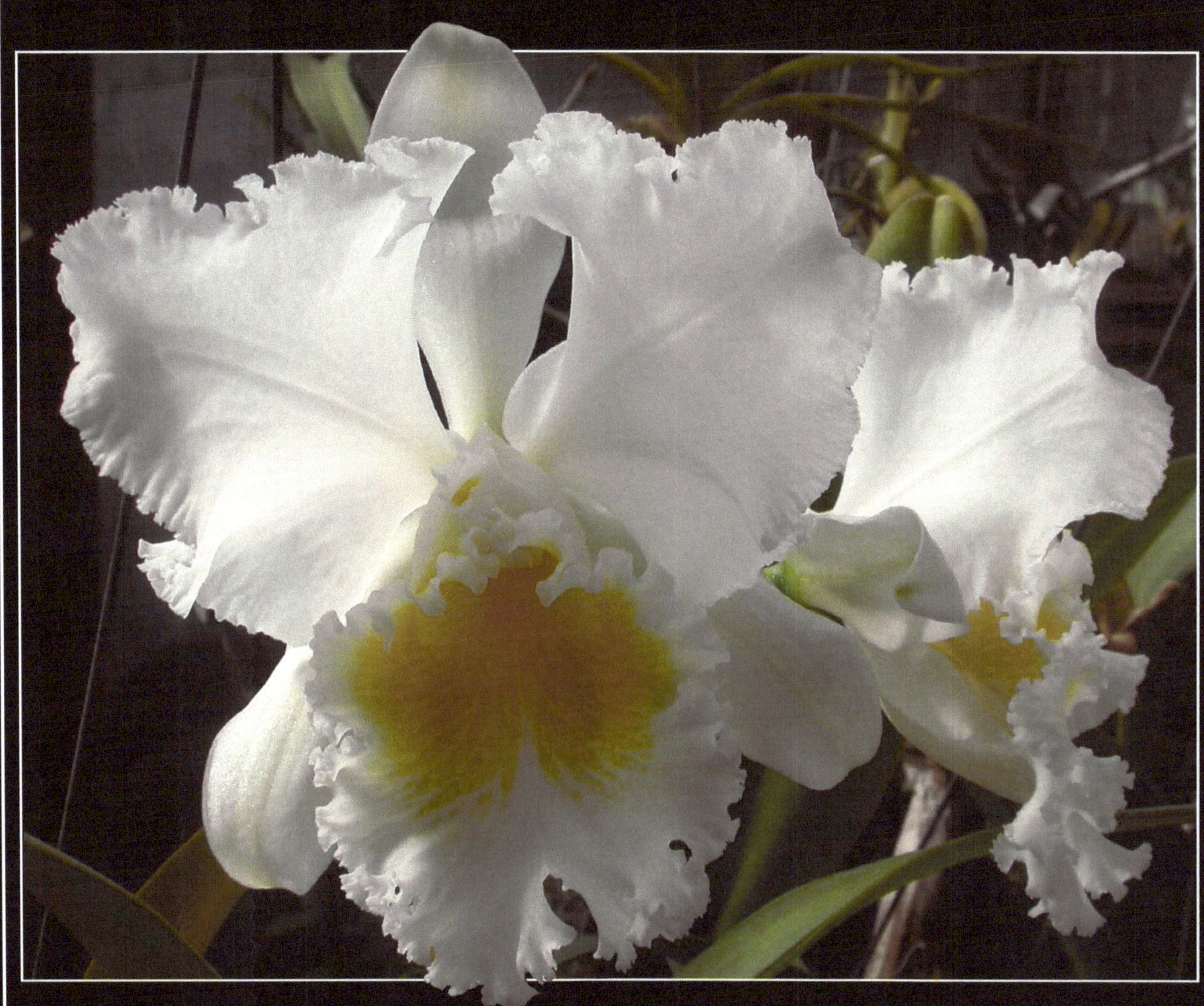

ABOVE
Cattleya Jose Marti 'Mother's Favorite' AM/AOS (C. Bob Betts x C. Bow Bells)

OVERLEAF LEFT
Paphiopedilum Magic Lantern (Paph. micranthum x Paph. delenatii)

OVERLEAF RIGHT
Miltassia Charles M. Fitch 'Izumi' AM/AOS

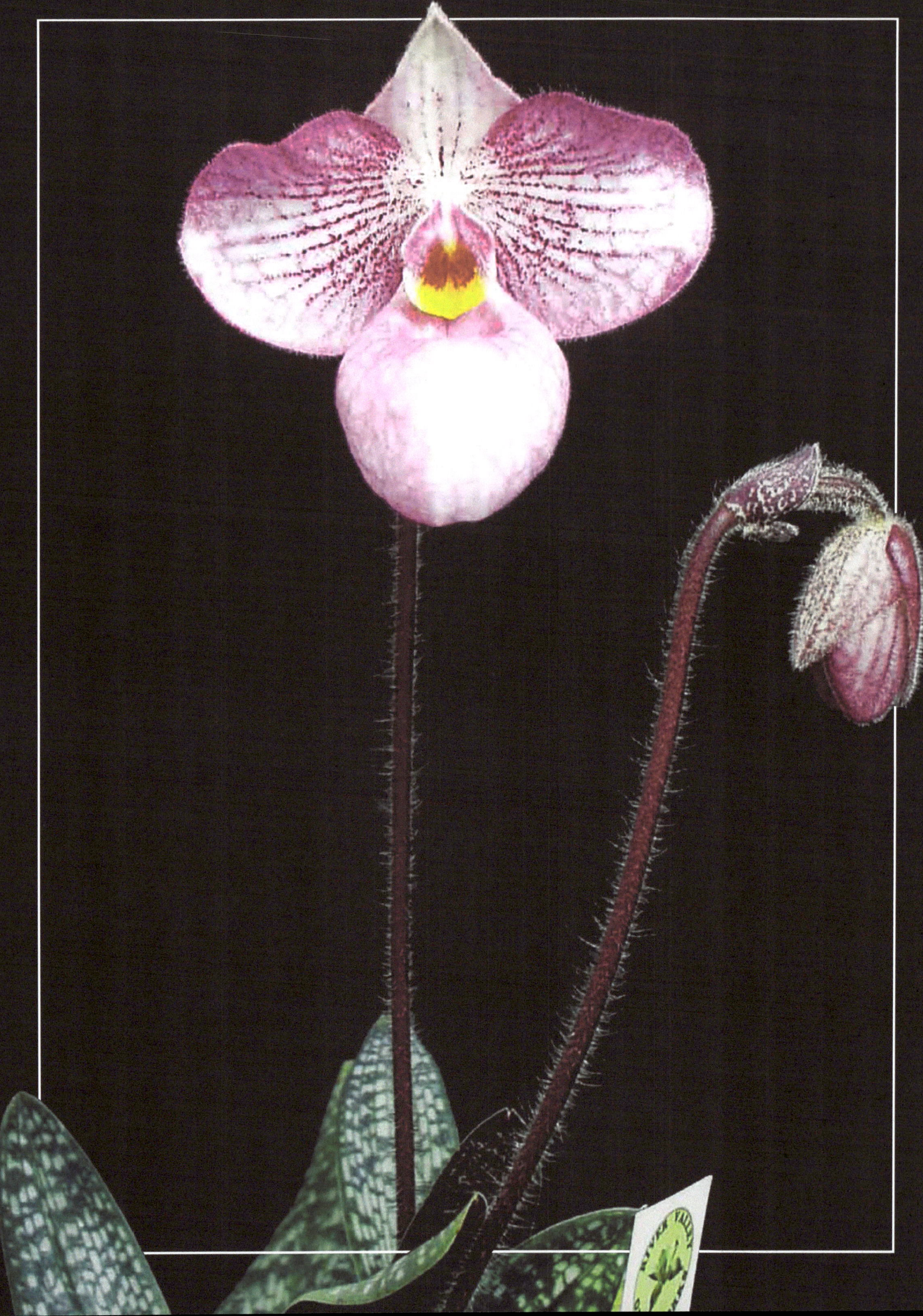

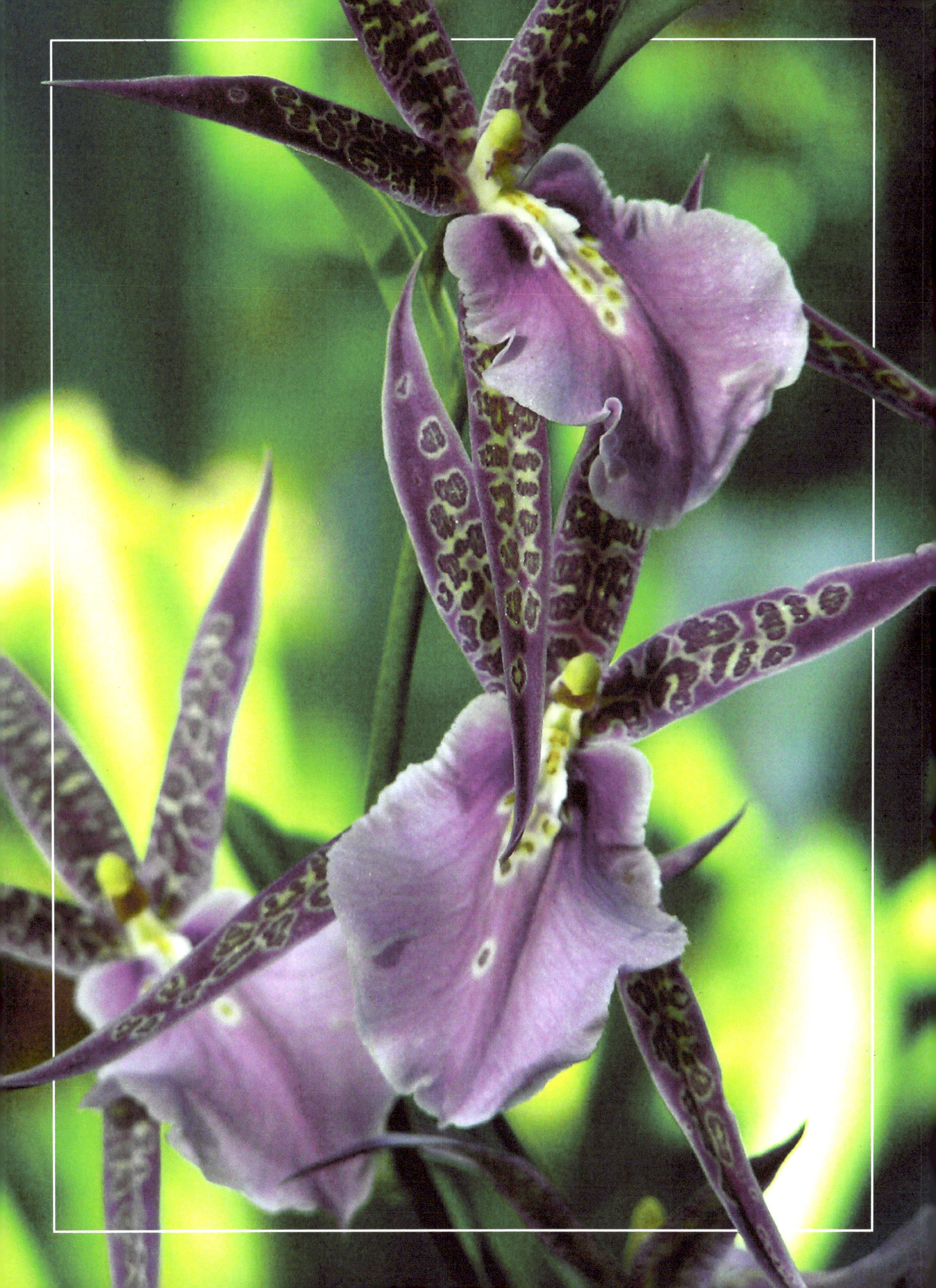

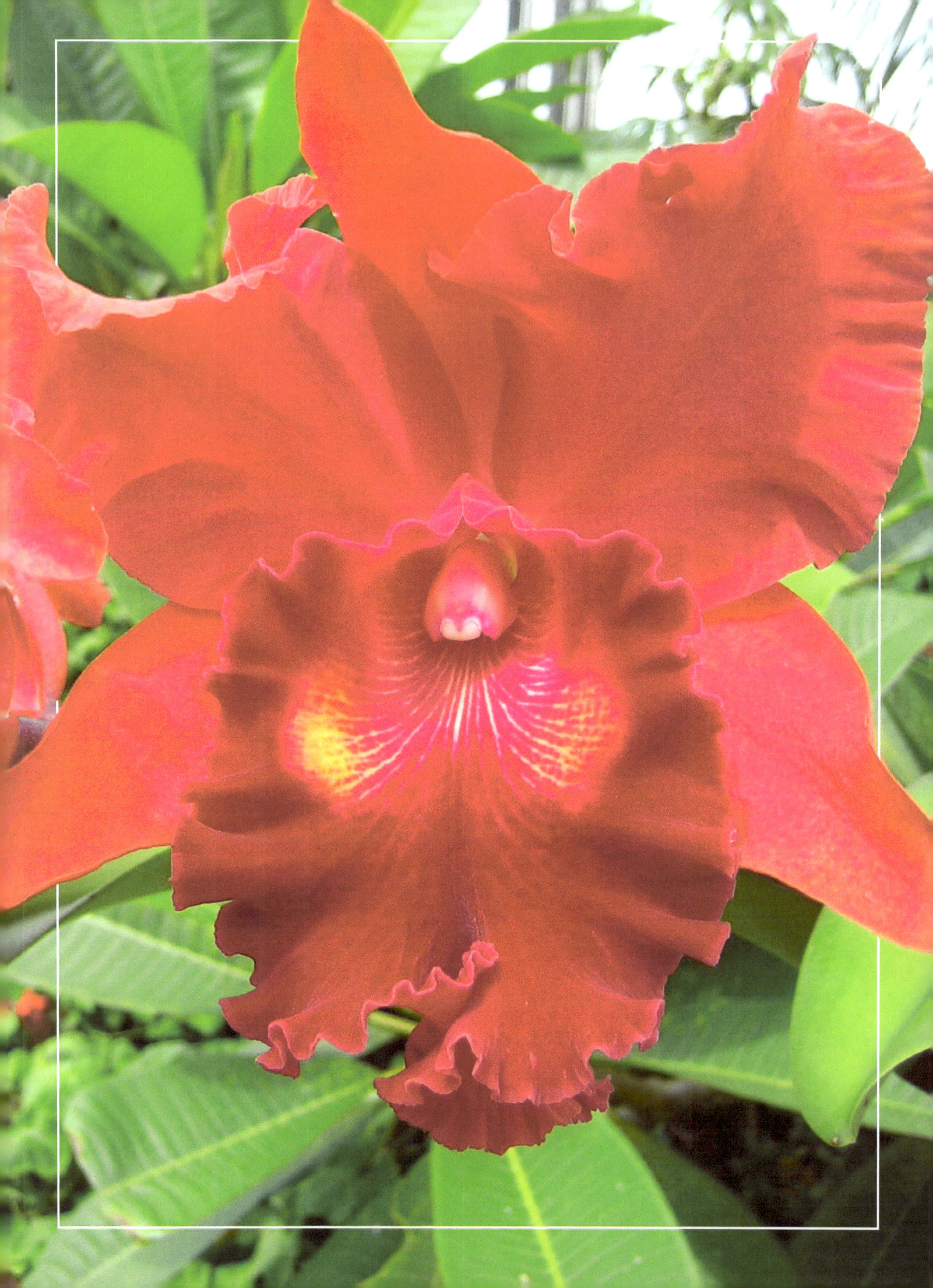

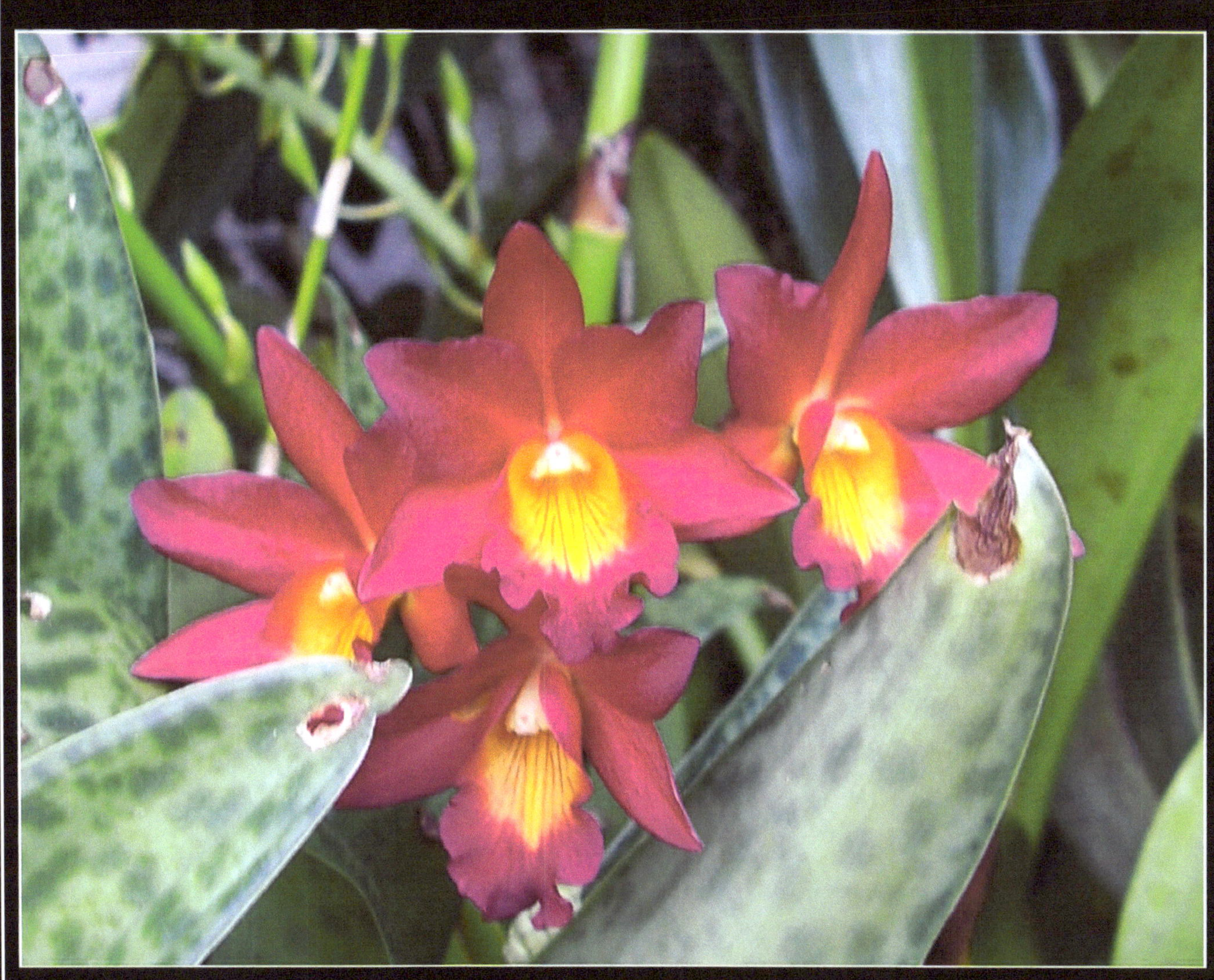

LEFT
Potinara San Damiano 'Halona'
(Pot. = Brassavola x Cattleya
x Laelia x Sophronitis)

ABOVE
Cattleytonia 'Why Not'
x Schomburgkia undulata

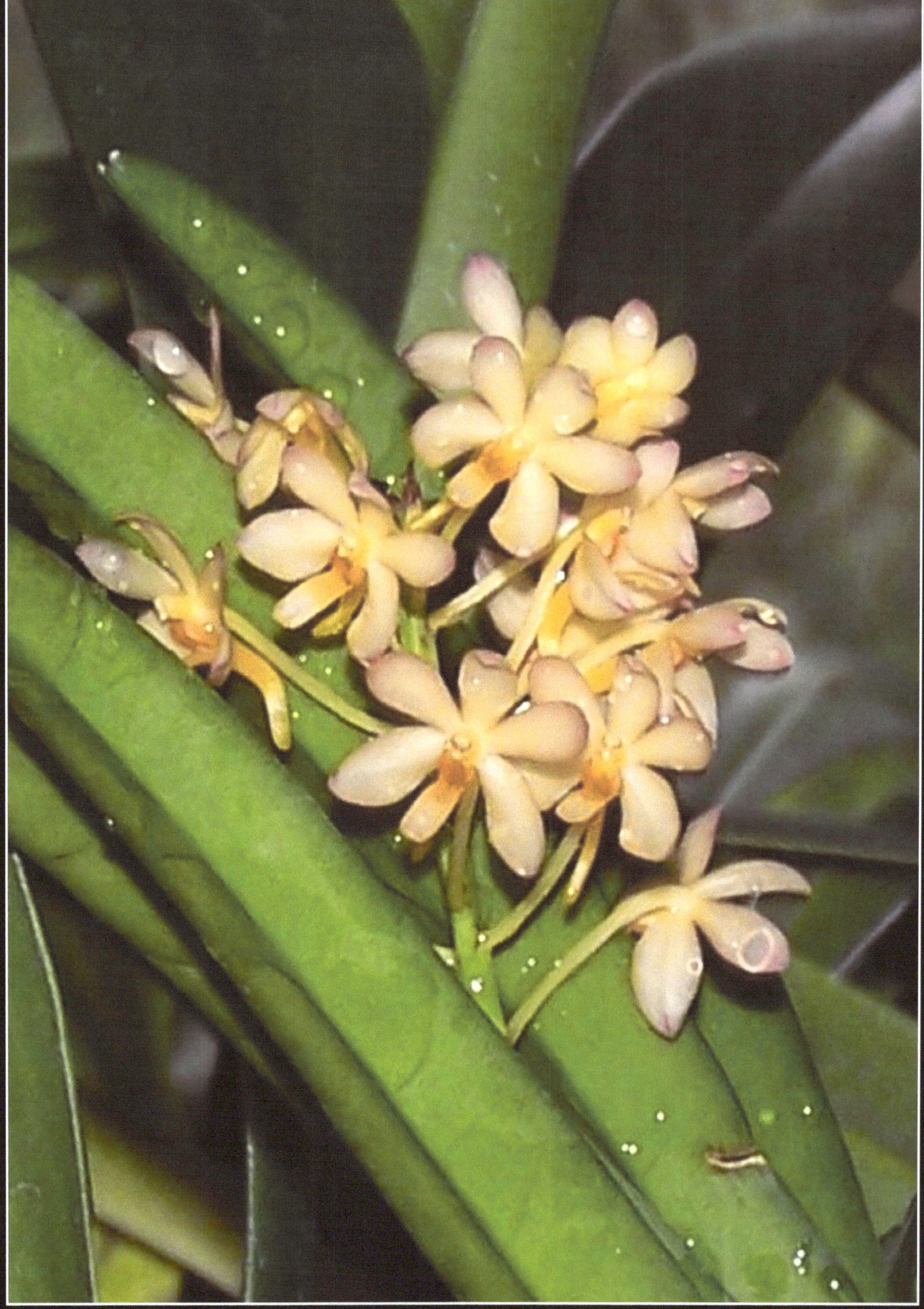

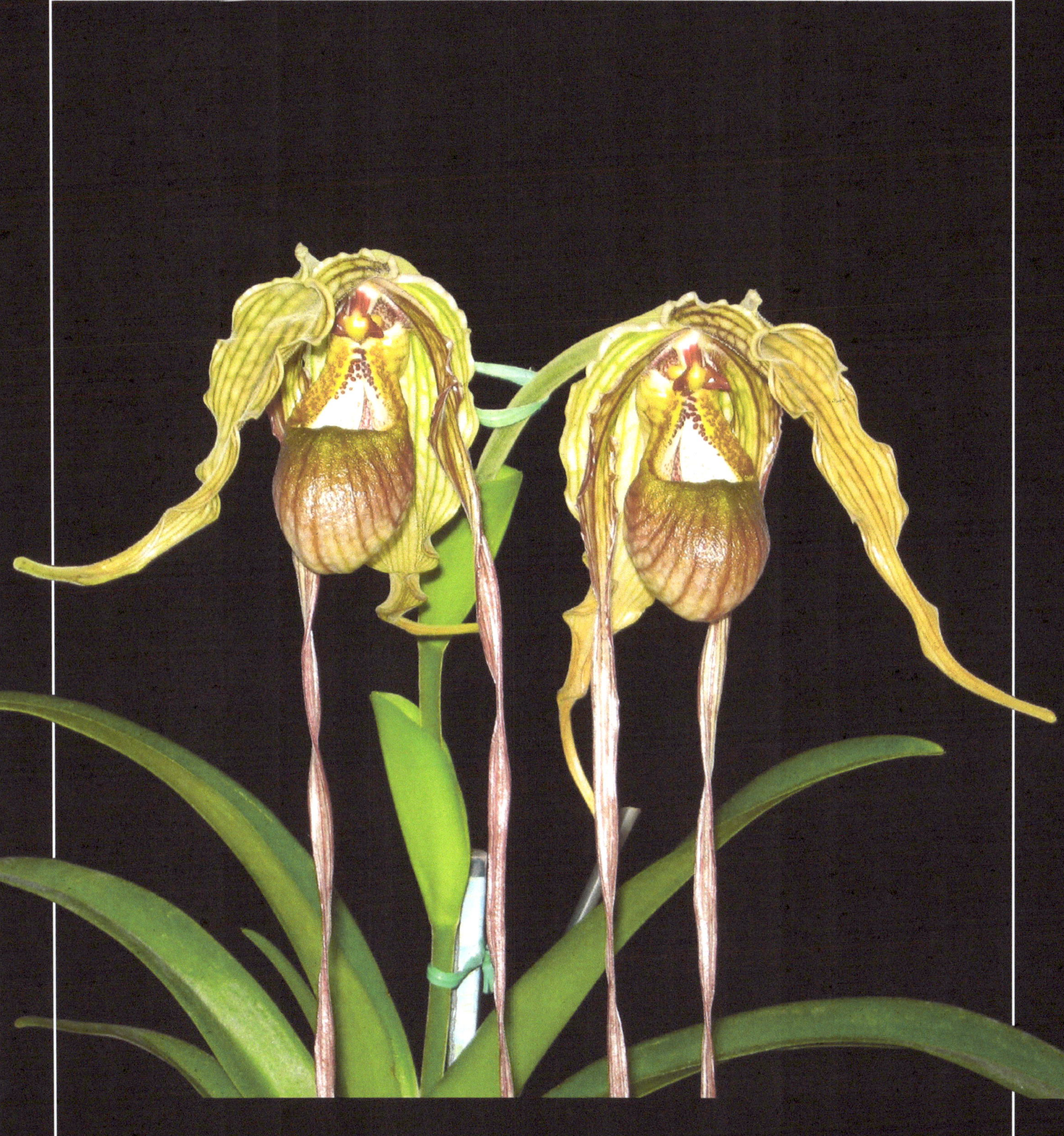

LEFT
Rumrillara Sugar Baby (Neostylis Lou Sneary x Ascocentrum miniatum)

ABOVE
Phragmipedium warscewiczianum

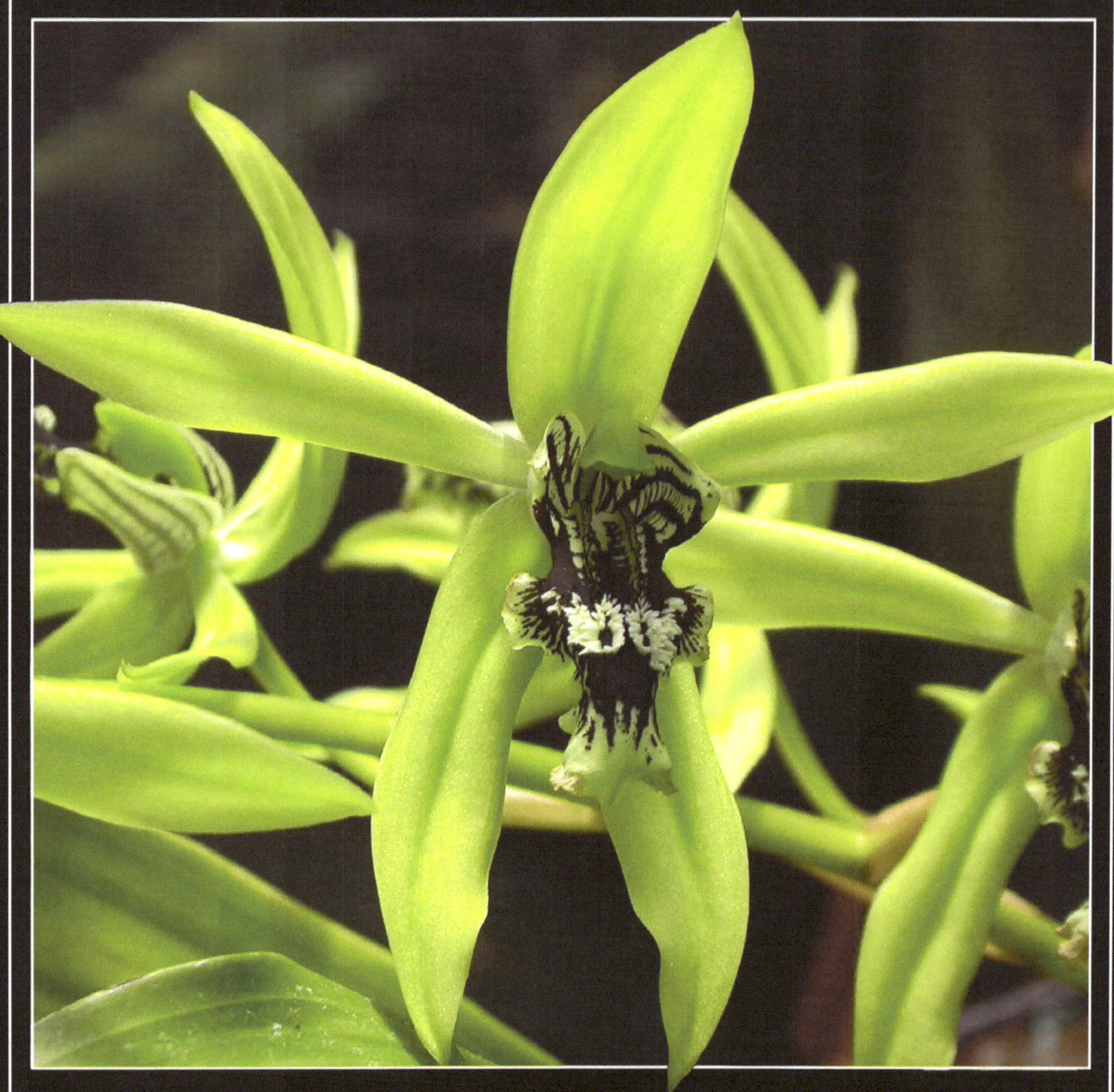

ABOVE
Coelogyne
South Carolina
(burfordiense X pandurata)

RIGHT
Encyclia radiata

OVERLEAF LEFT
Stanhopea wardii

OVERLEAF RIGHT
Laeliocattleya Iwanagara
Apple Blossom'Golden Elf'

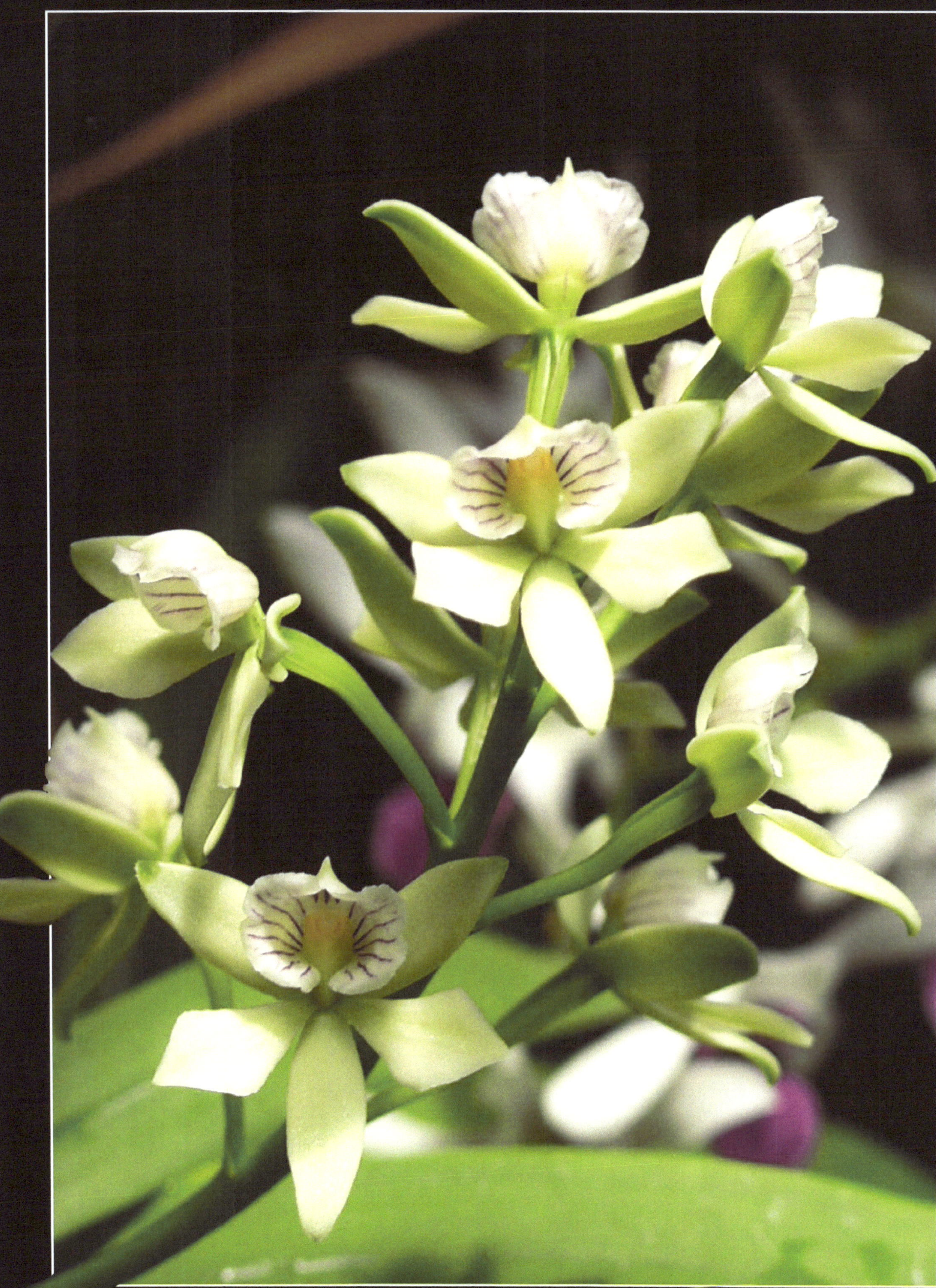

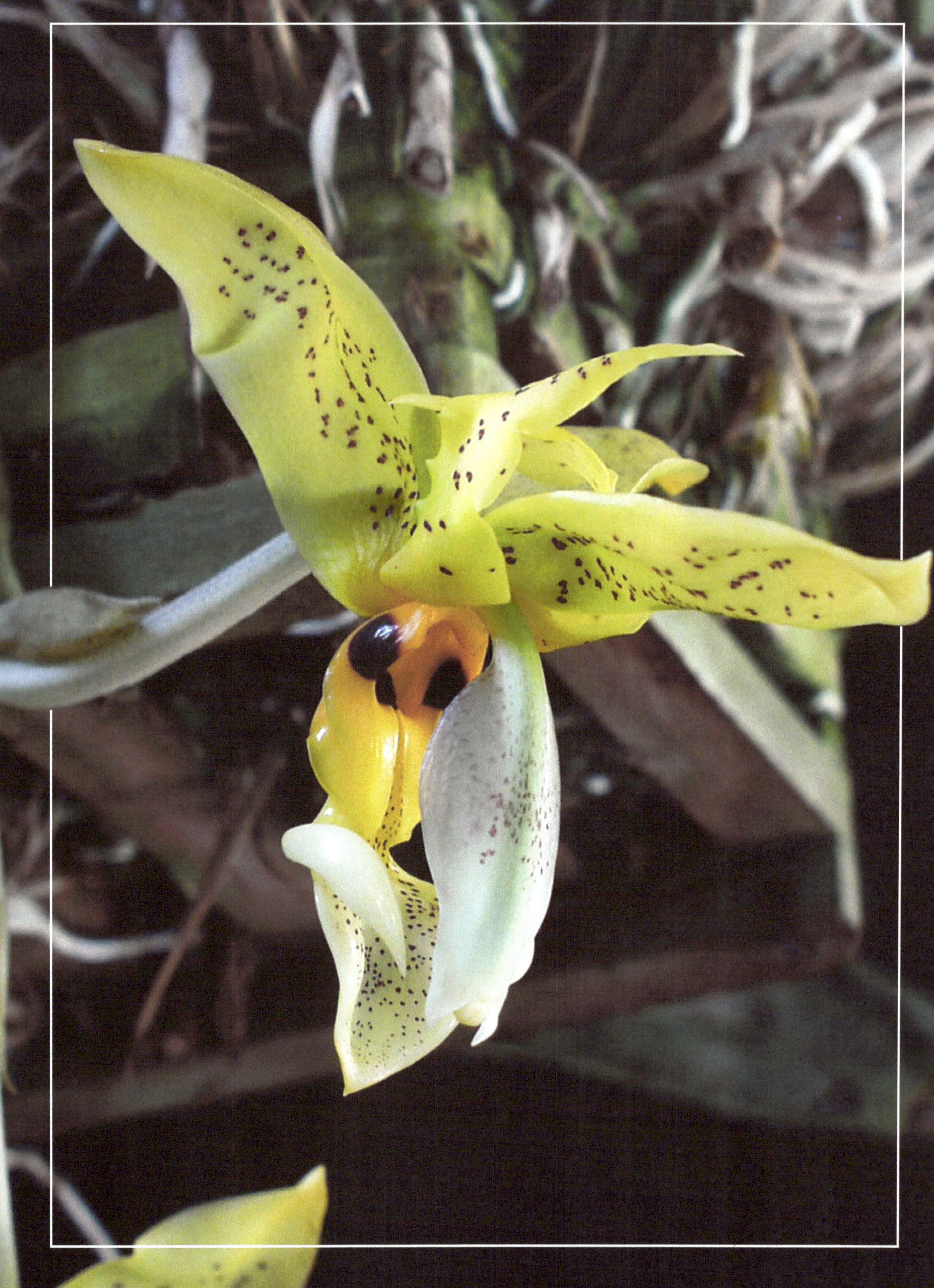

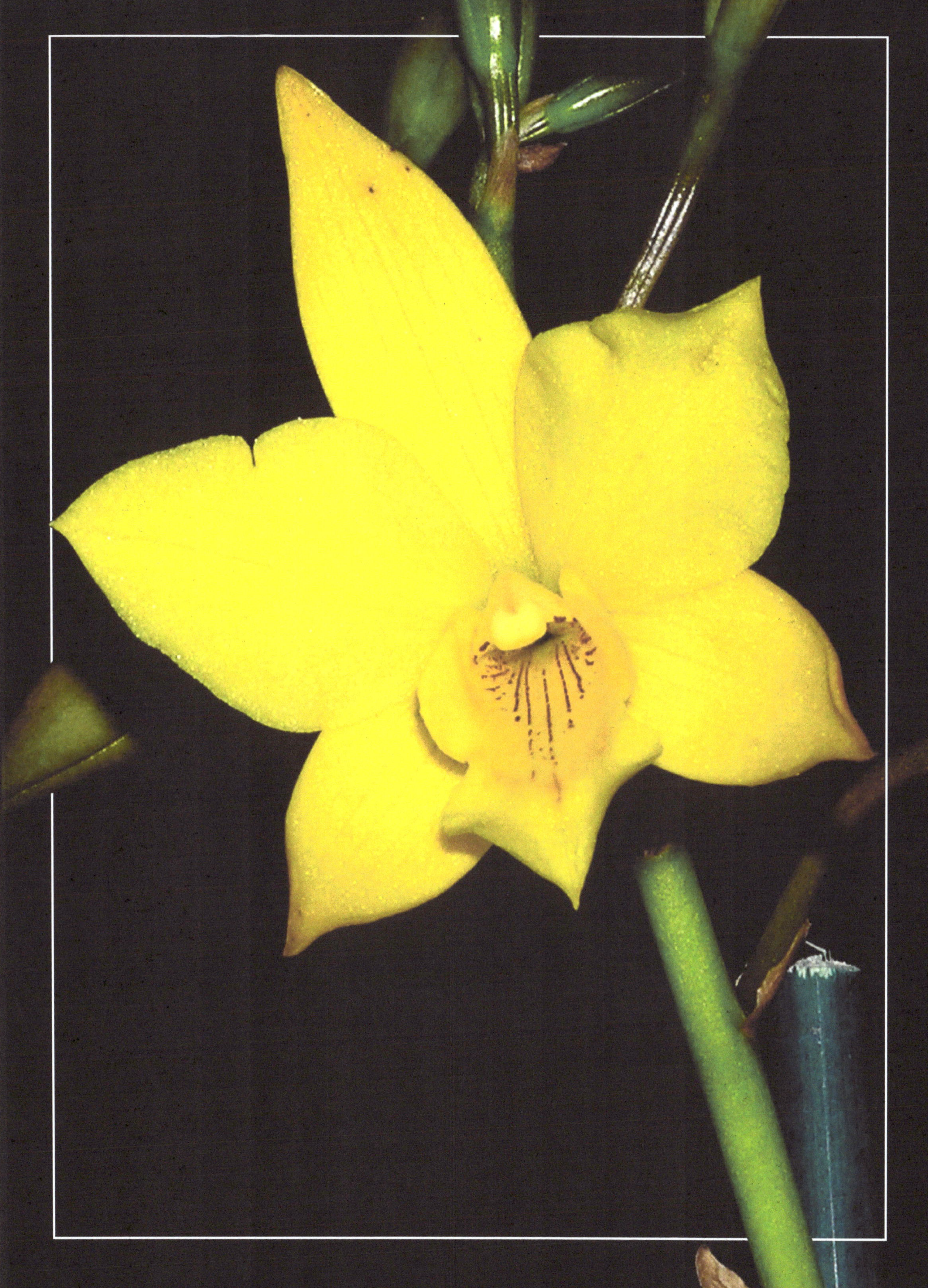

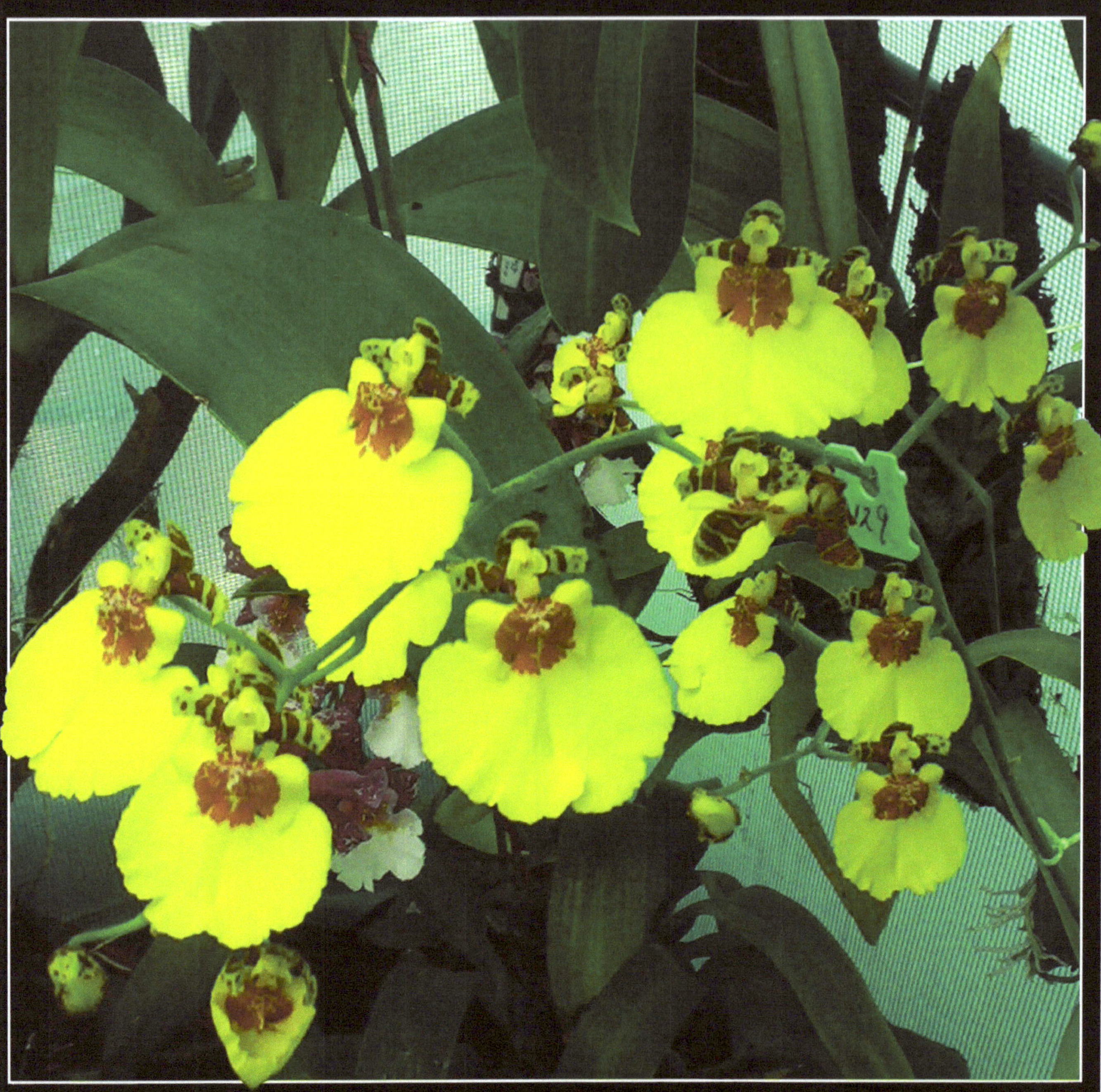

ABOVE
Oncidium varicosum
`Lemforde' AM/AOS

RIGHT
Rodricidium Just Dandy That's Grand
(Rcda. = Oncidium x Rodriguezia)

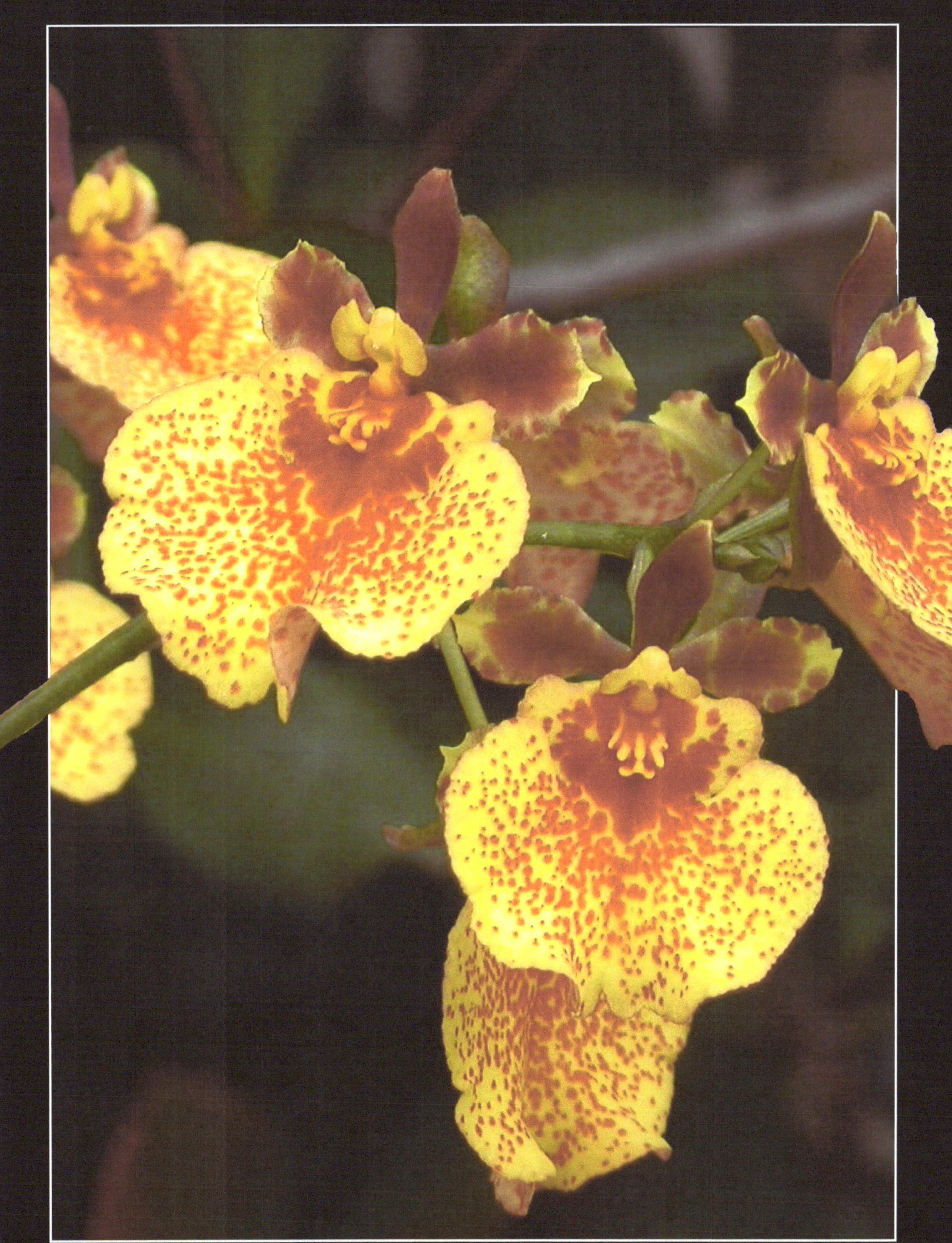

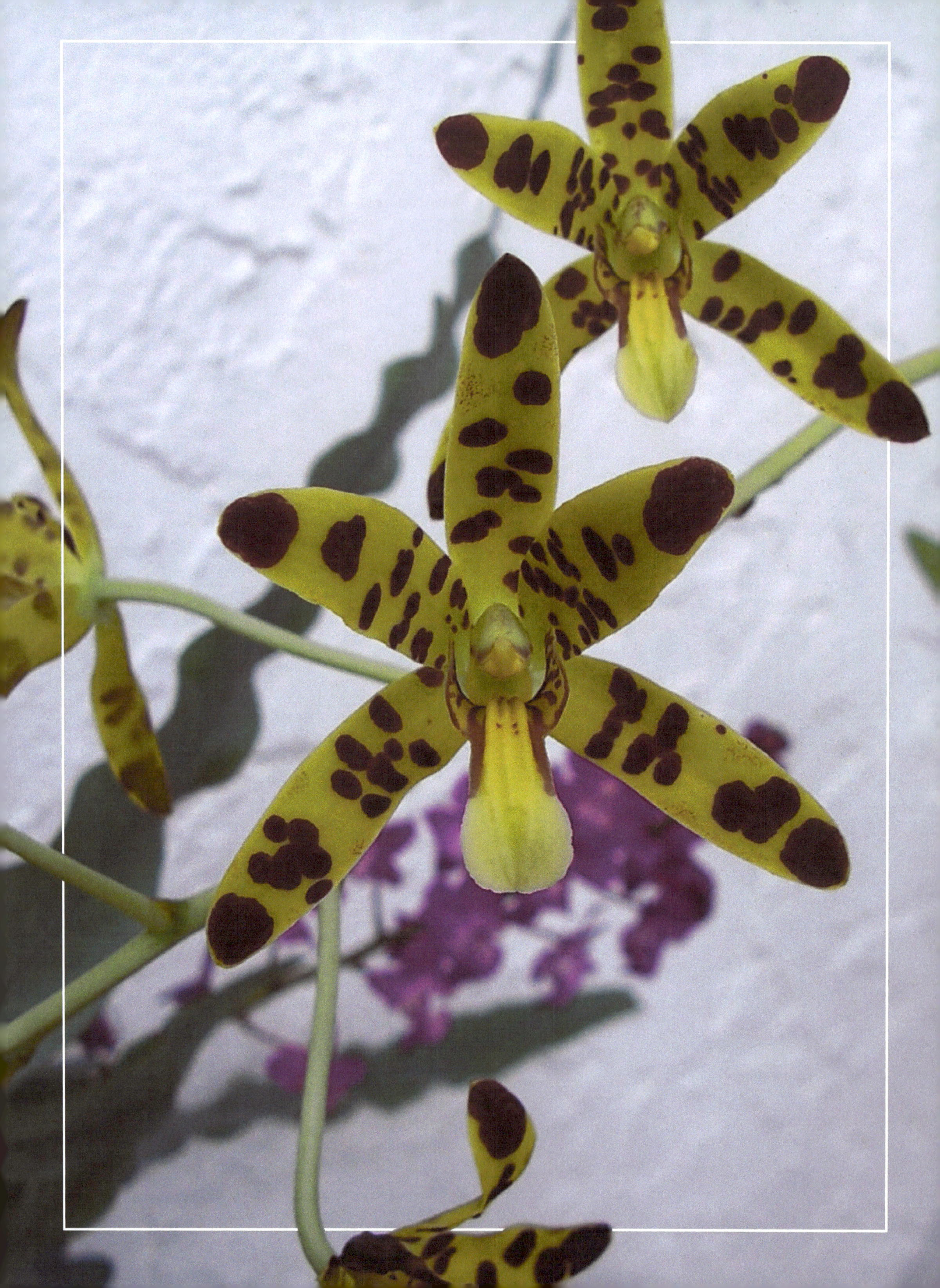

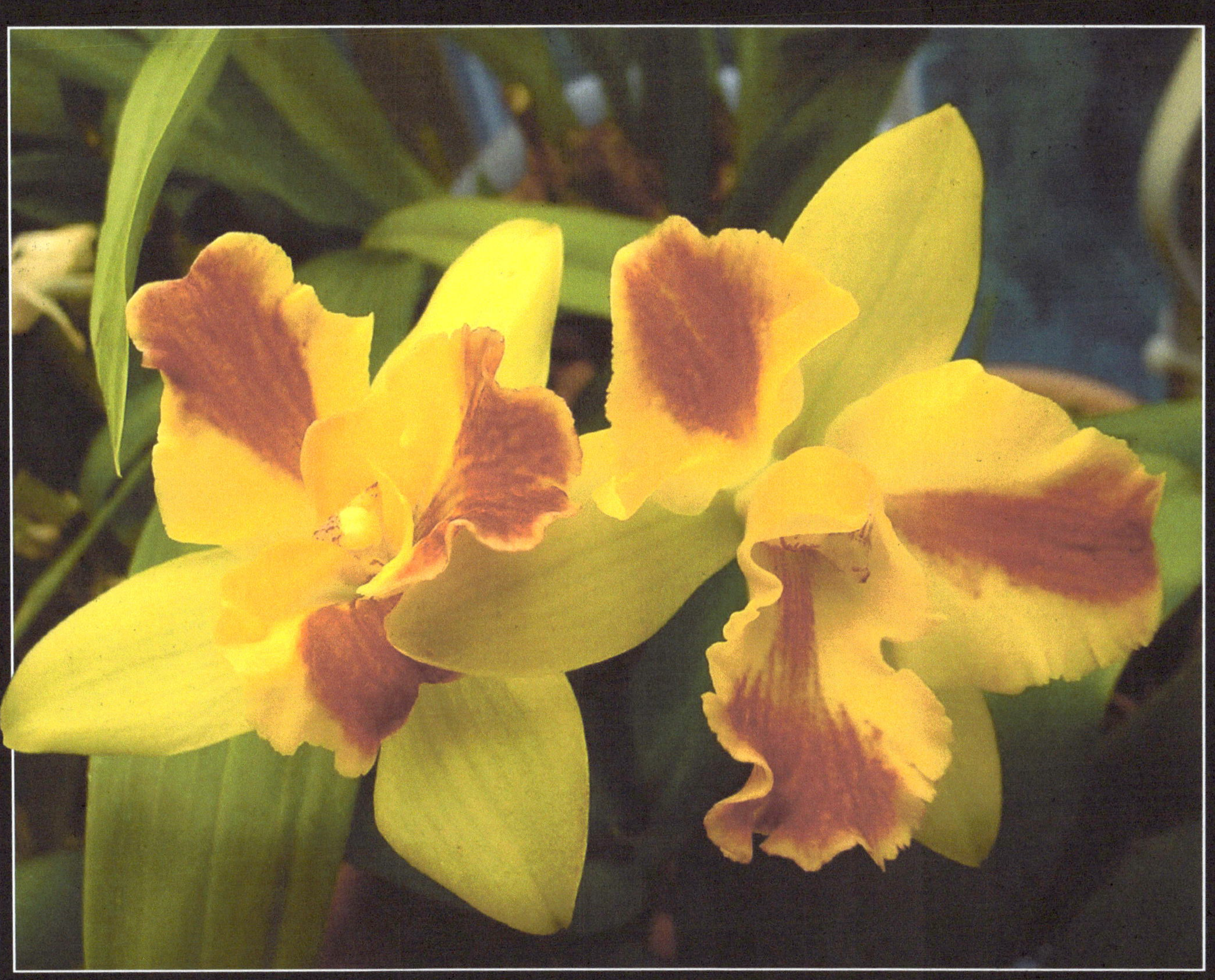

LEFT
Ansellia Gigantea Nilotica 'Wannakee' AM/AOS

Above
Potinara Burana Beauty 'Burana' AM/AOS

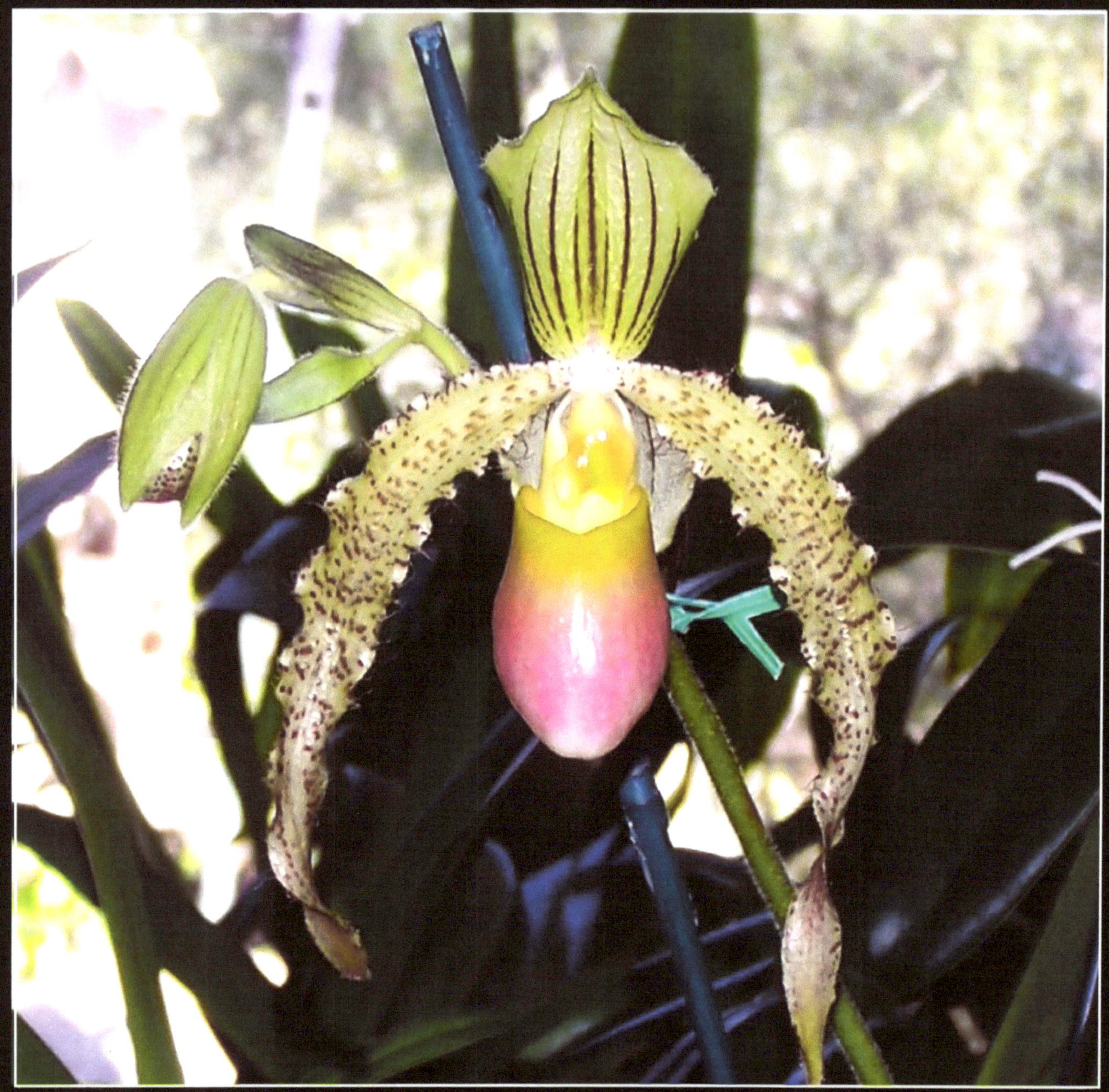

ABOVE
Paphiopedilum Oberhausen's Diament (primulinum x sanderianum)

RIGHT
Paphiopedilum Saint Swithin 'Kinglet' HCC/AOS (philippinense x rothschildianum)

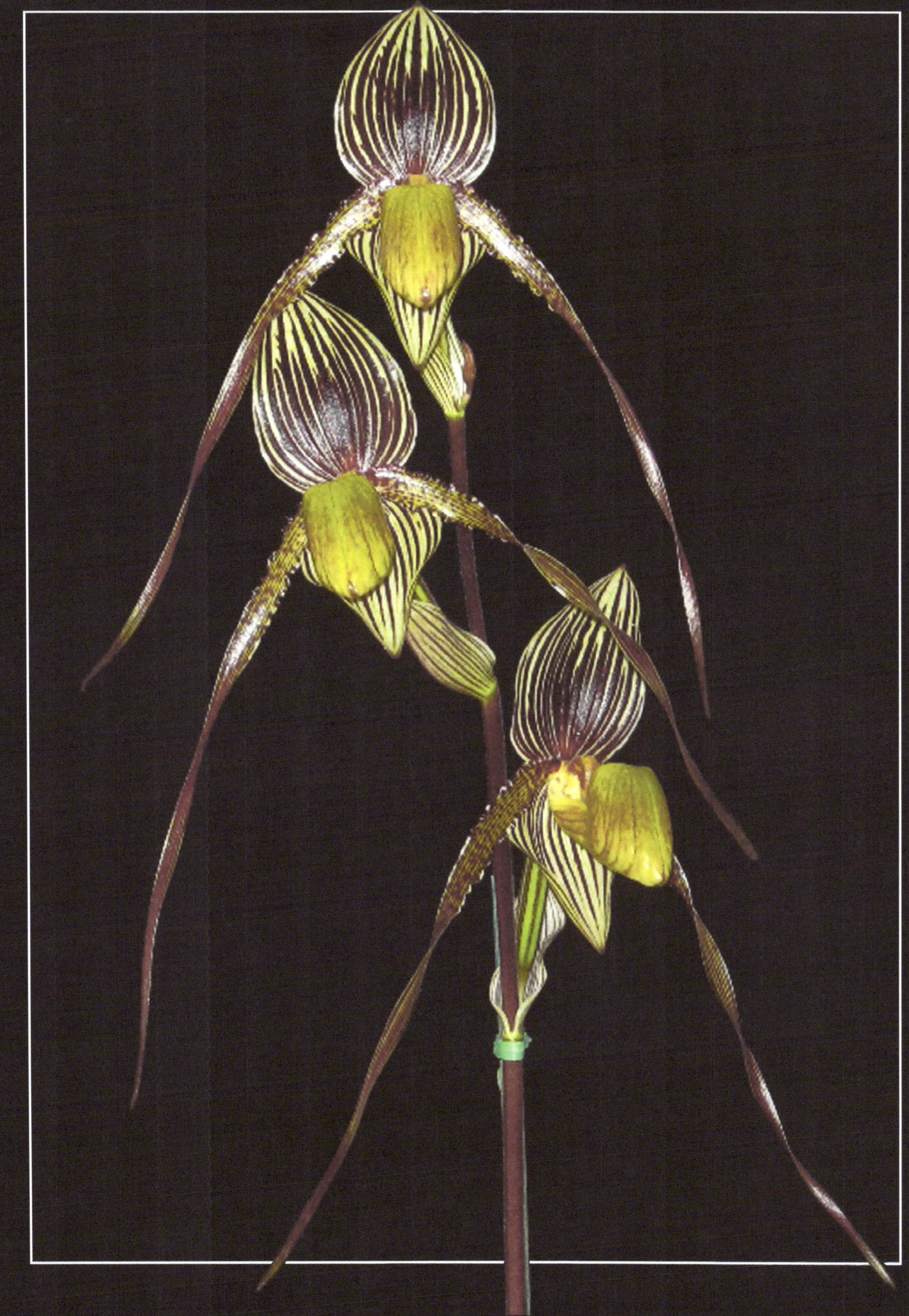

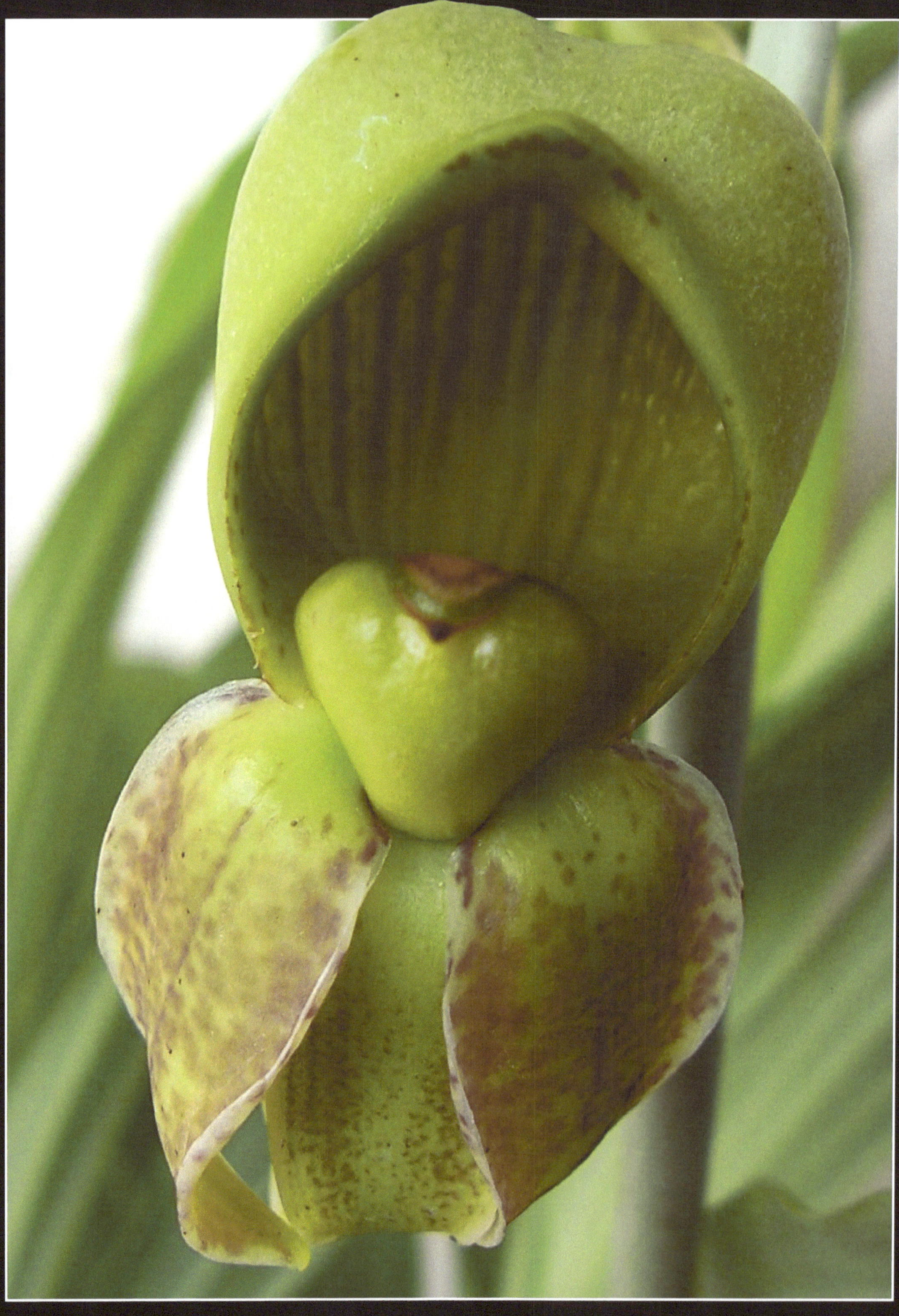

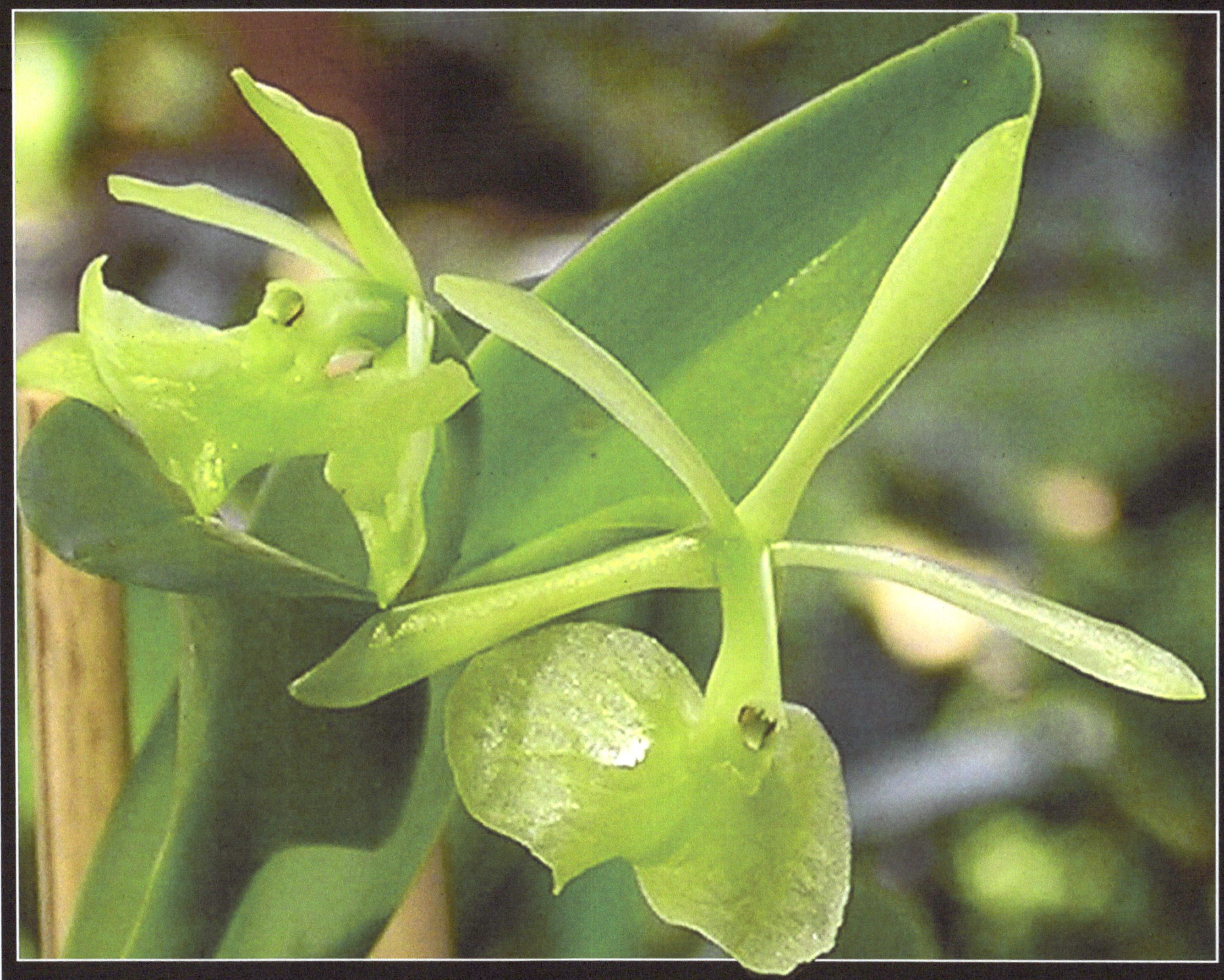

LEFT
Catasetum Callosum

ABOVE
Epidendrum difforme x sib

OVERLEAF LEFT
Phalaenopsis schilleriana

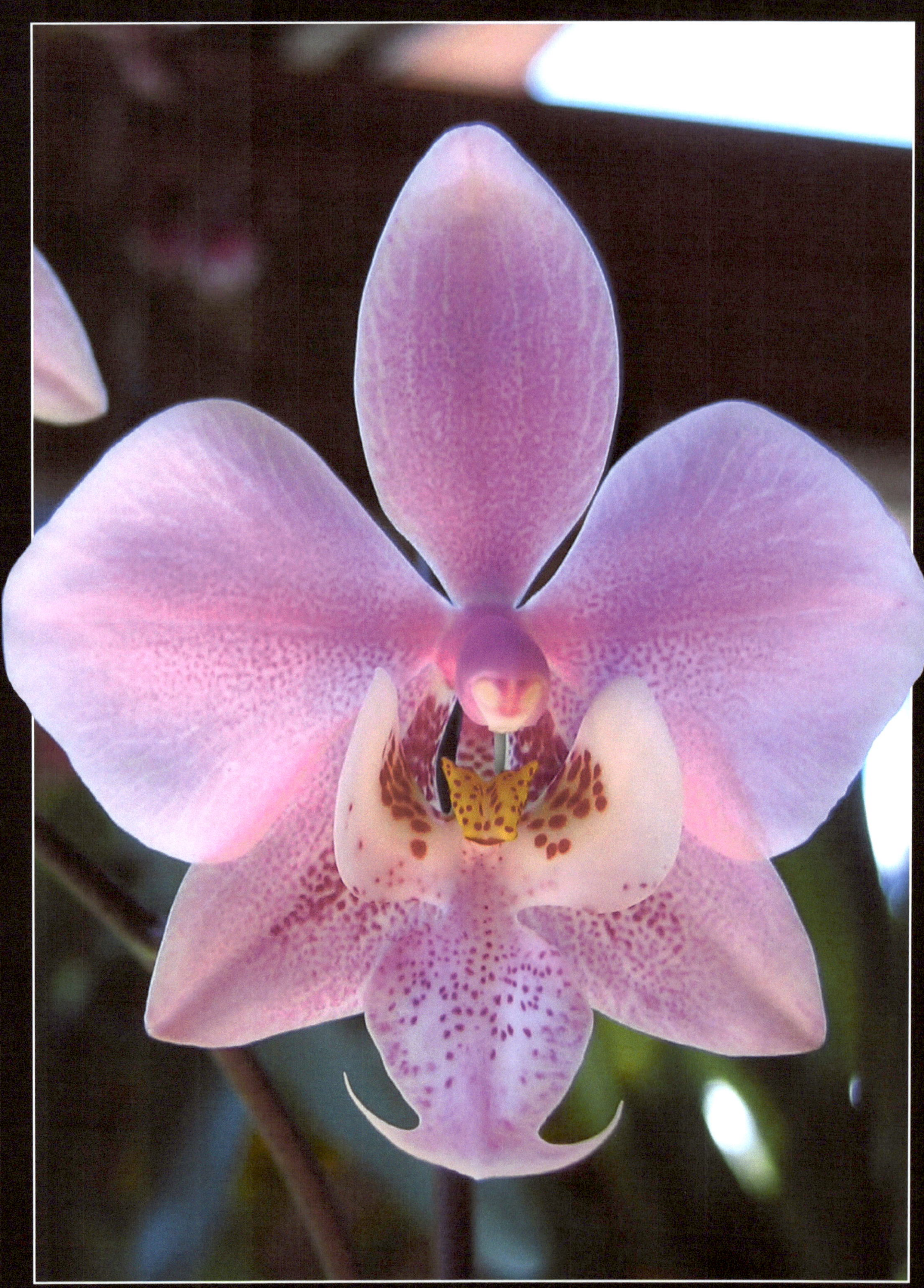

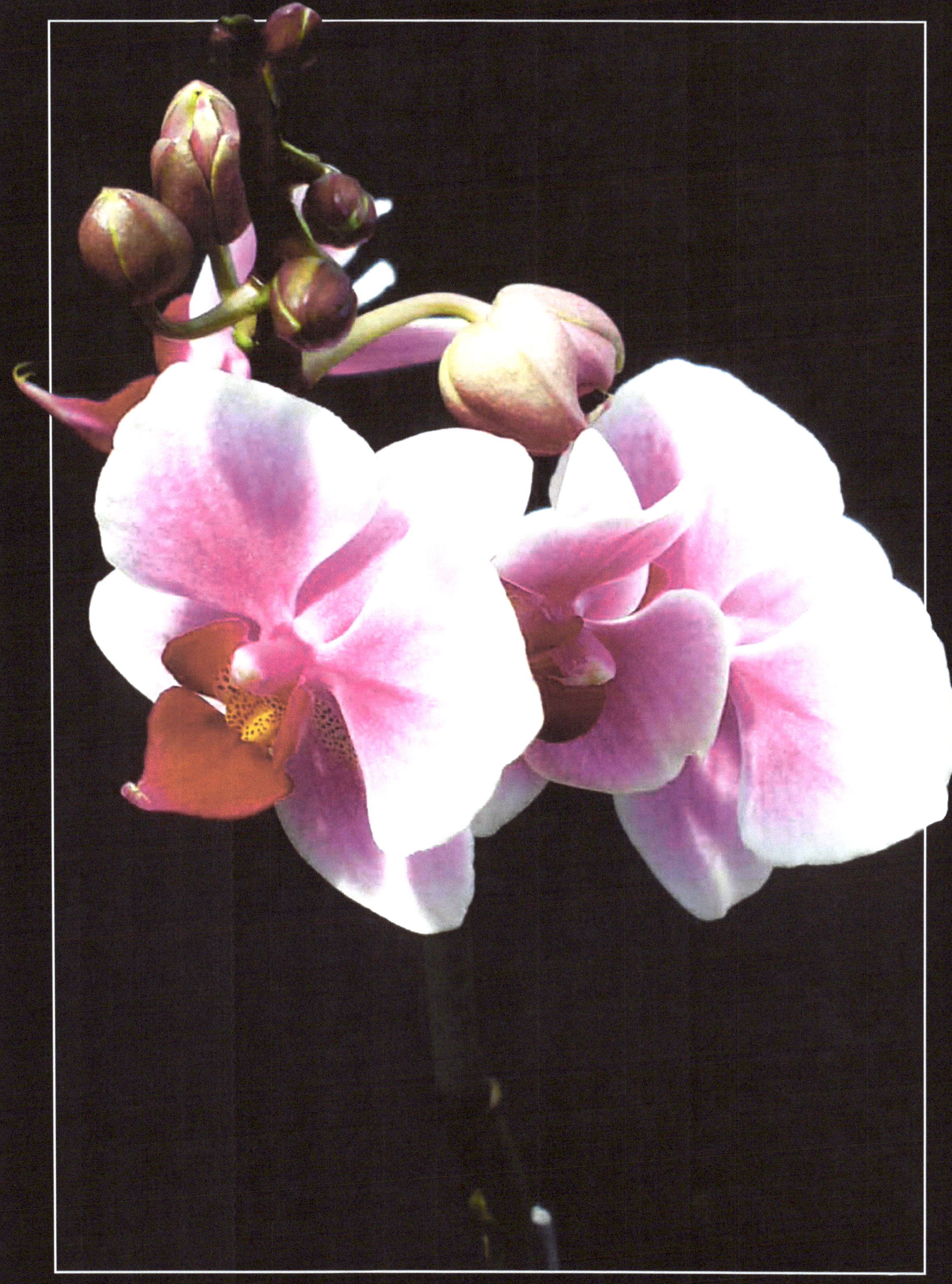

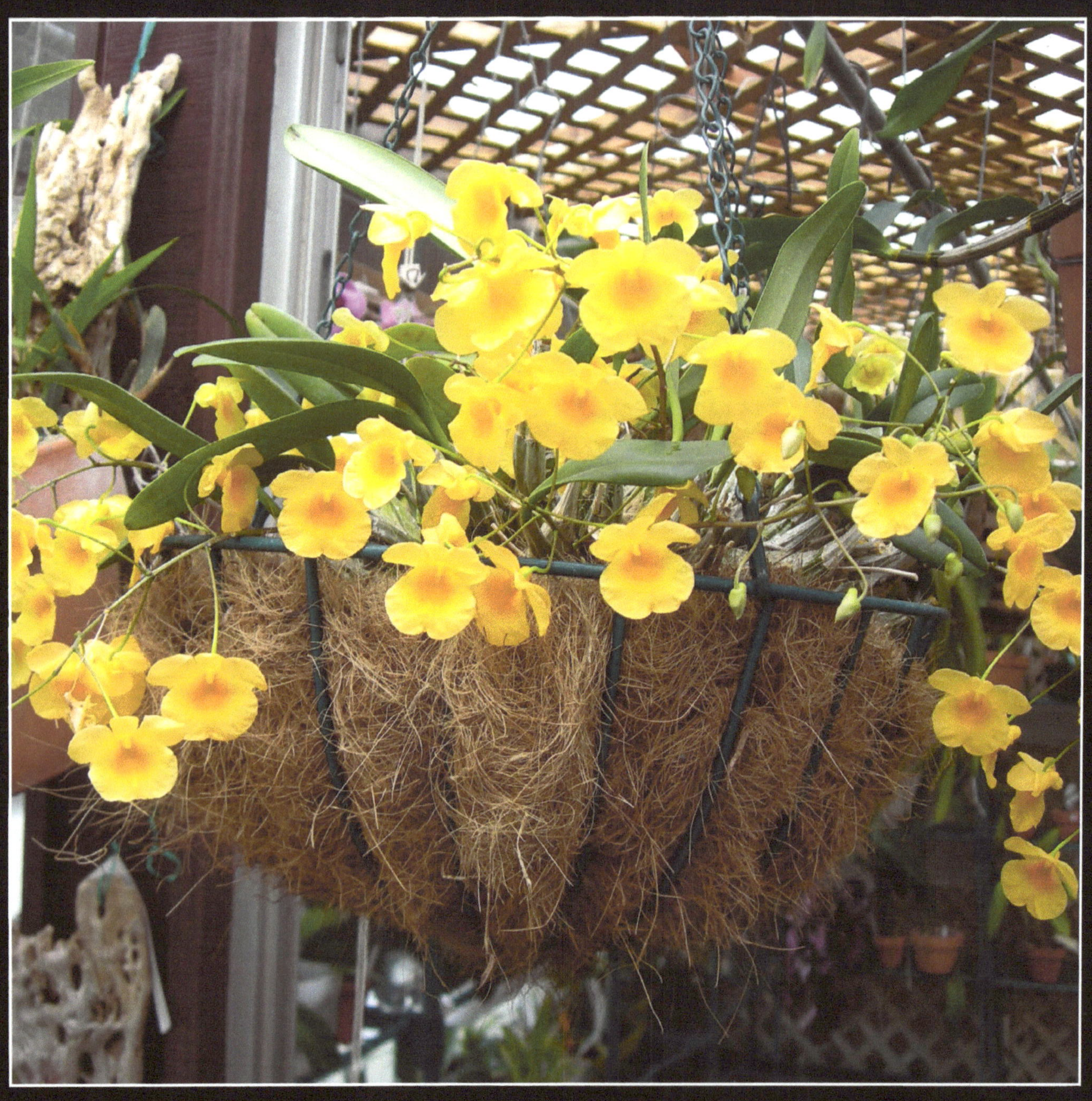

PREVIOUS OVERLEAF
Phalaenopsis Chimei Buddha X Phal. Salu Rose

ABOVE
Dendrobium lindleyi

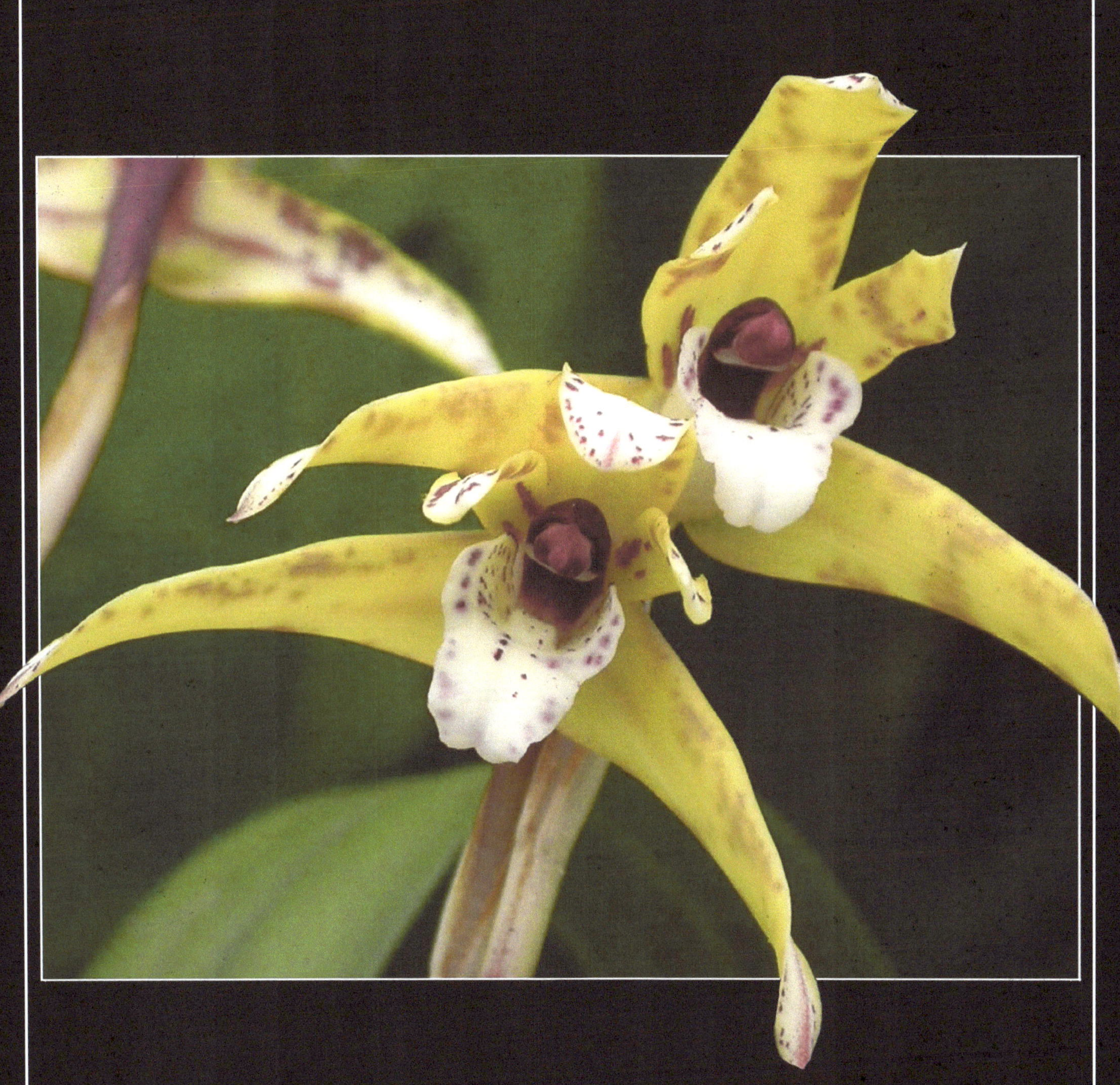

ABOVE
Maxillaria picta

OVERLEAF LEFT
Sophrocattleya Crystelle Smith (Cattleya loddigesii x Sc. Beaufort)

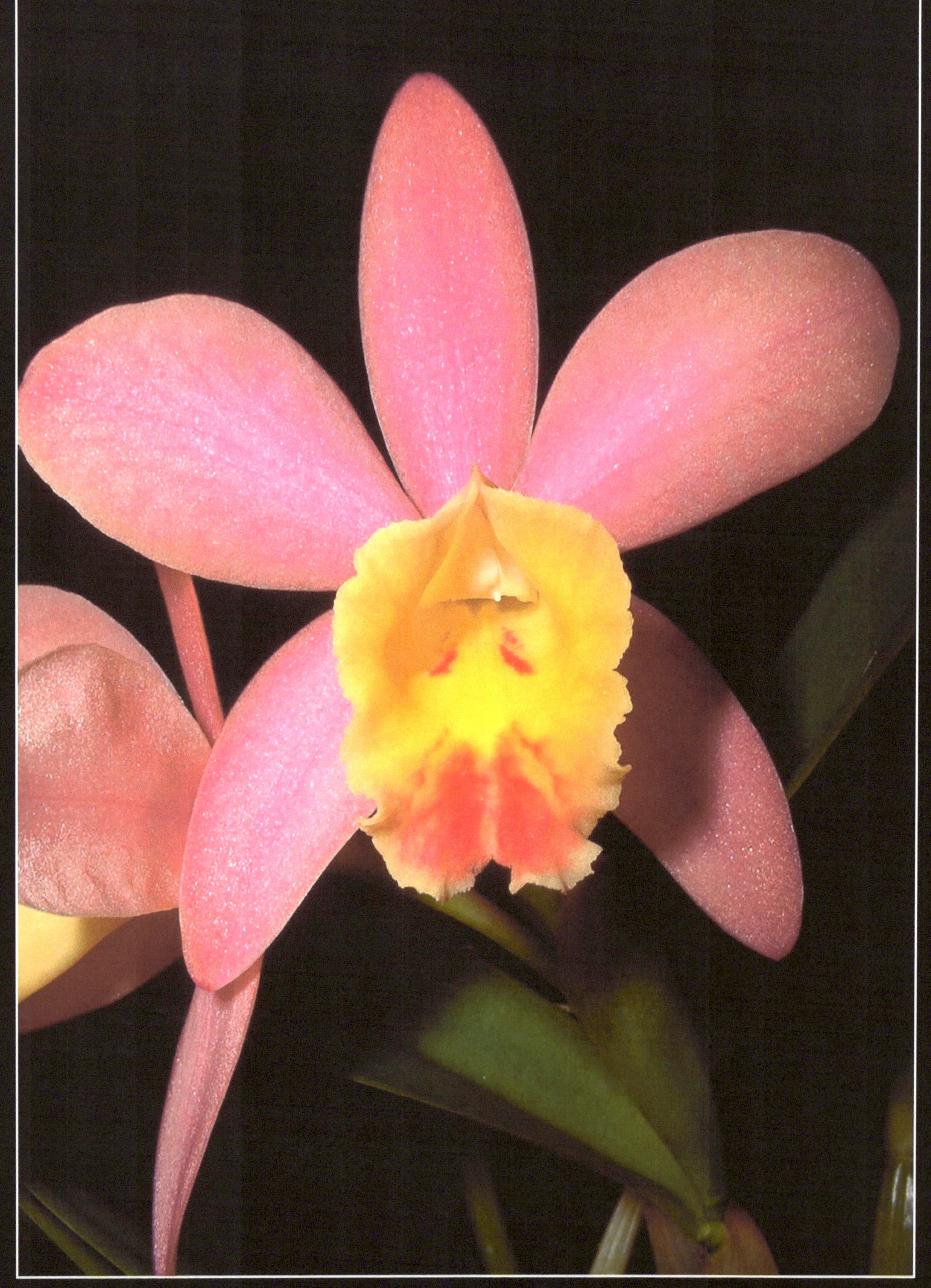

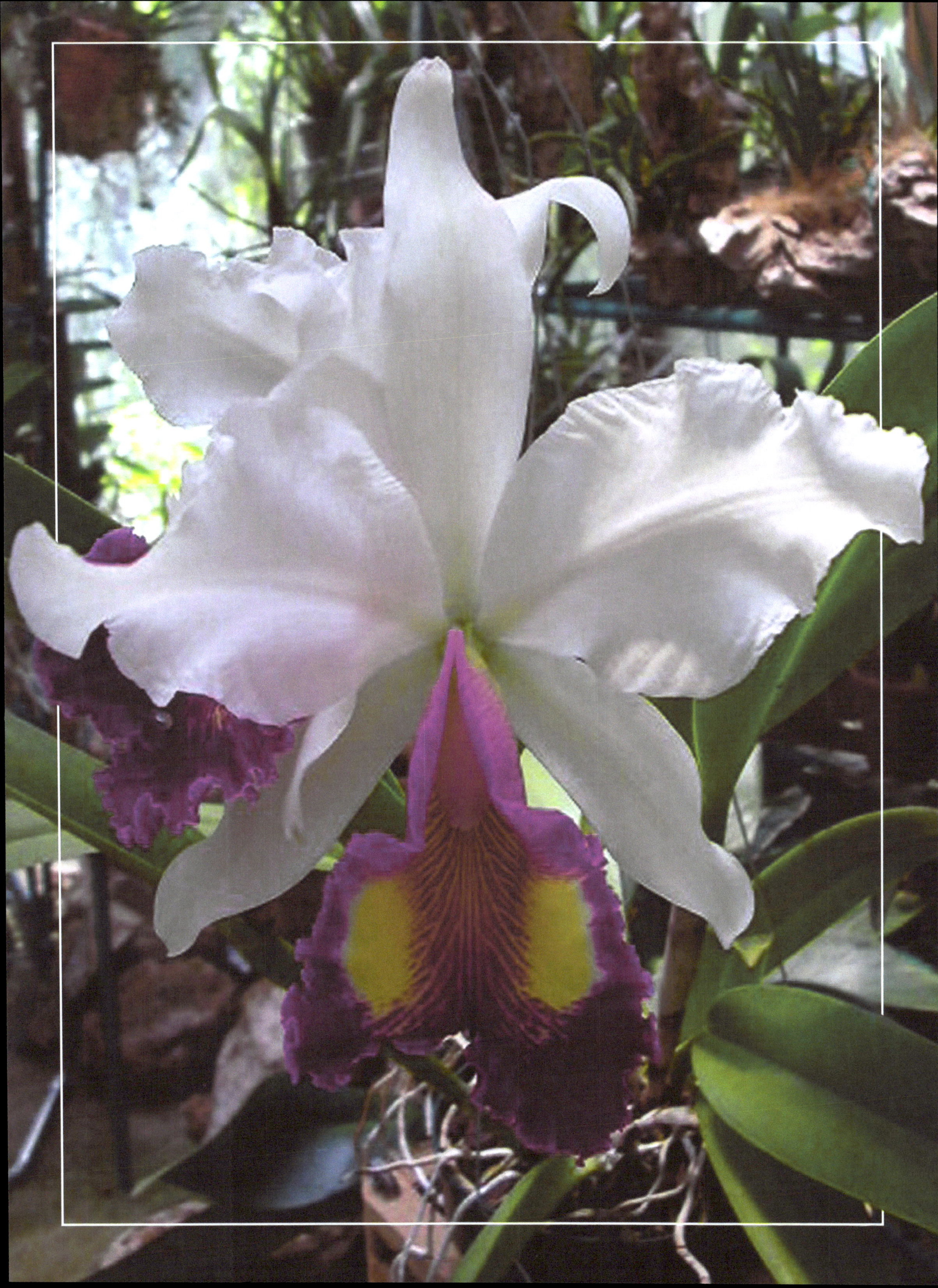

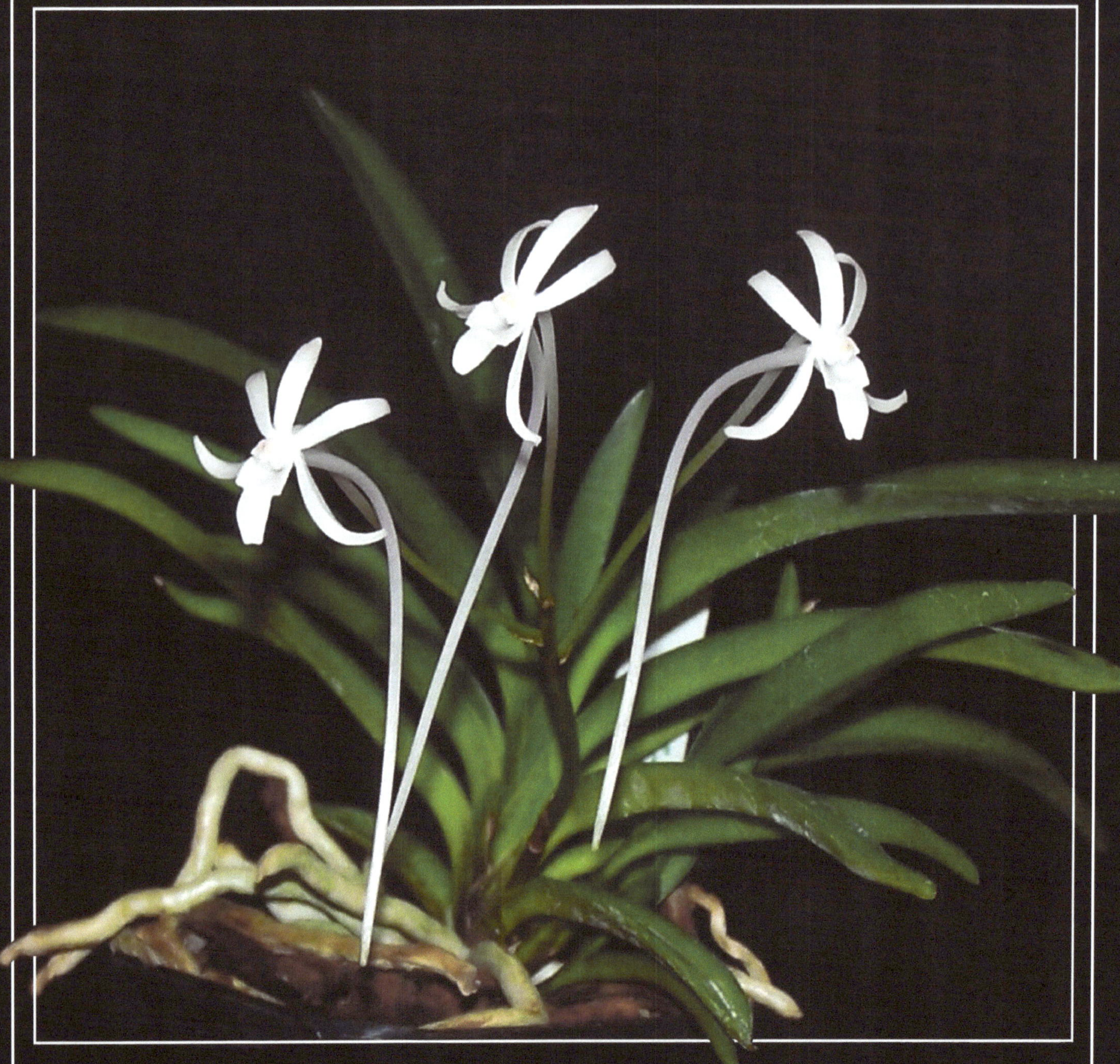

PREVIOUS OVERLEAF
Cattleya hardyana

ABOVE
Neofinetia falcata

RIGHT
Phragmipedium caricinum

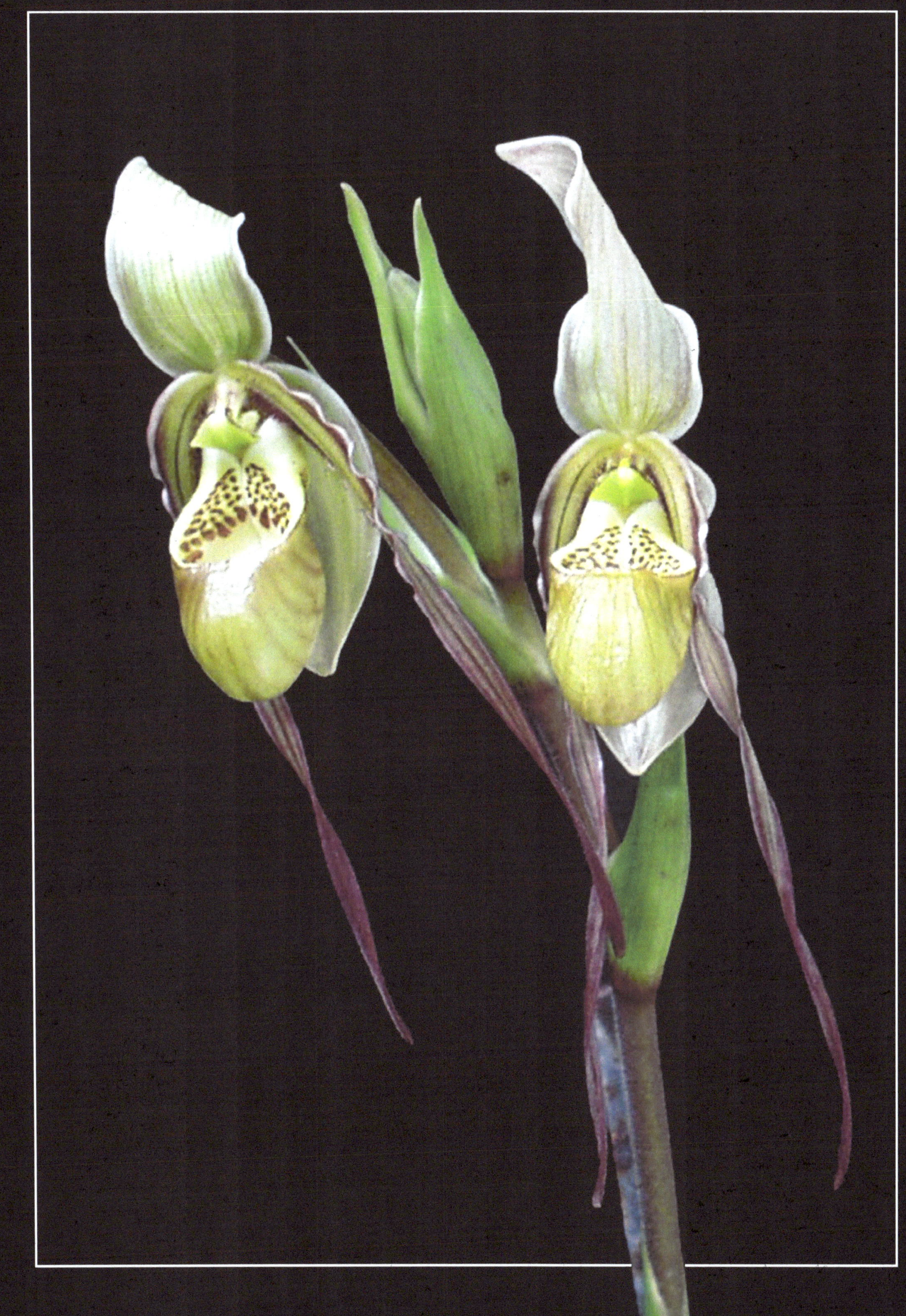

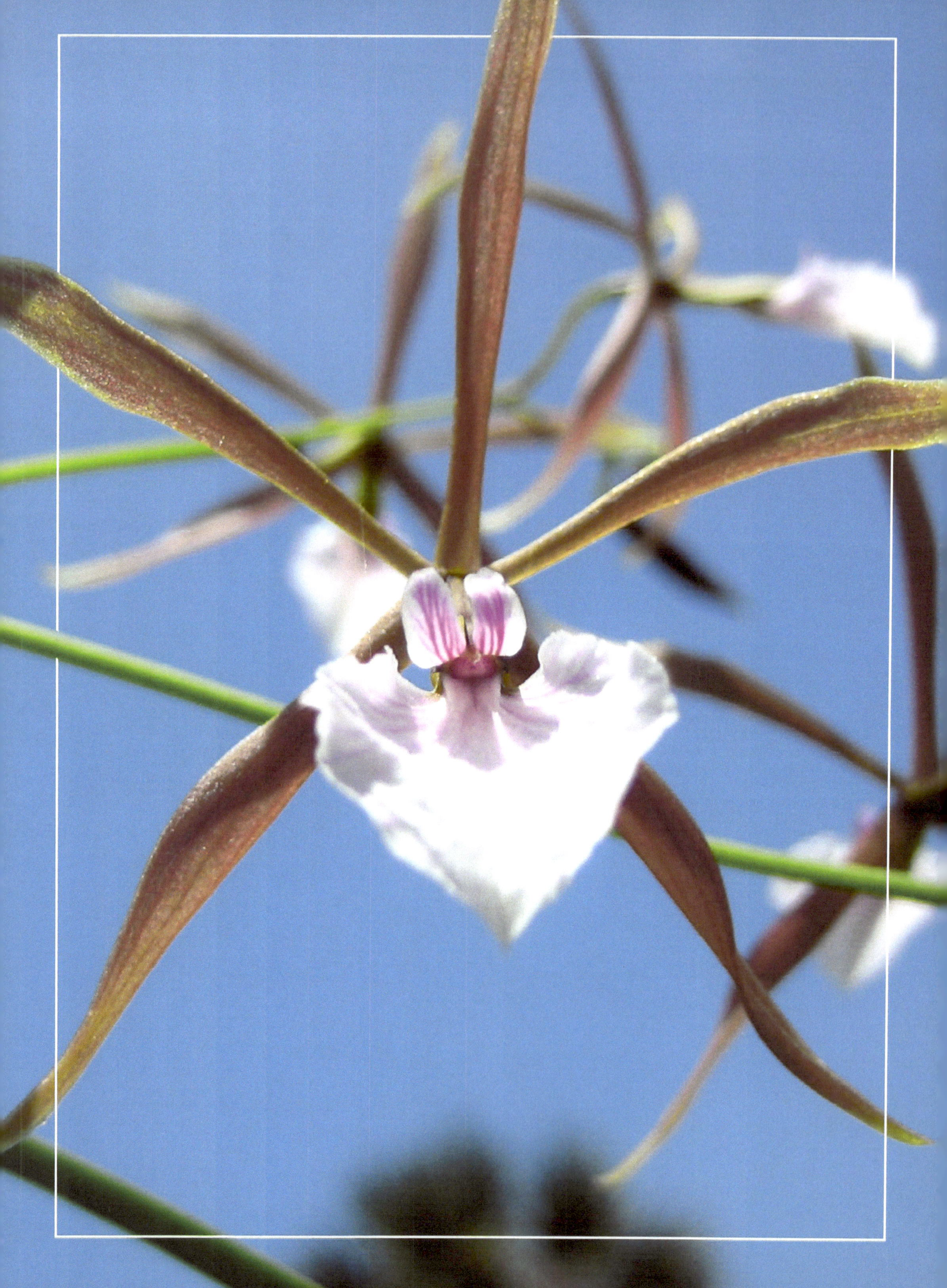

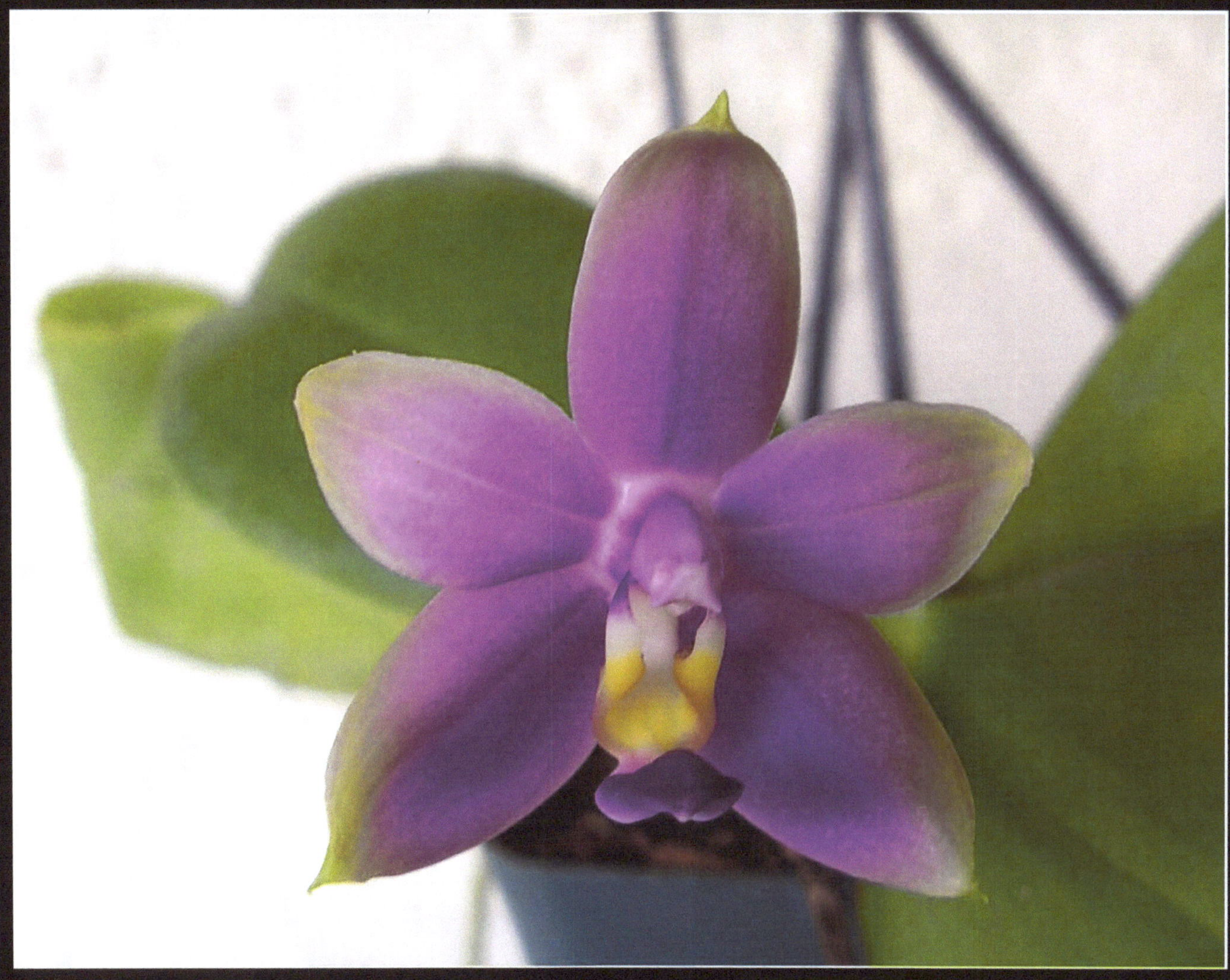

LEFT
Encyclia bractenses

ABOVE
Phalaenopsis violacea 'Krull's Navy Blue' AM/AOS

OVERLEAF LEFT
Masdevallia veitchiana 'Fairview'

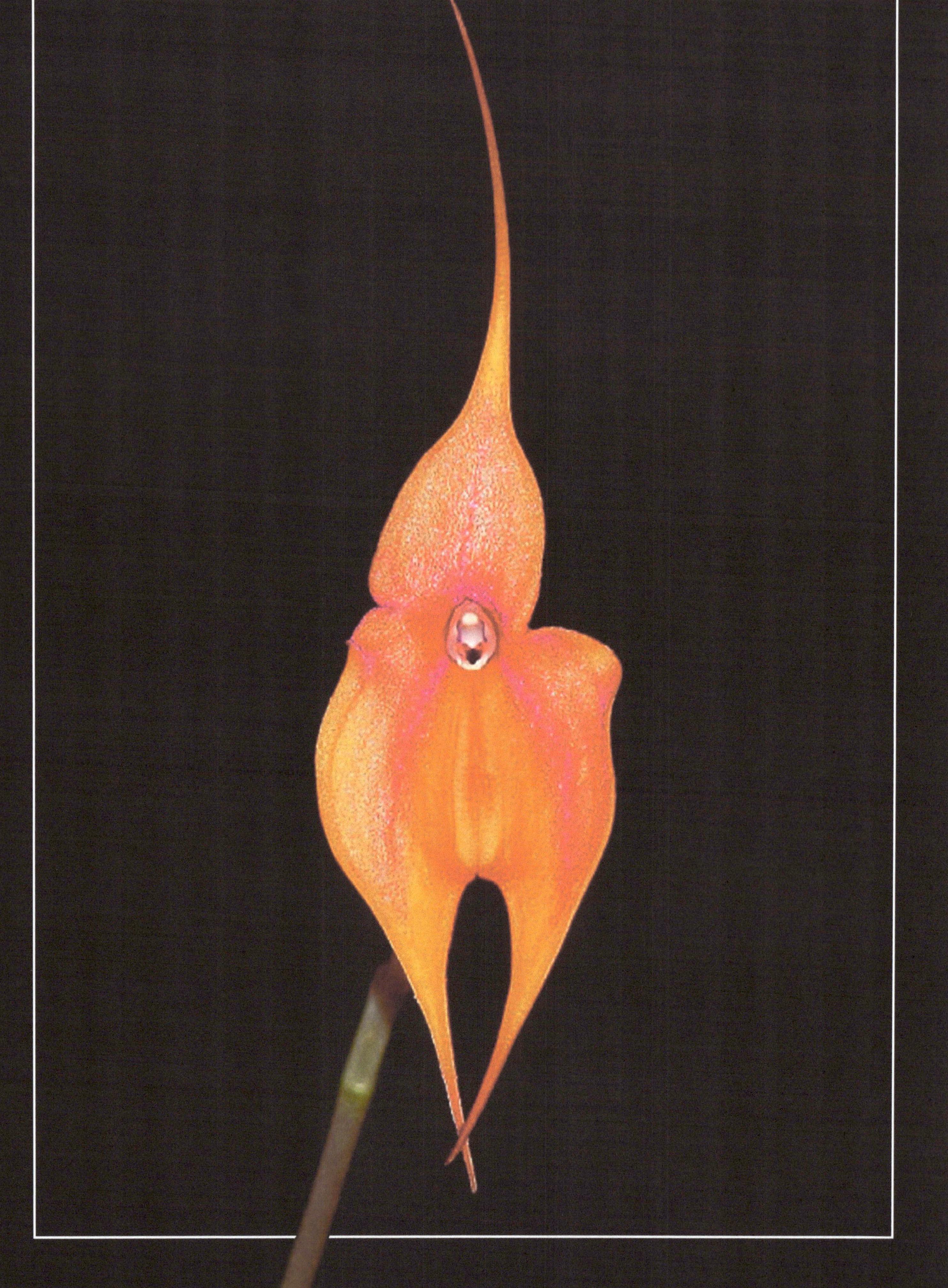

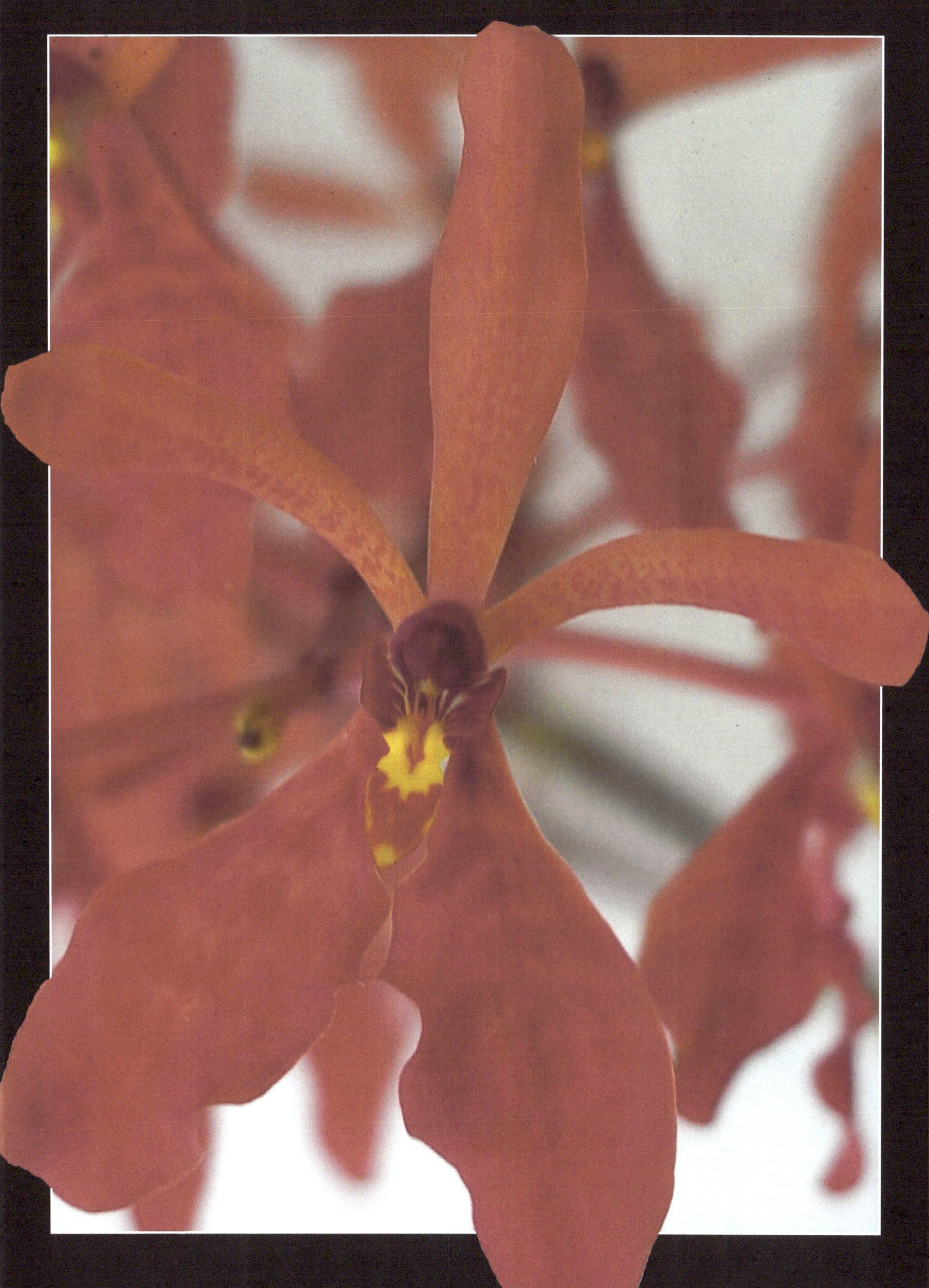

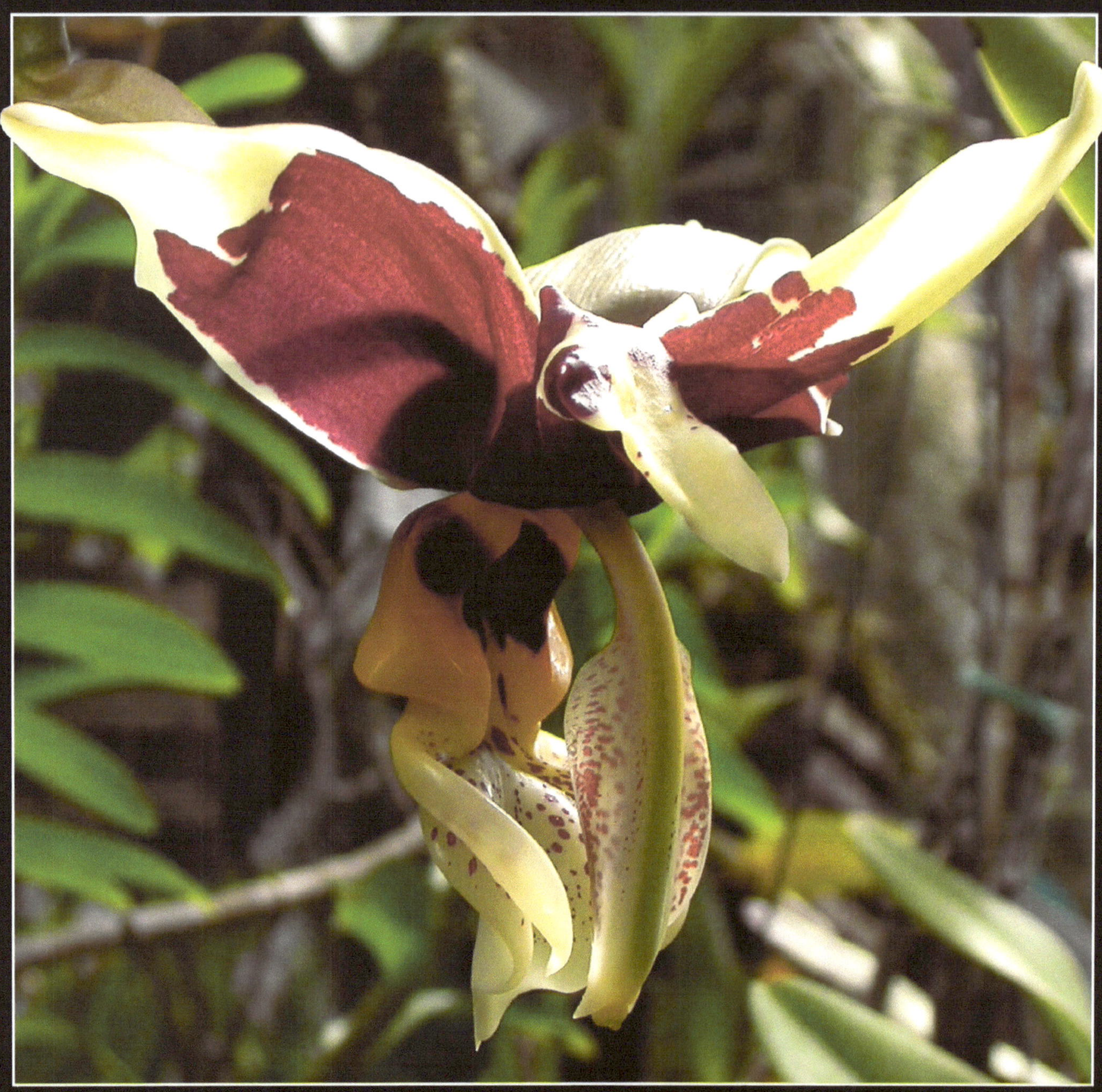

PREVIOUS OVERLEAF
Renanthera Nancy Chandler

ABOVE
Stanhopea Assidensis

RIGHT
Degarmoara Flying High (Mtssa. Jet Setter x Oda. Mcnabianum)

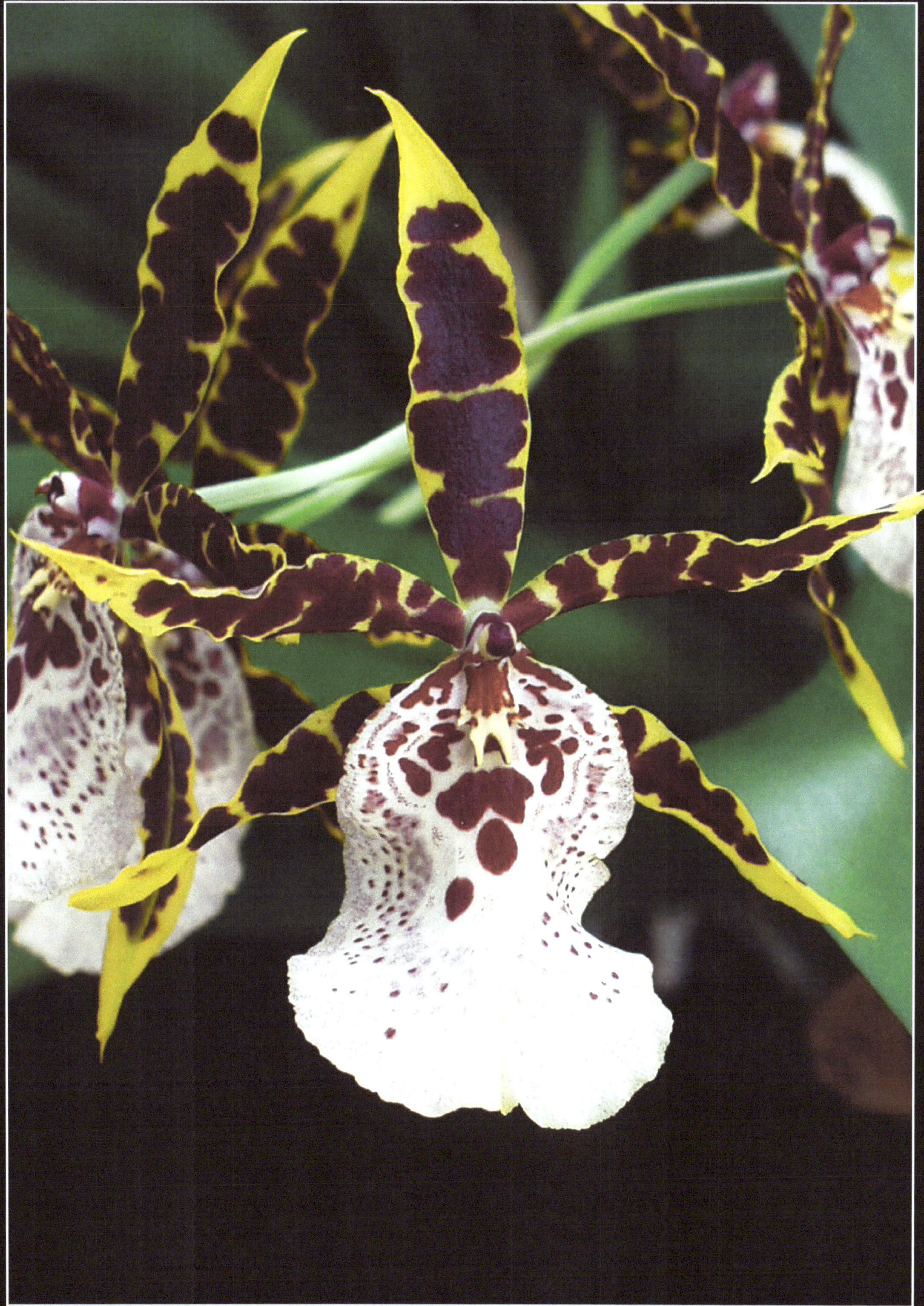

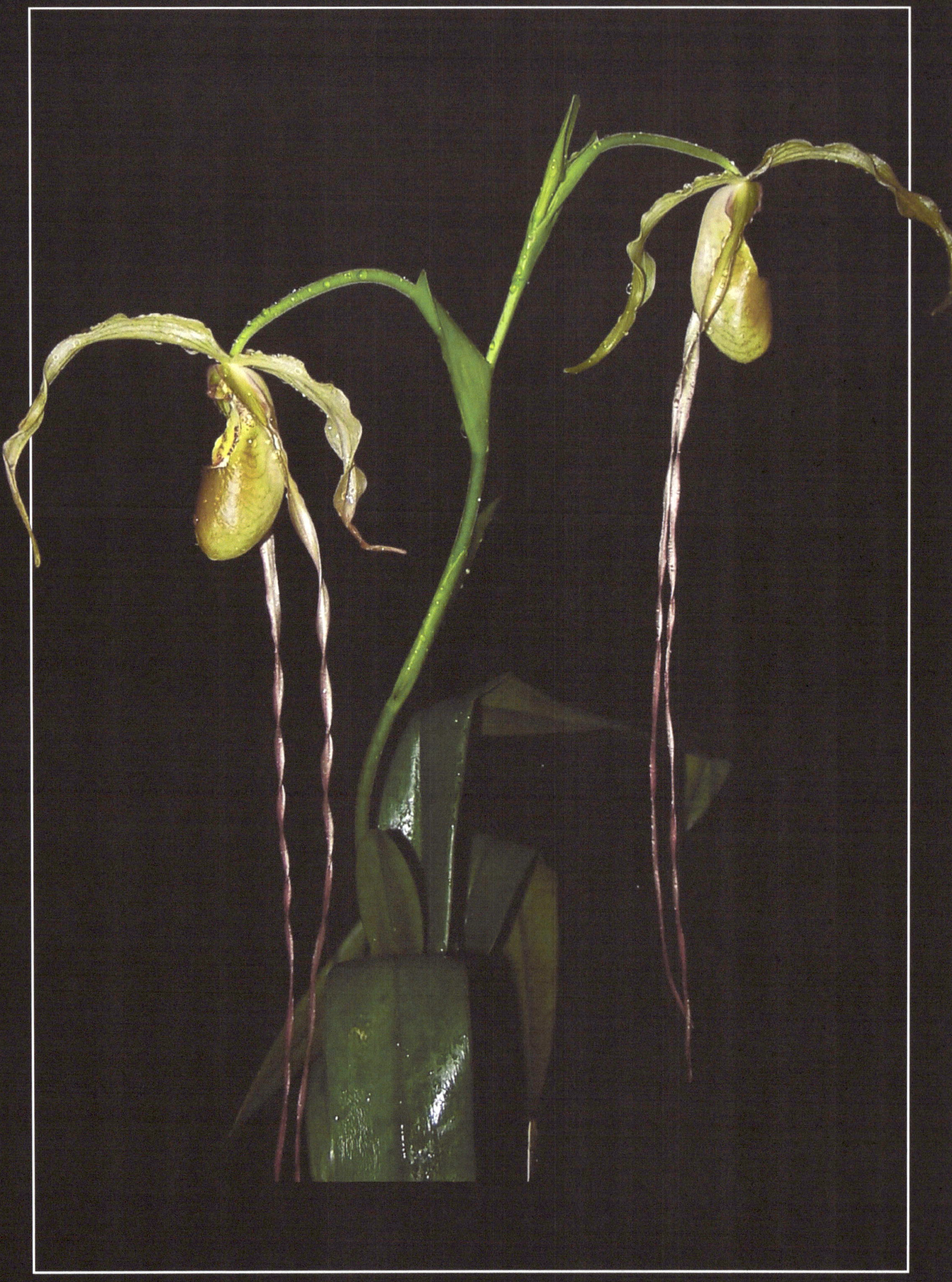

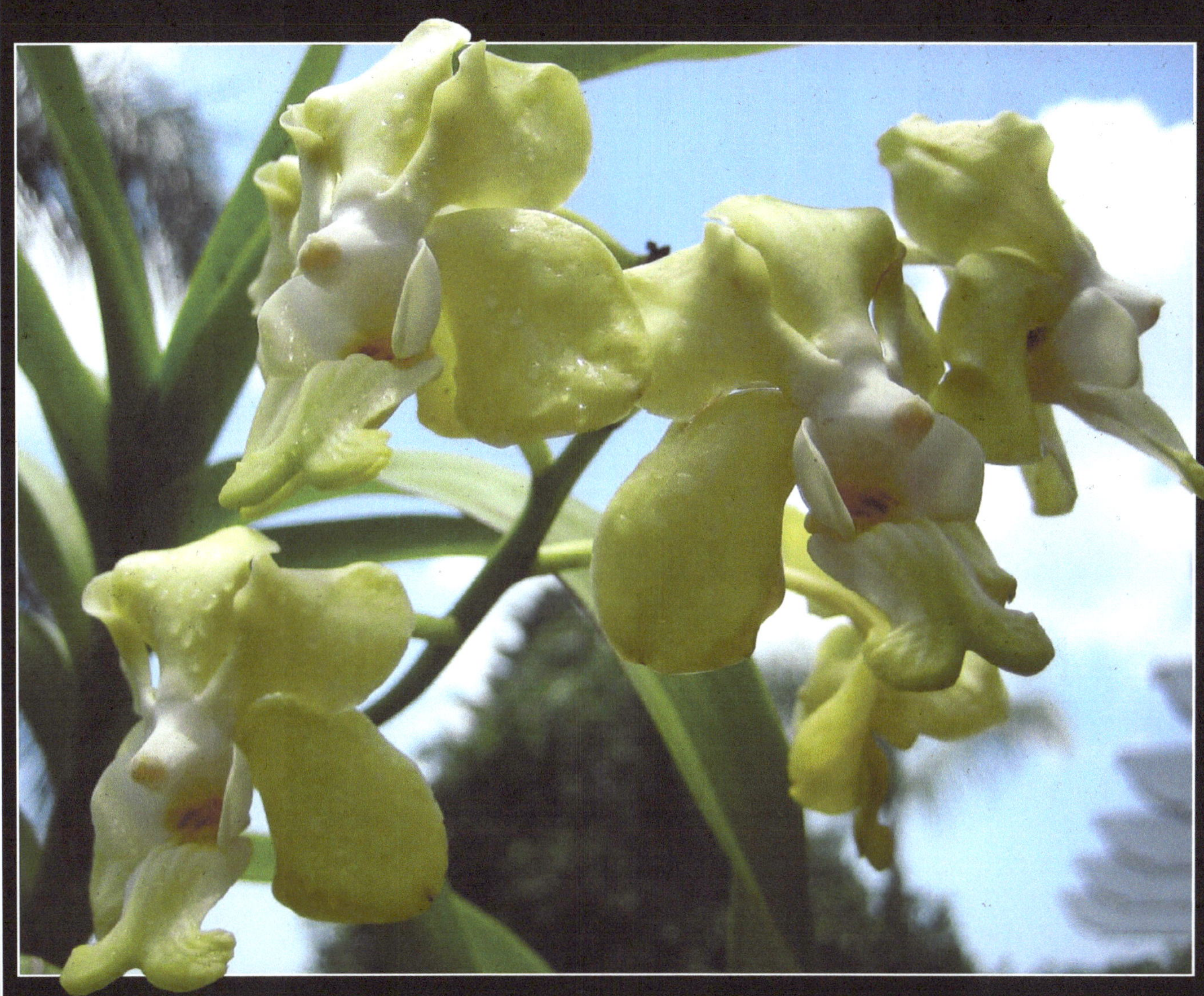

LEFT
Phragmipedium Giganteum 'My Janus'

ABOVE
Vanda dennisoniana

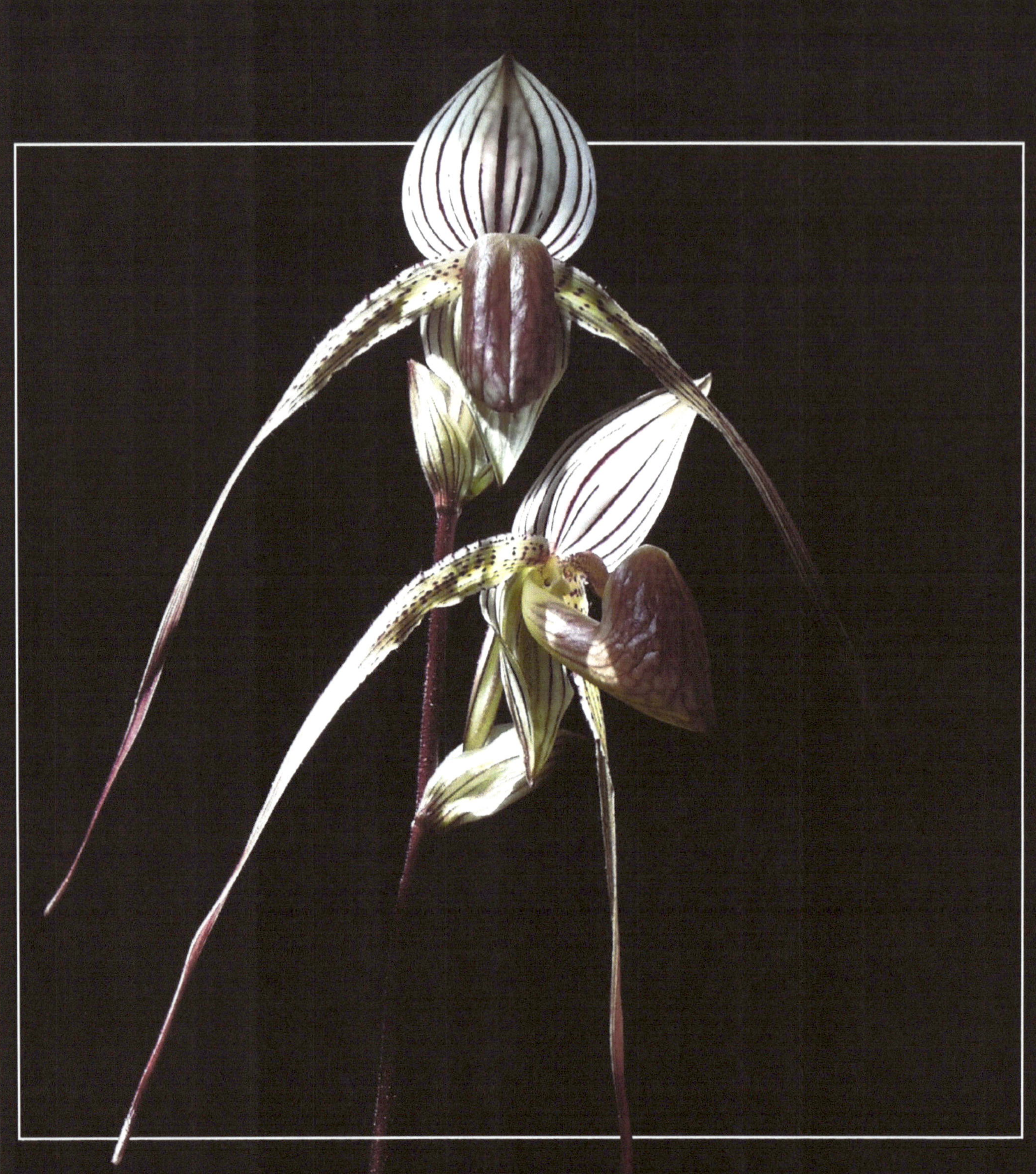

ABOVE
Paphiopedilum St. Isabel
(Paph. St. Swithin X Lady Isabel)

RIGHT
Cycnoches barthiorum
'Pink Dove'

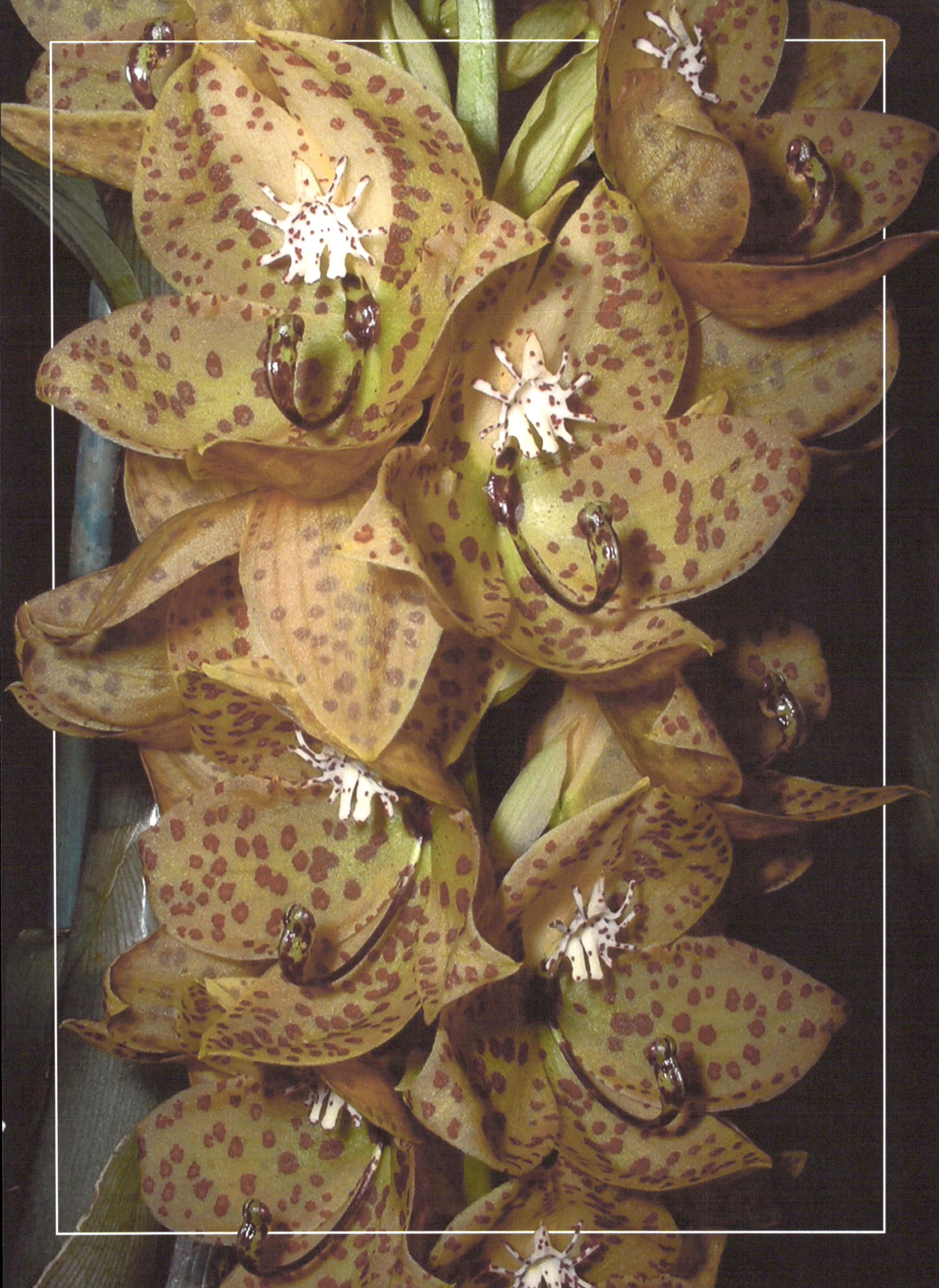

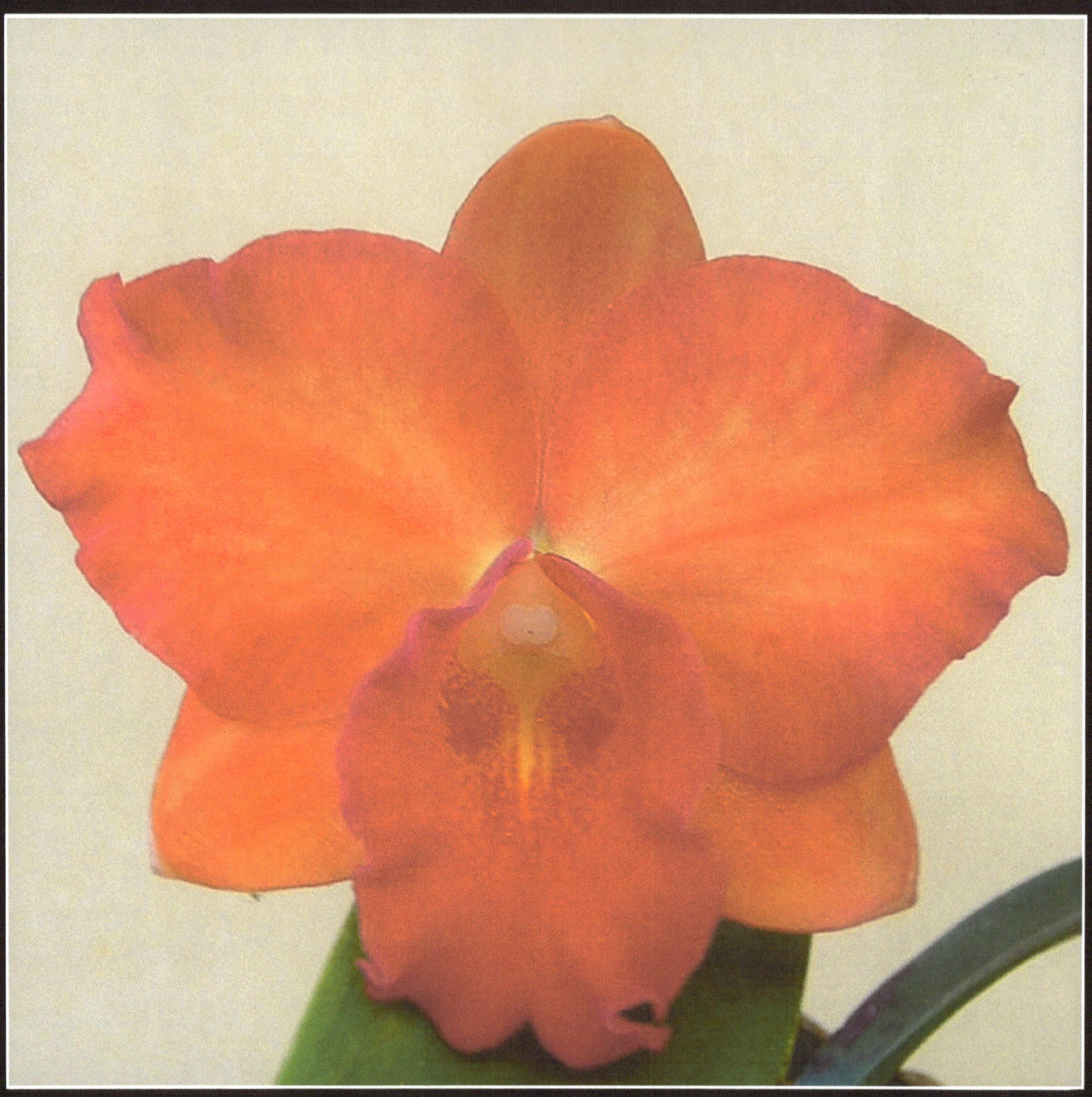

ABOVE
Potinara Exposé

RIGHT
Doritis pulcherrima chumporensis

OVERLEAF LEFT
Phragmipedium Penn's Creek Cascade (Phrag. Grande x Phrag. wallisii)

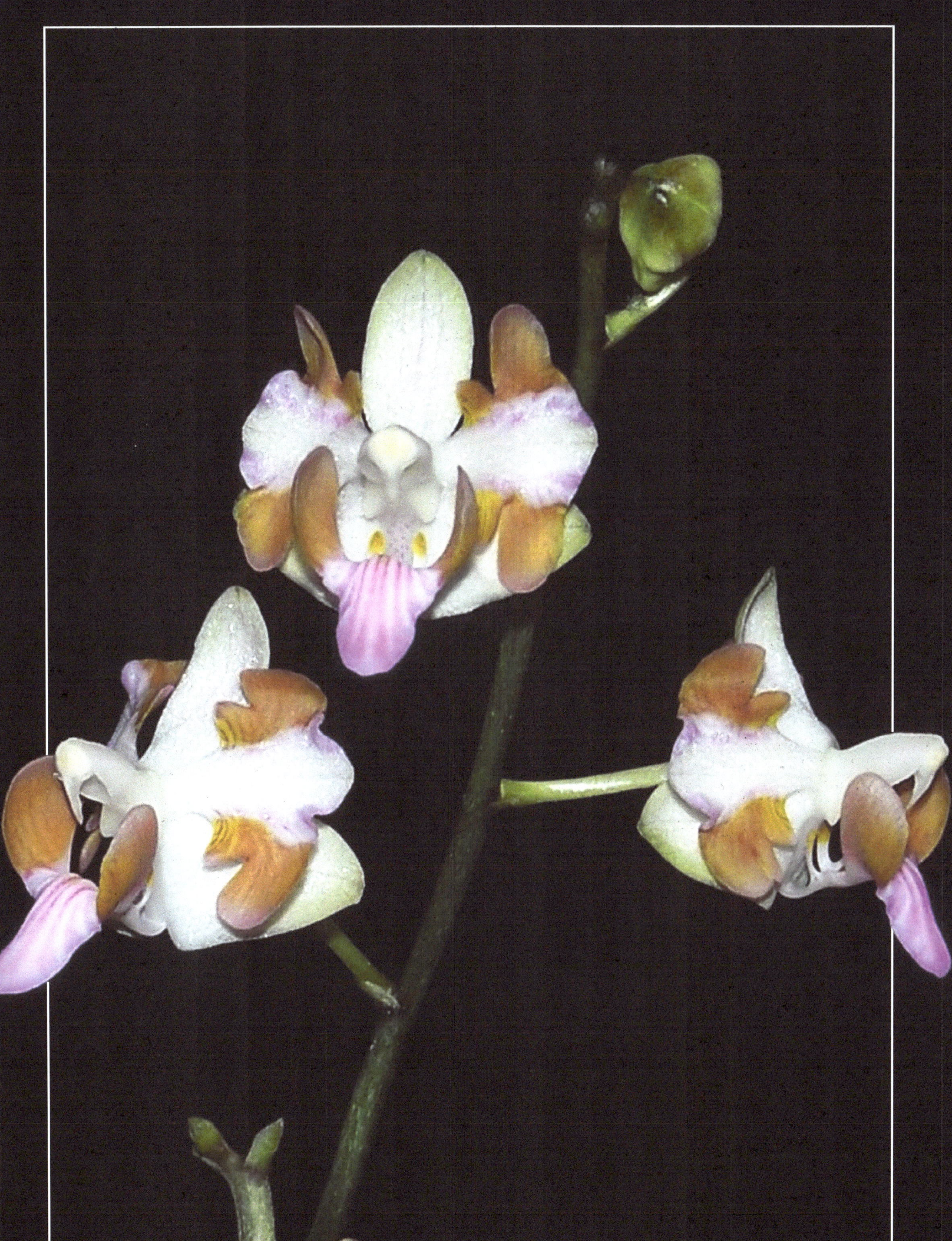

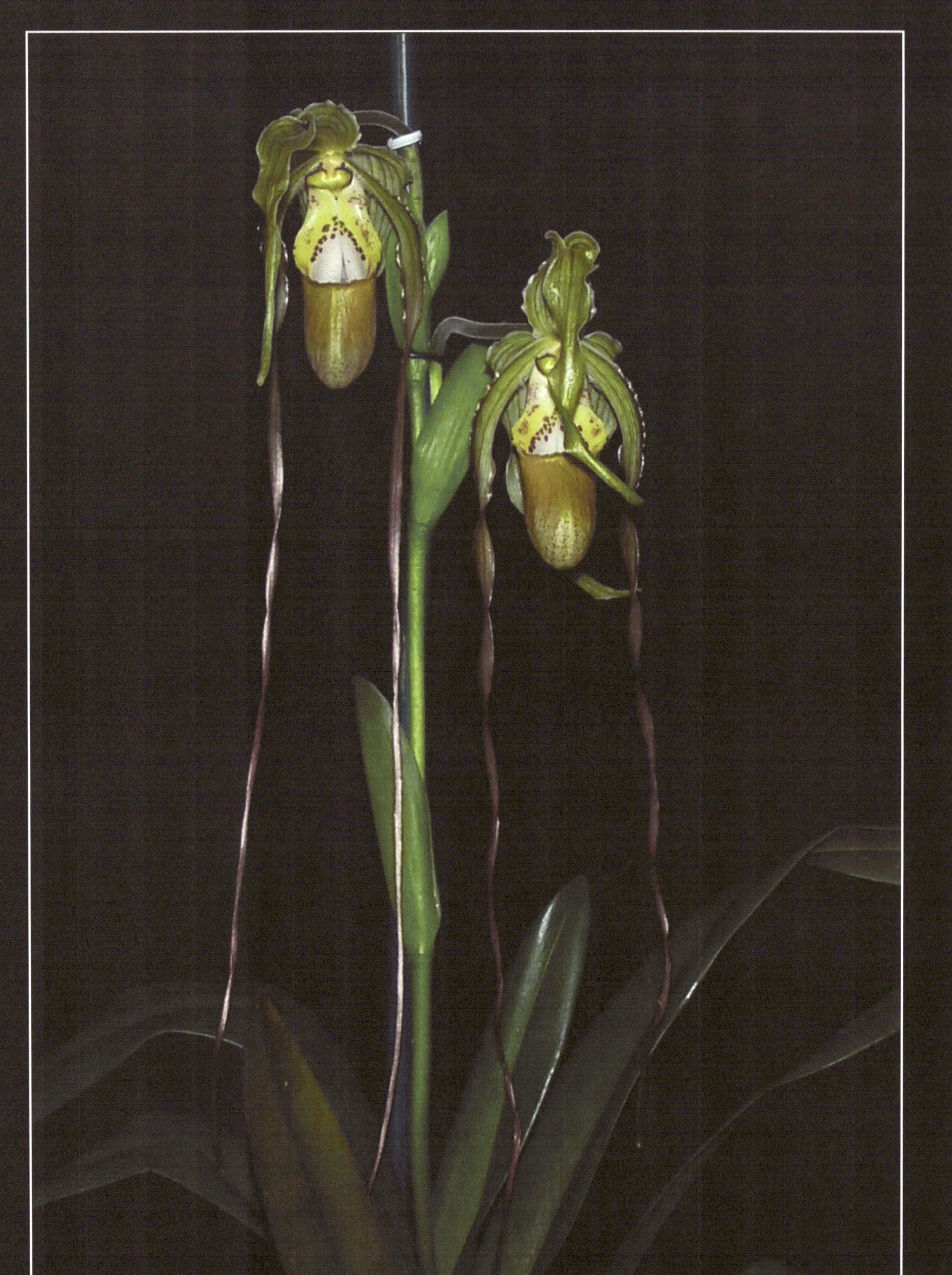

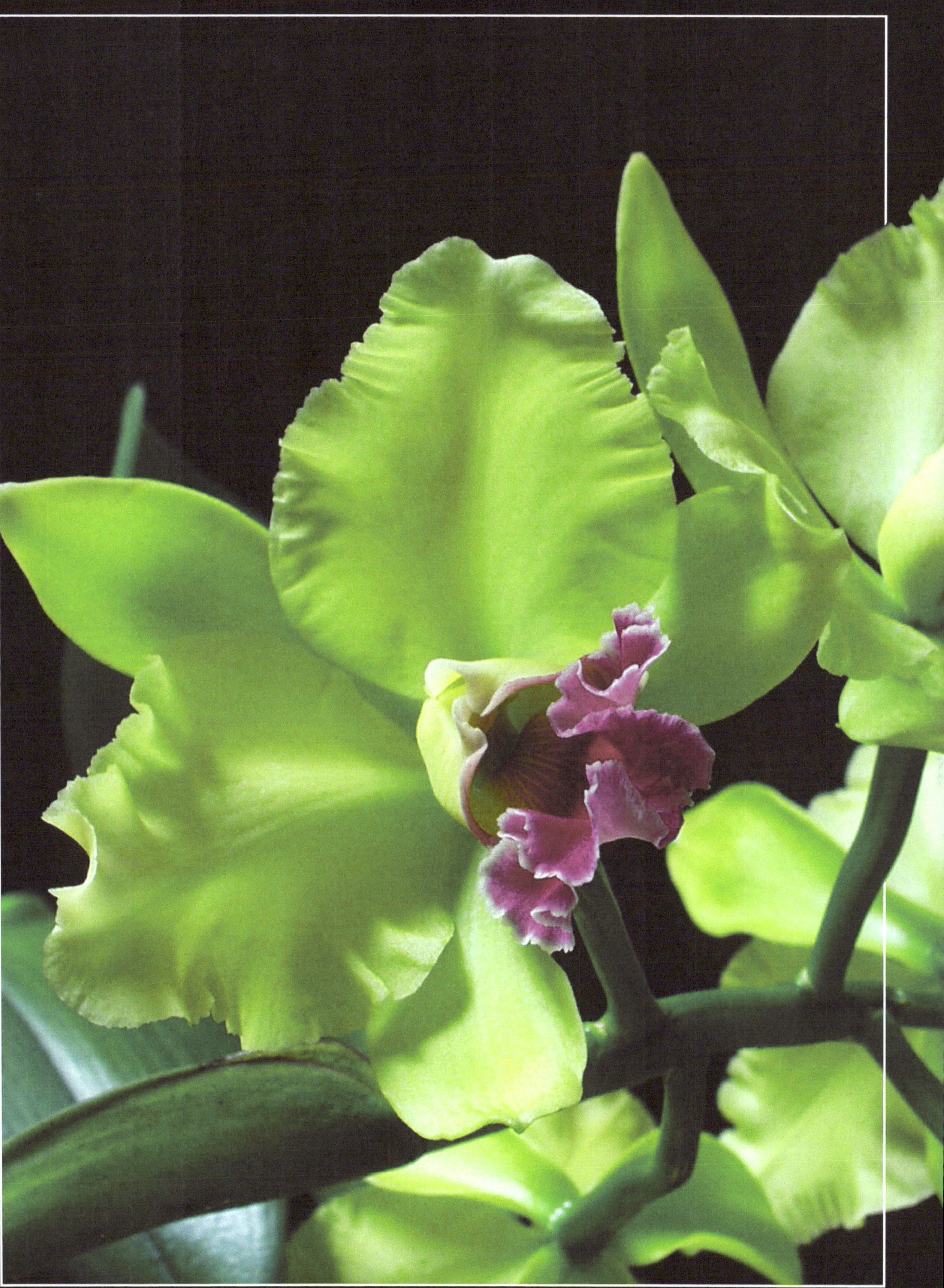

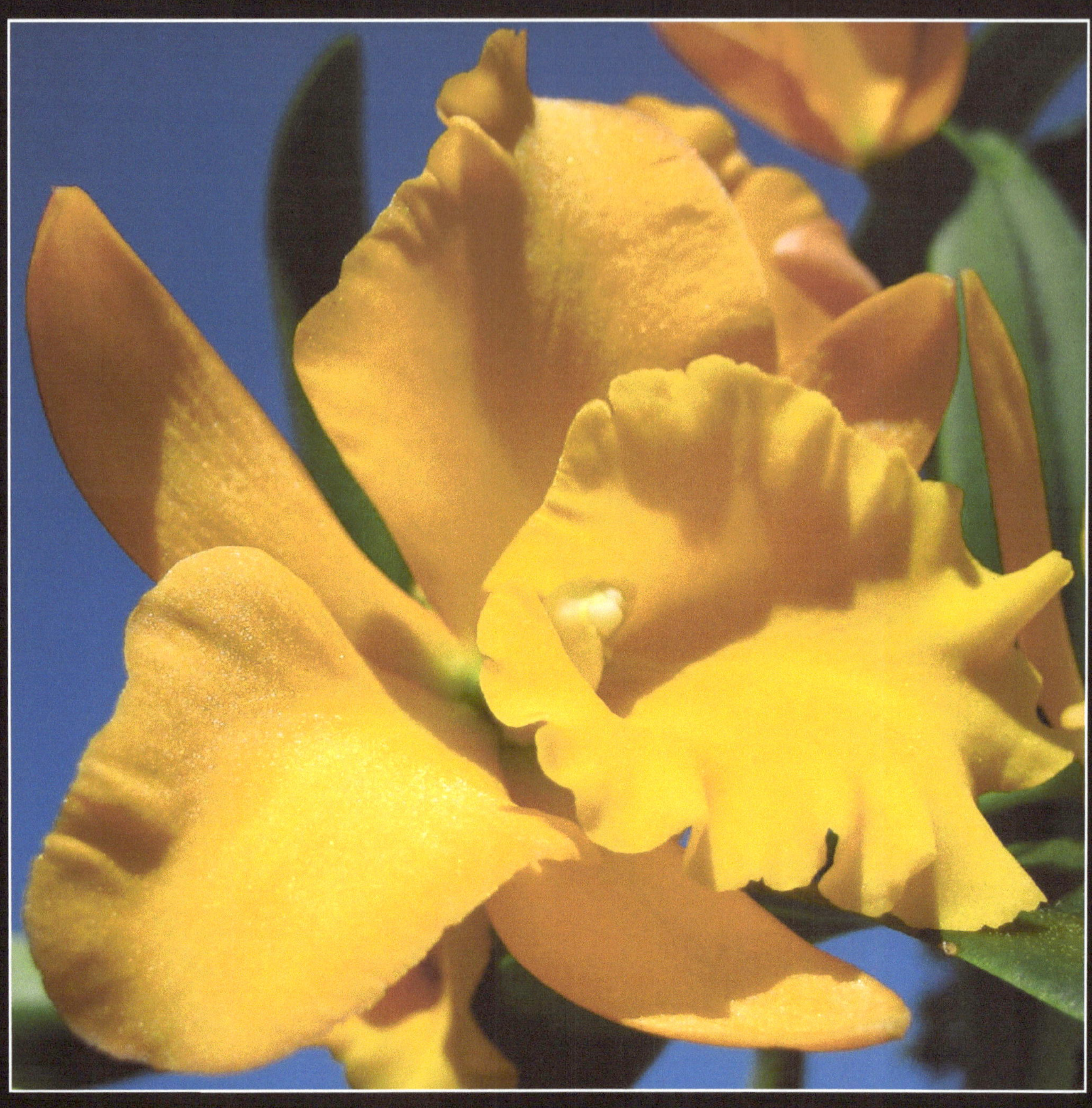

PREVIOUS OVERLEAF
Brassolaeliocattleya Memoria Helen Brown 'Sweet Afton' AM/AOS

ABOVE
Brassolaeliocattleya Orange Nugget

RIGHT
Paphiopedilum Bel Royal (rothschildianum x kolopakingii)

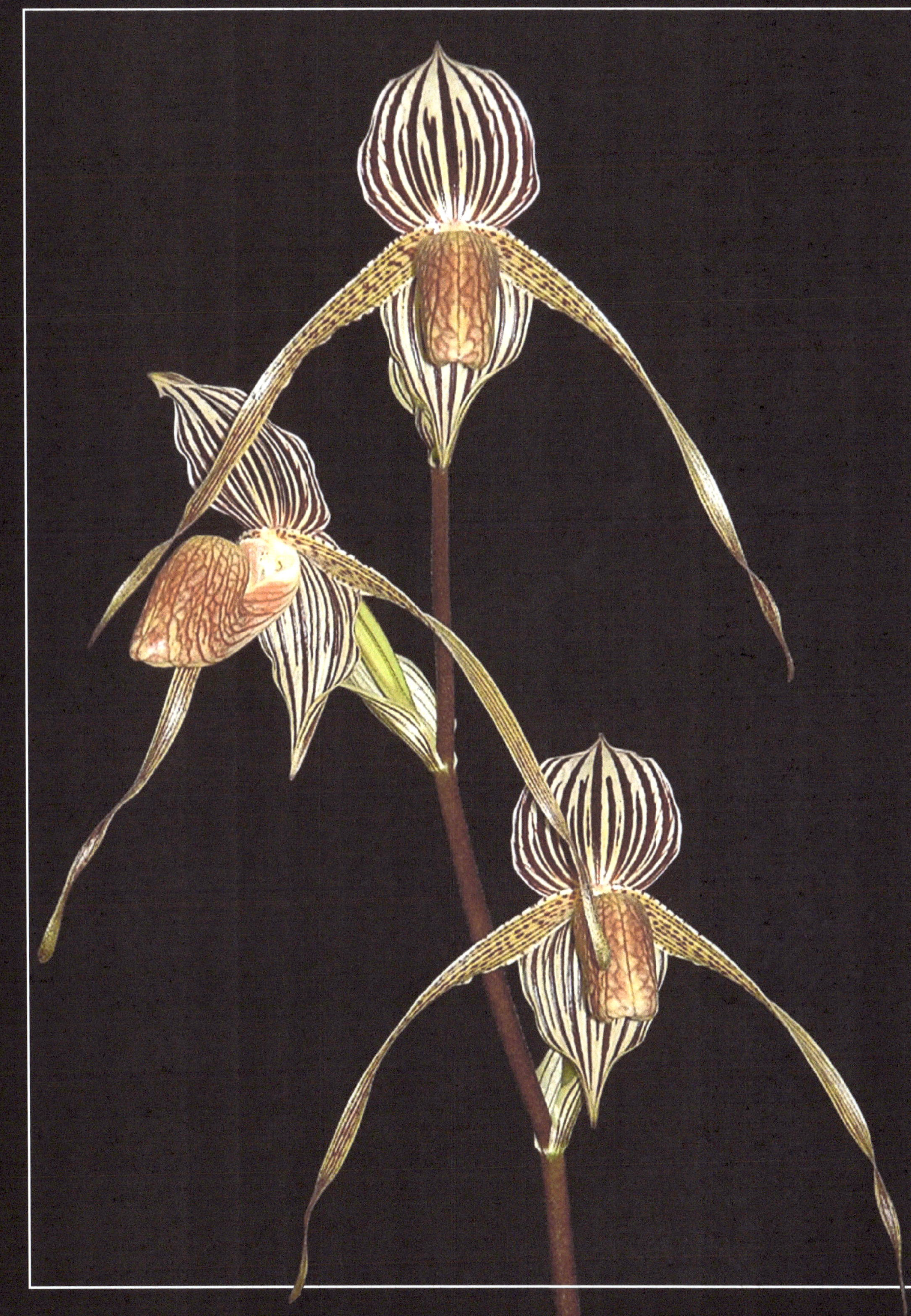

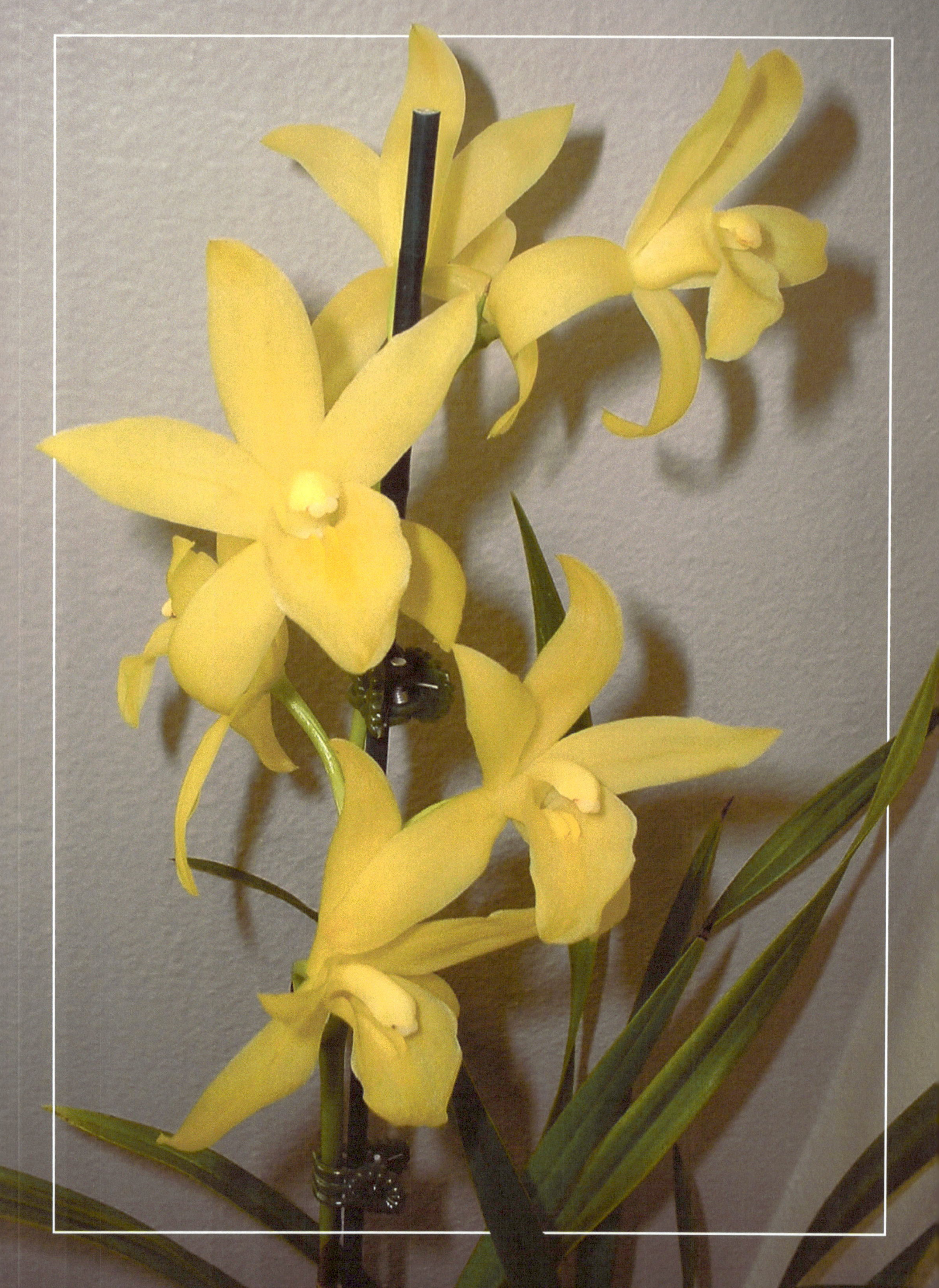

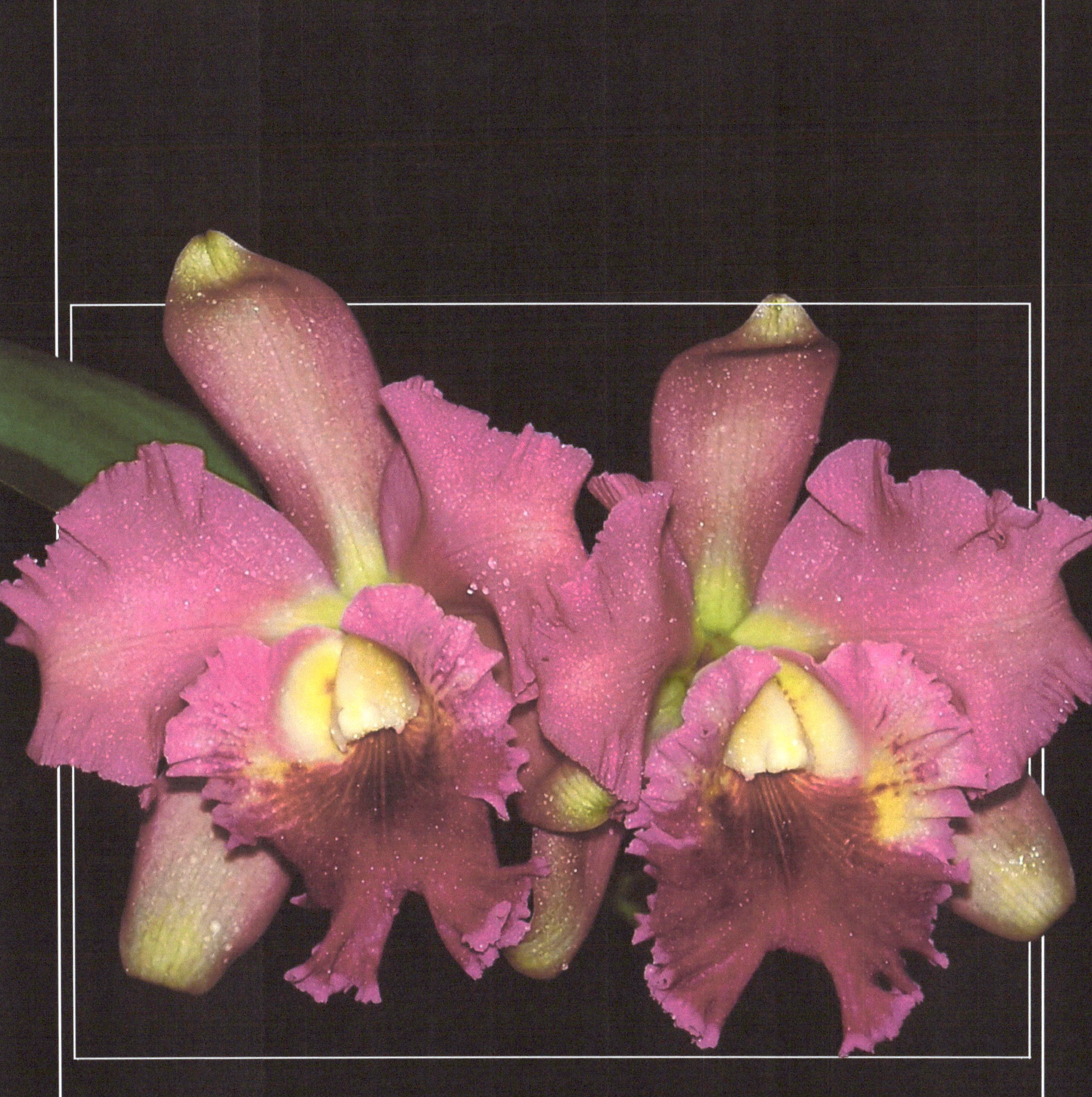

LEFT
Cymbidium Golden Elf 'Sundust' 4N

ABOVE
Brassolaeliocattleya Goldenzelle x Blc. Oh Susannah 'Lakeview'

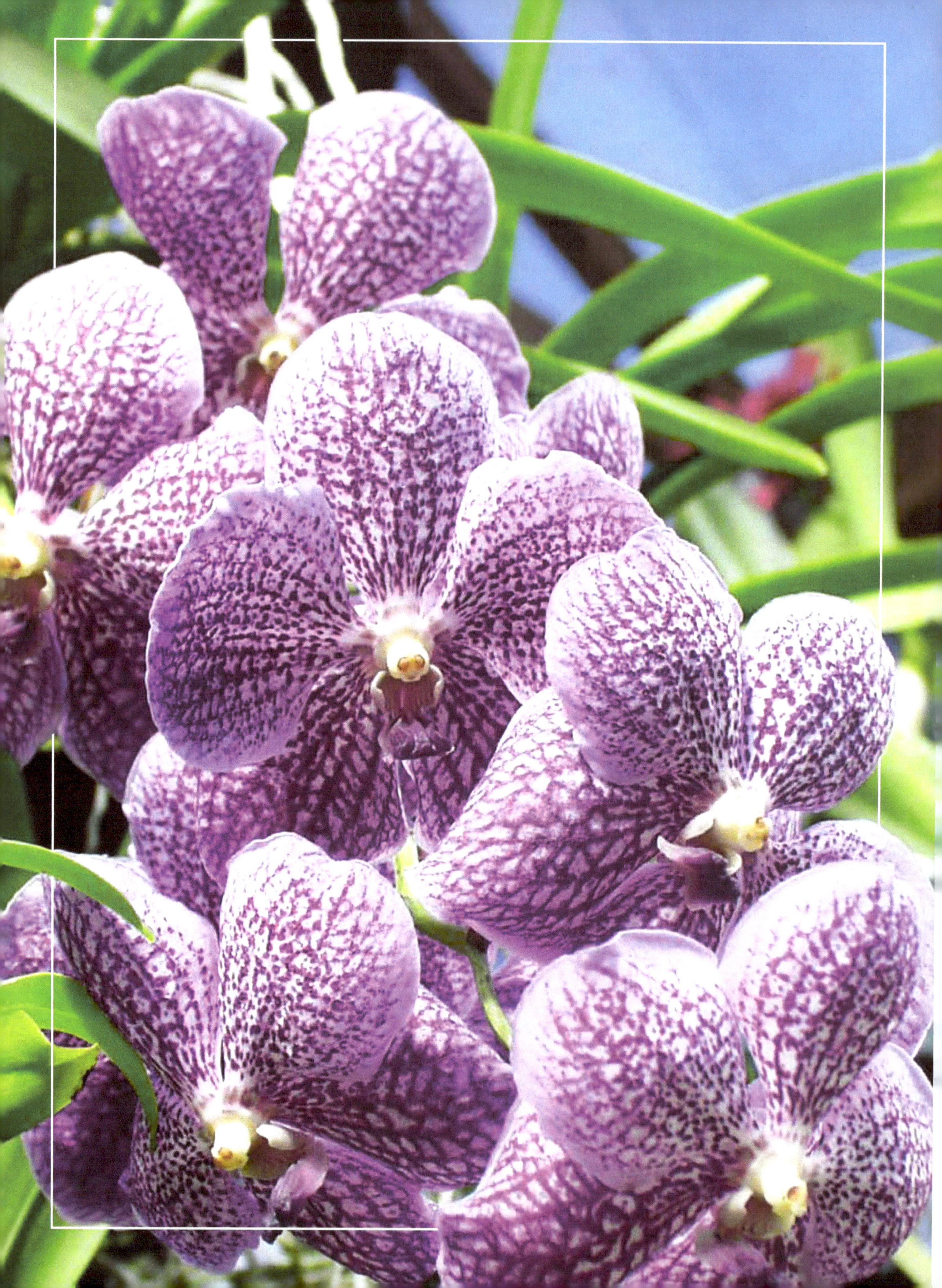

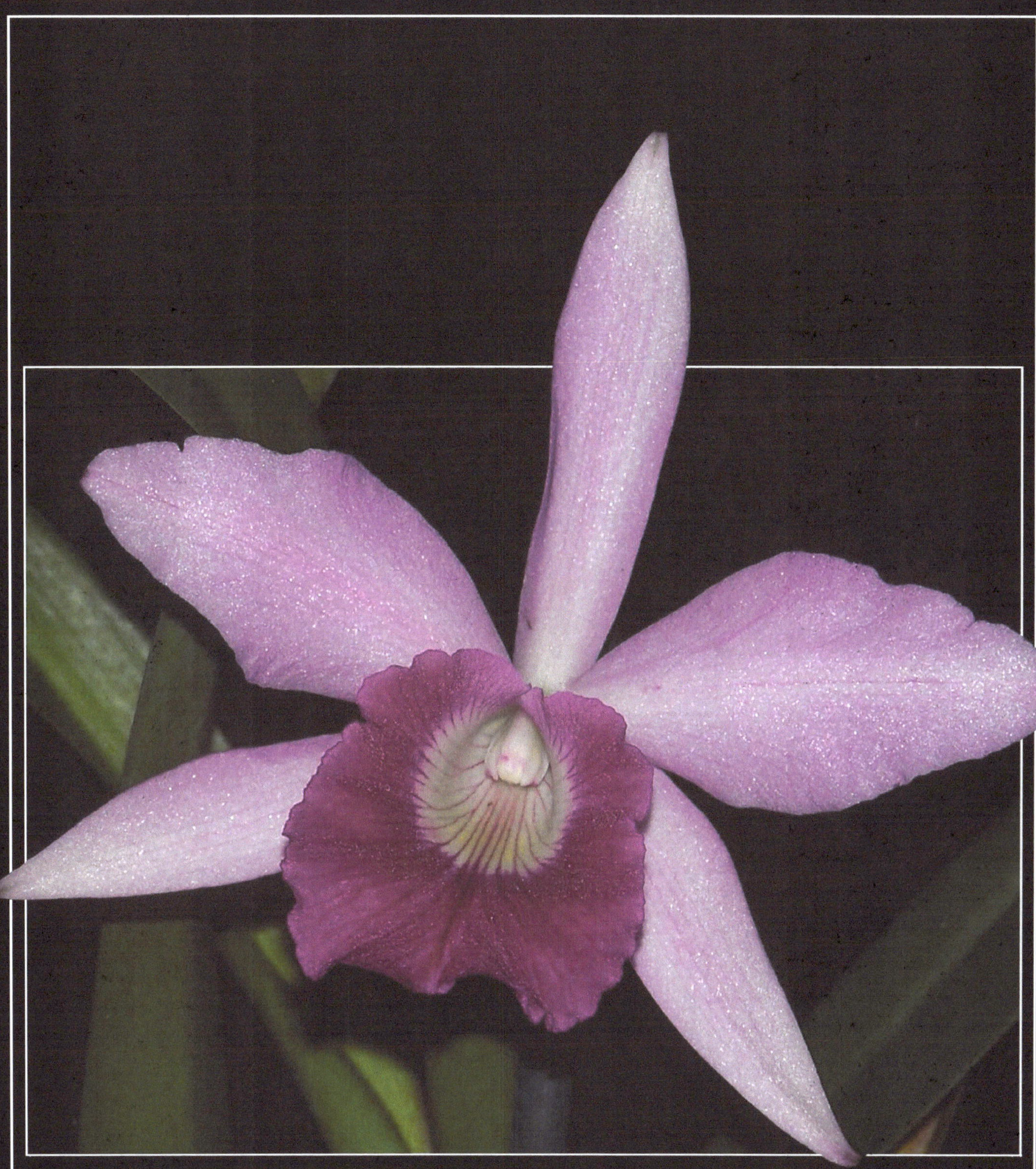

LEFT
Vanda Fuch's Delight

ABOVE
Brassolaeliocattleya
(Lc. Love Knot 'H & R'
x Brassolaelia Morning Glory 'H & R')

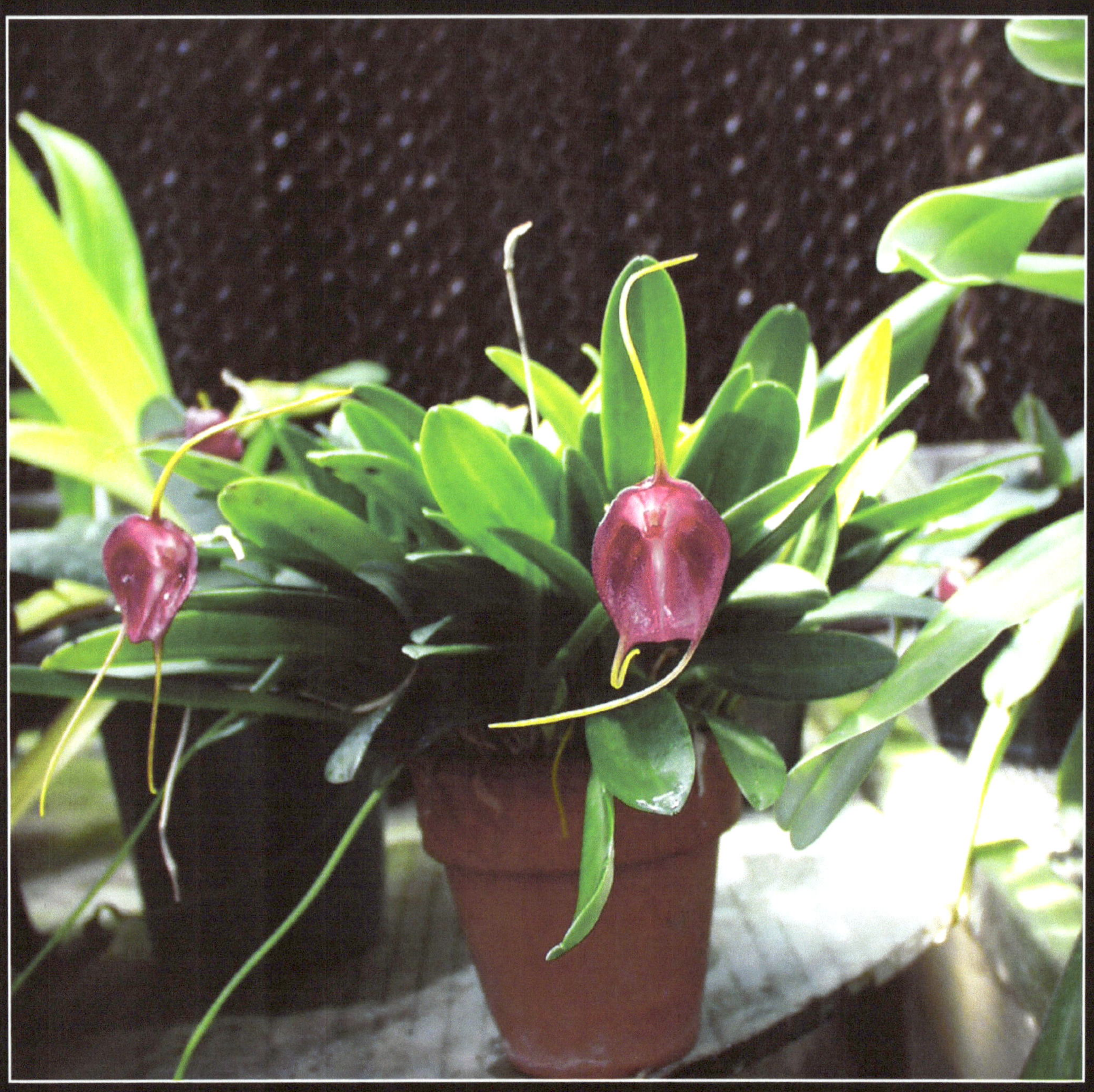

ABOVE
Masdevallia Pixie Shadow.
(M. infracta x M. schroederiana)

RIGHT
Dendrobium Victoria Regina

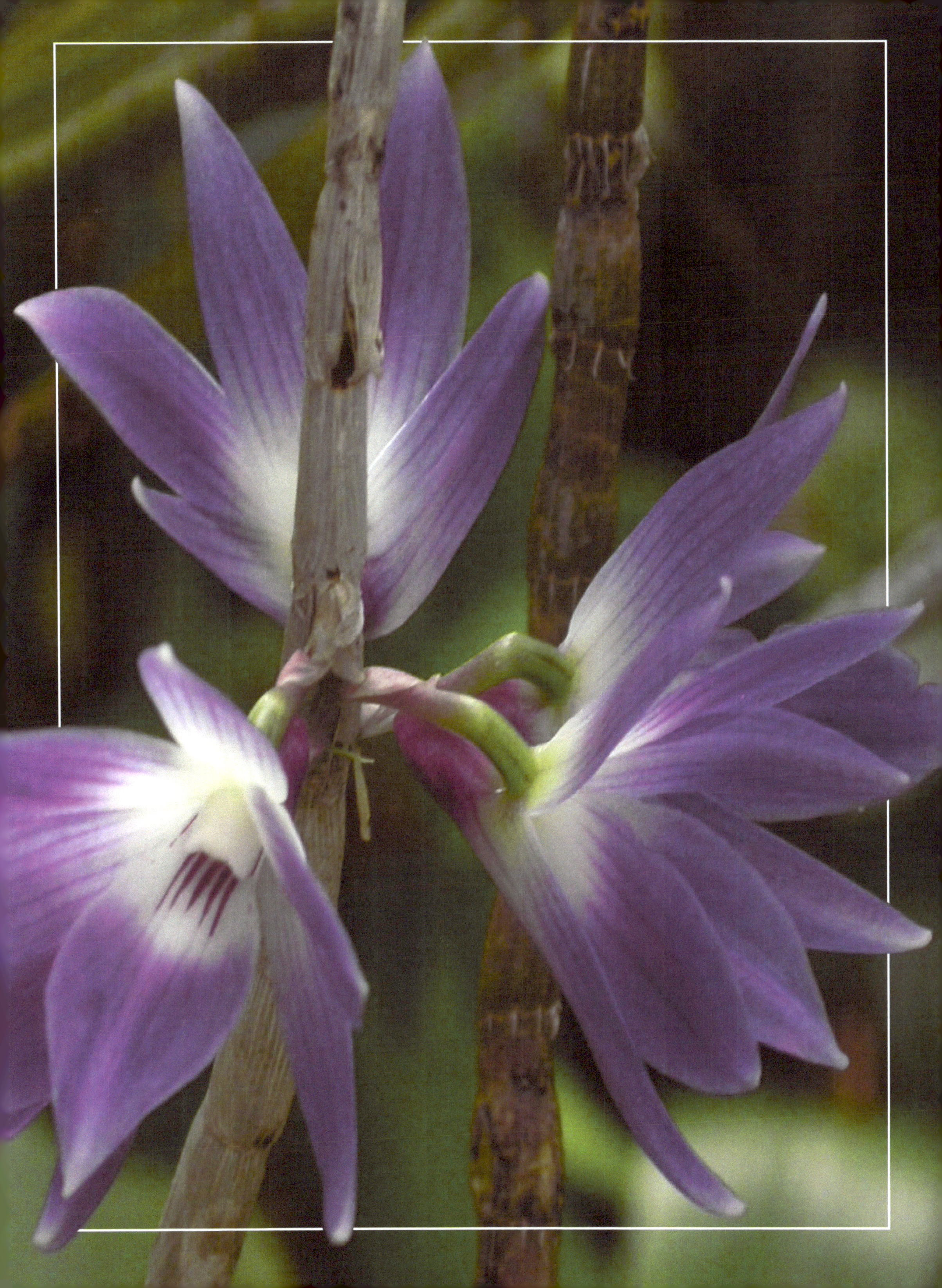

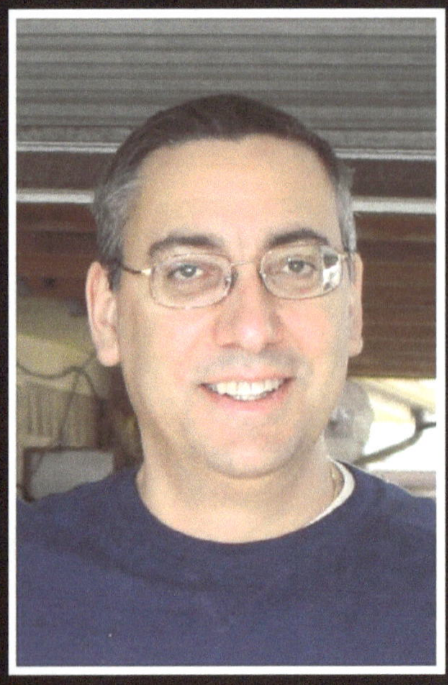

Name: Louis Aszod

Location: Clarksville, Arkansas

Hobbies: Orchids, writing, and travel.

Biography: When I was very young, my mother used to drag me with her to various nurseries where she would spend hours looking at plants to buy for our yard. One day, a particular nursery my mother favored had gotten in a very unusual looking piece of inventory. They had it displayed proudly on the front counter, and the stalks from which its leaves sprang were blanketed in vibrant, almost neon-bright orange flowers. This plant literally hypnotized me. I couldn't pull my eyes from it. I tugged at my mother's sleeve, and commanded that she buy it. I almost got a whooping right there—was I crazy? Did I not see how much that thing cost? Wailing, I was dragged away. It would take the passing of twenty-five years until I would get to see another orchid again, and although this orchid wasn't a nobile dendrobium, it still tugged at my sense of wonder and demanded that I take it home. A month and a half later, the plant was dead, but the orchid bug had bitten, and bitten hard. I bought how-to books. I bought plants.

Oh, I killed bunches more out of sheer ignorance and my stubbornness to keep trying unsuitable things for which I had completely inappropriate conditions. But one summer I got the chance to help professional growers divide and repot their collection of cattleyas, and I was paid in backbulb divisions. That summer opened the door to orchids for me. I learned how to listen to the plants, to let the plants guide my growing. They thrived. We have a greenhouse of our own now and an orchid collection numbering some 1000+ specimens—plenty to keep us busy. There is always room for "just one more," and the OrchidTalk forums and Orchid-Bids websites have given us the privilege of encountering wonderful people with whom to trade plants, exchange ideas, and grow. There is, and will never be, anything quite as satisfying.

Contributions to this publication: *Brassolaeliocattleya Memoria Helen Brown 'Sweet Afton' AM/AOS* pg. 77, *Cycnodes Wine Delight 'Jem' FCC/AOS* pg. 30, *Degarmoara Flying High 'Stars & Bars' HCC/AOS* pg. 69, *Epidendrum floribundum* pg. 05, *Masdevallia Pixie Shadow* pg. 84, *Paphiopedilum Hsinying Fairbre* pg. 09, *Paphiopedilum St. Isabel* pg. 72, *Stanhopea wardii* pg. 46, *and Vanda Fuch's Delight* pg. 82. Text pgs. 98 - 107.

Name: Tim Balgos

Location: Sydney, Australia

Hobbies: Orchids (of course), Gardening, Bushwalking, Camping, Beach, Music, Theatre, Food, Wine, Computers, and finally sitting around the house doing nothing!

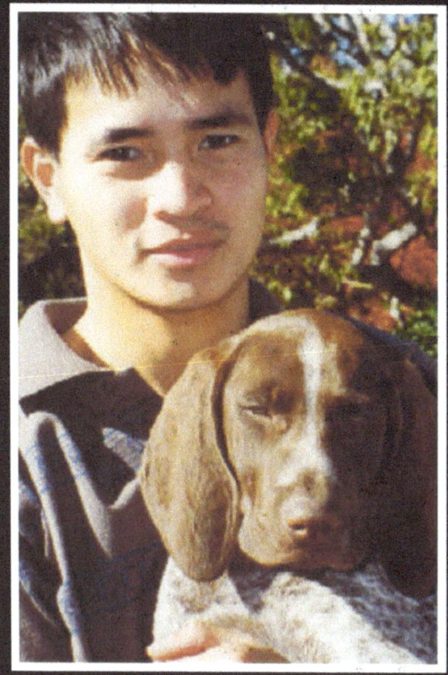

Biography: I have been growing 'seriously' for the last 2 and a half years. This has coincided with joining an Orchid Society. My first recollection of orchids making a life changing impact would be when I was in my early teens and my parents took me to one of the Orchid Shows at the Sydney Botanic Gardens. Held at the expansive grounds, the show left such an impression on us, that not long afterwards some Cymbidiums were purchased. Many of these plants, over 20 years old now, are still growing in their garden. Of course, that meant that when I chose the type of orchids I was going to grow it was not going to be Cymbidiums (rebellious child that I am, there must be a Freudian explanation for it, but that would take up far too many counseling sessions.)

So, it was that 'my' first orchid was the Australian native Dendrobium kingianum, a plant which surprisingly is still with me despite the neglect. Since then, the acquisition has increased in what seems to be an exponential rate. The collection comprises mainly of Paphiopedilums and Phragmipediums, Australian Dendrobiums and Cattleyas. Some other genera such as Dendrochilum, Stanhopea, Coelogyne, Pterostylis, various Vandacaeous and Pleurothallids are represented by one or two plants. Another surprise, is that I have begun acquiring Cymbidiums (I assure myself that it is ok, after all, it's only one or two, hmmm… six). Many of my plants were acquired as a result of raffle prizes and tables sales at the orchid societies I have joined or frequented. I have been a member of Five Dock RSL Orchid Society, where I am a committee member and the webmaster, and the Species Orchid Society of NSW for over two years. What of the future? Hopefully many more moments spent with orchids!

Contributions to this publication: *Paphiopedilum Coos* pg. 20, *Sunipia bicolor* pg. 08, *and Potinara Exposé* pg.74.

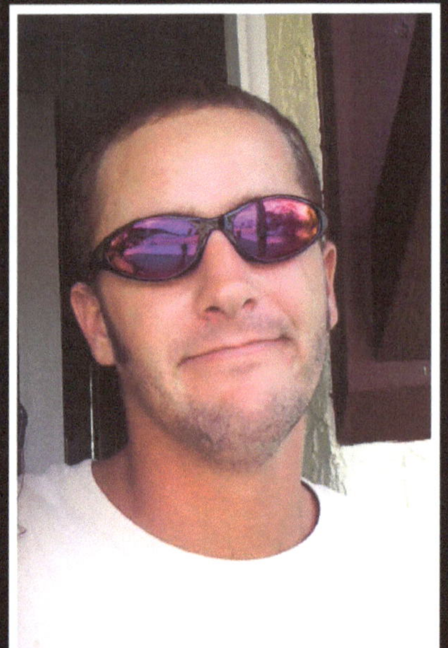

Name: Aaron Brothers

Location: Rotonda, Florida

Occupation: Aluminum Contractor

Hobbies: Saltwater Fly Fishing and Orchids.

Biography: I was born and raised in Islamorada, Florida, located in the fabulous Florida Keys. I have been growing orchids most of my life, and was introduced to them by my wonderful grandmother, Dolores. Thanks to her teachings and guidance, I have been able to amass a wonderful collection of many different species of orchids.

I prefer to grow schomburgkias and laelias, but also have a good collection of many different species and hybrids. Currently, I have been doing a lot of work trying to cross schomburgkias and cattleyas to create some cattleyas that will have a much higher tolerance to light, therefore making wonderful landscape plants that will thrive down here in the South Florida sun.

Contributions to this publication: *Ansellia Gigantea Nilotica 'Wannakee' AM/AOS* pg. 50, *Cattleya Bacti 'Grape Wax'* pg. 19, *Catasetum Callosum* pg. 54, *Cattleytonia 'Why Not' x Schomburgkia undulata* pg. 41, *Cymbidium Fred's Beauty* pg. 10, *Laeliocattleya Netresiri Waxy 'Jairug'* pg. 14, *Phalaenopsis violacea 'Krull's Navy Blue' AM/AOS* pg. 65, *Renanthera Nancy Chandler* pg. 67, *Schomburgkia Brysiana 'Robert x self'* pg. 29, *and Schomburgkia exaltata* pg. 33.

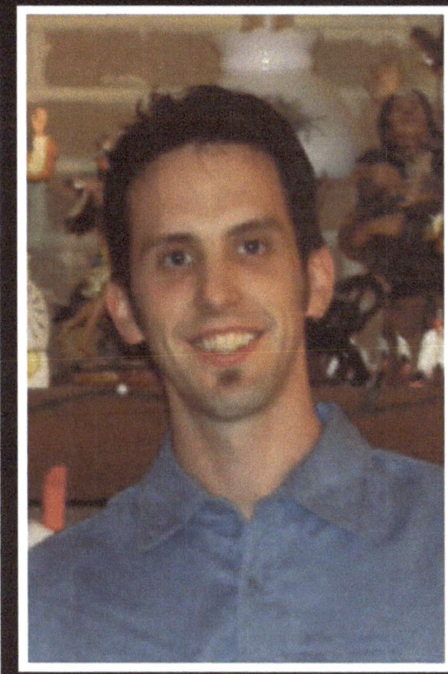

Name: Bruce B. Brown

Location: Clarksville, Arkansas

Occupation: College Professor

Hobbies: Computers, travel, photography, gardening, orchids, drawing, and design.

Biography: I have a Master of Fine Arts in Drama from the University of Virginia. I received my Bachelor of Arts from Southeastern Oklahoma State University. My theatre designs have been seen at many regional theatres including Findlay Summer Stock, Heritage Repertory Theatre, the Oklahoma Shakespearean Festival, as well as the Kennedy Center in Washington D.C., to name a few. I have been growing orchids for the past twelve years.

In addition to my theatre training, I have a passion for travel and learning. I recently returned from a trip to Egypt where I spent two weeks studying ancient Egyptian art and history. In the summer of 2001 I visited Malta and its Neolithic ruins and in 2000 I spent 14 days touring Italy from Verona and Juliet's balcony to the Roman Coliseum of Caesar. In 1998 I toured Greece where I questioned the oracle at Delphi on new year's eve and raced on the original Olympic field in Athens.

As far back as I can remember, I have always been interested in plants and flowers. As a child, I grew vegetables and roses. Then, after moving away to college, I grew houseplants –mostly tropical. Today, Louis and I have well over 1000 orchids in the greenhouse we built in 1996. I grow an ever-increasing variety of orchids and tropical plants. I serve as the Vice President of my local orchid society and learn as much as I can about these plants through my friends online at RVO's OrchidTalk Forum.

Contributions to this publication: *Encyclia radiata* pg. 45, *Odontocidium Tiger Crow 'Golden Girl' HCC/AOS* pg. 35, *Paphiopedilum Magic Lantern* pg. 38, *Phalaenopsis Chimei Buddha x Phal. Salu Rose* pg. 57, *Phragmipedium Albopurpureum 'Sir Arthur' AM/AOS* (title page), *Phragmipedium Belle Hougue Point* pg. 100, *and Phragmipedium caricinum* pg. 63.

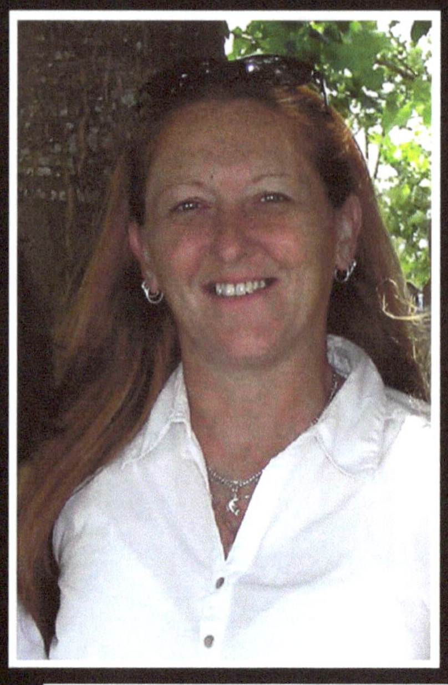

Name: Valerie L. Burns

Location: Okeechobee, Florida

Occupation: Doing what I like to do!

Hobbies: Photography, orchids and growing plants.

Biography: I became interested in orchids when my youngest daughter gave me one, invited me to an orchid show and sale in May 2005, and then gave me the link to the RVO OrchidTalk forums.– after that I was hooked!

The first year of orchid growing brought both the best and the worst this hobby has to offer. I saw great flowers from my plants, but I also saw some things no orchid grower should have to witness. I started out with mostly Phalaenopsis and Dendrobium orchids, then fell in love with Cattleyas and Vandas. I also have some Potinaras, Miltonidiums and Oncidiums. In the future, I would like to try a fragrant phalaenopsis, but my absolute, all time favorite orchid to grow and bloom would have to be the fragrant and colorful Cattleyas in my collection. Specifically, my *Laelioattleya Trick or Treat* (featured on page 32) with its orange flowers is at the top of my favorites list.

Its been a challenging experience, and though I'm still not an orchid expert, I am learning, thanks to all the people on RVO.

Contributions to this publication: *Brassidium Fly Away 'Taida'* pg. 06, *Epidendrum difforme x sib* pg. 55, *Laeliocattleya Trick or Treat* pg. 23, *Laeliocattleya Iwanagara Apple Blossm 'Golden Elf'* pg. 47, *Miltassia Charles M.Fitch 'Izumi' AM/AOS* pg. 39, *Paphiopedilum Maudiae Alba x Paph. Mitylene Alba* pg. 34, *and Vuylstekeara Aloha Sparks 'Ruby Eyes' 12-13.*

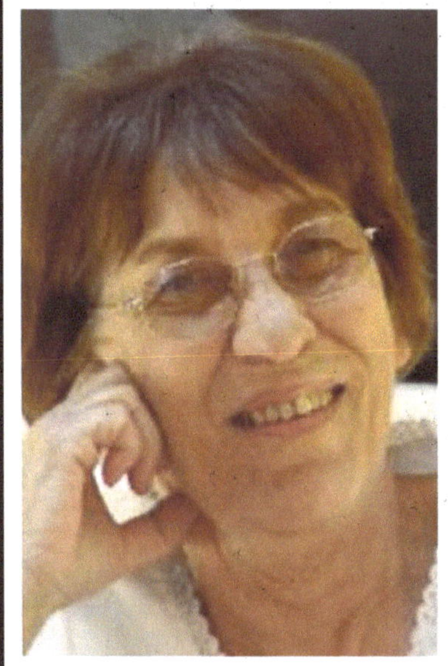

Name: Virginia 'Gin' Carter

Location: Lebanon, Missouri

Occupation: Retired

Hobbies: I enjoy growing orchids and other plants. I also raise birds, and enjoy riding horseback.

Biography: I was born in Richmond, California. I lived in northern California for twenty-nine years before moving to Southern California. When my husband retired, we moved to Southern Missouri. We have lived here for twenty-five years.

I became interested in Orchids sometime in the late 60s or early 70s. I had a neighbor in Southern California who received two Cymbidiums as gifts. She set them out in the So. Ca. sun and I found a couple of bulbs that had a little green –that was my first attempt with orchids. Next, I bought a couple of cattleya seedlings in bags from a large discount store. I got them not knowing it would be four or five years until there was a chance of them blooming. They bloomed right before we moved to Missouri.

After moving, I went to work in a pet shop and started raising birds. My favorite bird is an Alexandrine Ringneck. I like all of them really; each is so different in temperament.

My favorite orchids are Vandas; although, I also like a lot of the species that are unusual. Right now I have Cattleyas, Phalaenopsis species, Vandas, Coryanthes, Paphiopedilums, Phragmipediums, and an assortment of specie plants.

Contributions to this publication: *Coryanthes alborosea* pg. 36, *Phalaenopsis Violacea var. coerulea* pg. 26, *Dendrobium lindleyi* pg. 58, *and Cattleya hardyana* pg. 61.

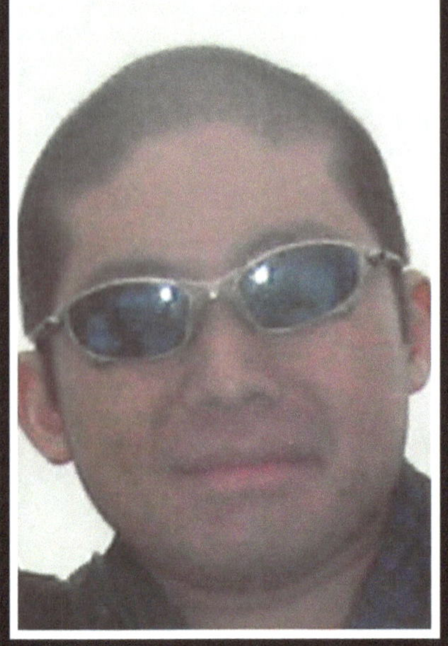

Name: Jason Chang, M.D.

Location: Manhattan, New York

Occupation: Medicine Resident

Hobbies: Orchids and fishing.

Biography: Born in 1978, I was first exposed to orchids in high school, recalling them as "those expensive plants that my mother would buy (and not grow very well)." After a number of facetious comments directed at my mother's green thumb, or lack thereof, I was challenged to grow the plants properly. A visit to the local library produced the requisite starting information and, after blooming a few plants, I began to grow them in earnest, gravitating first to the showy large-flowered cattleya hybrids and vandas. Eventually I was drawn to the exotic paphiopedilums and phragmipediums, the tropical "lady-slipper" orchids which form the bulk of my collection today. The orchids followed me to the dormitories of Princeton University and later the NYU School of Medicine, and now to a sun-drenched and obscenely-overpriced Manhattan apartment.

I am currently finishing up a residency in internal medicine at NYU and am contemplating a career in medical oncology. When not working or tending to the orchids, I can usually be found on a boat somewhere along the NY/NJ shores, drinking beer and trying to catch "the big one."

Contributions to this publication: *Paphiopedilum Bel Royal* pg. 79, *Paphiopedilum Saint Swithin 'Kinglet' HCC/AOS* pg. 53, *Phragmipedium besseae* pg. 15, *Laelia purpurata* (front cover), *Masdevallia veitchiana 'Fairview'* pg. 66, *Vanda Sansai Blue 'Meechai' AM/AOS* pg. 27, *and Phragmipedium warscewiczianum* pg. 43.

Name: Clint M. Dawley

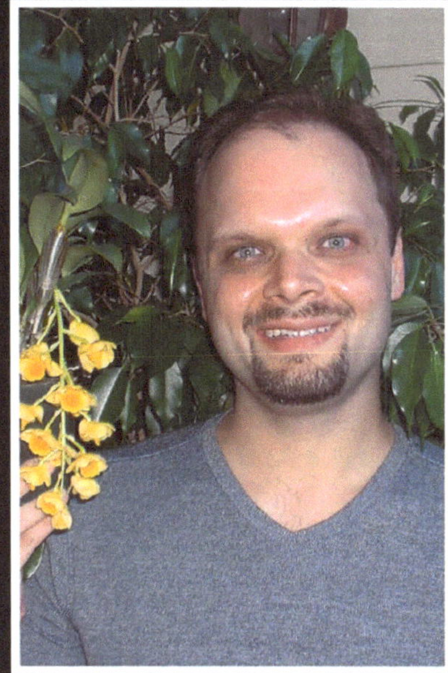

Location: Fort Worth, Texas

Occupation: Database Manager

Hobbies: Reading, dancing, figure skating, and gardening.

Biography: My fascination with plants started at about age 4 or 5. From this young age, some of my first memories are fond ones of planting my grandmother's vegetable garden. I remember stomping watermelon seeds in Athens, Texas as my grandmother dug the holes. I was surprised to see them sprout and even more surprised to eat them several months later.

I have always grown a houseplant or two or ten, depending on space limitations. I've only been growing orchids for about 10 years now, with my first one being a grocery store phalaenopsis. After killing this plant and picking up a couple of others, I mastered the culture of this genus, but it was a few more years before I discovered my favorites - the Venezuelan and Columbian cattleyas and their vast hybrids.

For me, orchid cultivation unlocks some of the secrets of evolution. Orchids are honed by natural selection to attract specific insect cross-pollinators. Clues to each individual orchid's pollinator can be inferred from floral shape and even scent! I currently have about 75 orchids on my sun porch and under lights in an east-facing bay window.

I live in Fort Worth, Texas with my two fine felines (Fritz and Sasha) and my partner of eleven years, Cody.

Contributions to this publication: *Brassolaeliocattleya Dora Louise Capen 'Lea' HCC/AOS* pg. 07, *Sophrocattleya Crystelle Smith* pg. 60, *Cycnoches barthiorum 'Pink Dove'* pg. 73, *Dendrobium Super Ise Abundance x Super Star Shapely* pg. 25, *Odontonia Memoria Martin Orenstein 'Lulu' HCC/AOS* pg. 21, *Potinara Burana Beauty 'Burana' AM/AOS* pg. 51, *Sophrolaeliocattleya Precious Beauty* (table of contents), *Cymbidium Golden Elf 'Sundust' 4n* pg. 80, *and Zygoneria Adelaide Meadows 'Fat Cat'* pg. 17.

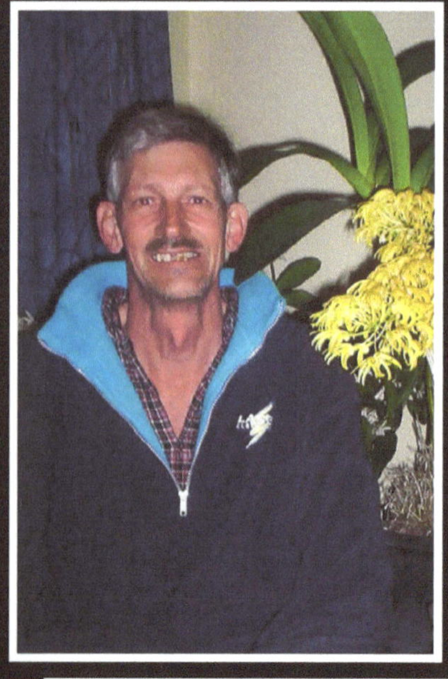

Name: Murray Gyde

Location: Henderson, Auckland, New Zealand

Occupation: Service Electrician

Hobbies: Orchids, fishing, wharf and surf.

Biography: At the time of writing I am 49, seperated, and have my 14 year old son living with me. I have been growing orchids since 1982 when I moved from Christchurch, New Zealand up to Auckland with my parents. The First plants that I bought were Cymbidiums (flax with a bulb at the base, as we call them). From these, I rapidly expanded into other genera, some of which grew and flowered, though, many others did not.

I eventually moved to Brisbane, Austrailia to live and started a collection there that was fun and taught me a lot about growing orchids. Anyway, Aussie didn't work out for me so I returned back to New Zealand where I started my third orchid collection.

I am now growing a large number of the Odontoglossum alliance but have not forgotten other genera, like Dendrobium, Cattelya and Laliea. I hope that all who look at this book and admire the plants and flowers are inspired.

Contributions to this publication: *Bifrenaria aureo-fulva x harrisoniae* pg. 18, *Laelia perrinii* pg. 32, *and Oncidium varicosum 'Lemforde' AM/AOS* pg. 48.

Name: Cindy R. Hicks

Location: Rotonda West, Florida

Occupation: Artist and Homemaker

Hobbies: Gardening, orchids, Cooking, Pottery and Sculpting.

Biography: Following in both of my grandmothers' foot steps, I have been an avid cook and gardener all of my life. When I married my husband, Terrence, he also joined in my interests. Our desire to garden year around prompted us to move to Florida in 2003 where we started landscaping our back yard. There, we put in a lathe house for our orchids that quickly became an unending quest for the many different types of orchids that are yet to be added to our collection.

Contributions to this publication: *Brassolaeliocattleya Orange Nugget* pg. 78, *Dendrobium Farmeri* pg. 16, *Encyclia bractenses* pg. 64, *Maxillaria Tenuifolia* pg. 31, *Potinara San Damiano 'Halona'* pg. 40, *and Vanda dennisoniana* pg. 71. *(Pictured in the photo above is Molly Taco.)*

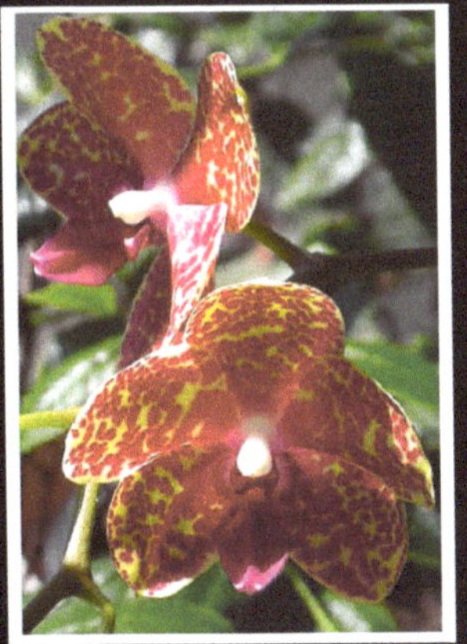

Name: Hiep-Hoa T. Nguyen

Location: Pasadena, California

Occupation: Biotech Executive

Hobbies: Triathlon, Swimming, Diving, Skiing, Running, Biking, Orchids, Gardening, Photography, Traveling and many others.

Biography: BS in Chemical Engineering and Chemistry. Ph.D in Chemistry.

Contributions to this publication: *Cattleya Jose Marti 'Mother's Favorite' AM/AOS* pg. 37, *Coelogyne South Carolina* pg. 44, *Dendrobium thyrsiflorum* pg. 22, *Dendrobium Victoria Regina* pg. 85, *Maxillaria picta* pg. 59, *Rodricidum Just Dandy That's Grand* pg. 49, *Stanhopea Assidensis* pg. 68, *and Trichocentrum Nathakhum* pg. 28. *(Phalaenopsis Dou-dii Rose x Phal. Golden Sun - pictured above.)*

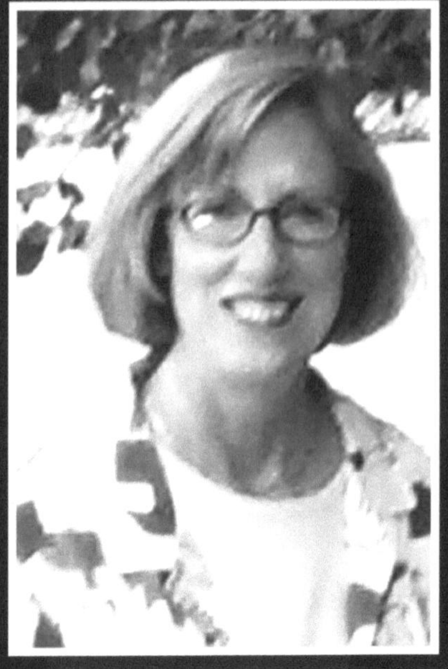

Name: Lynda Schwemmer

Location: Buena Vista, Colorado

Occupation: Artist

Hobbies: In addition to orchids, I am interested in all types of art and music. I love to read. I enjoy hiking in the mountains and spending time with my growing family. I want to do much more traveling.

Biography: Raised and educated in the great plains states, I got the opportunity to move to Colorado as a result of one of my husband's engineering assignments; there was no looking back.

After our two children graduated from high school, I finally had time to pursue my interest in art and began doing watercolor. I was introduced to silk painting during a winter in New Mexico, and that quickly became my medium of choice. I have enjoyed showing my work in small galleries in the central Rockies.

While searching for images for a silk painting project featuring orchids, I became aware of the orchid world. One thing led to another, and soon I was starting my own collection. I am still amazed that I can successfully grow and bloom exotic orchids in the windowsills of my mountain home, with its cool, arid conditions.

I am concentrating on orchids that grow easily here and have long lasting flowers–mainly phals and oncids, but also a selection of cattleya types and more and more slippers. Having these plants in bloom helps me get through our long winters. But I am very interested in finding a winter residence in Florida!

Contributions to this publication: *Phalaenopsis schilleriana* pg. 56.

Name: Diane Suprock

Location: Thousand Oaks, California

Occupation: Project Manager, Biotech Industry

Hobbies: I am an avid birdwatcher, travelling to all parts of the world to view the amazing variety of these beautiful creatures. I also, of course, enjoy growing orchids, African Violets, and just about anything else for which I can find space.

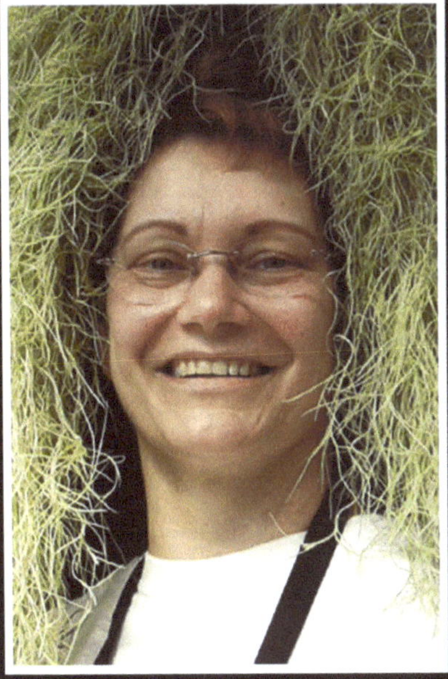

Biography: As a business professional with a BSBA and MBA, I have worked in many different industries doing operations mangement and consulting. I am currently employed by the largest Biotech Company in the world, where I have the opportunity to manage large scale projects that take me around the globe.

I inherited my love of orchids and all plants from my parents, especially my mother, who, for many years, grew orchids in her greenhouse. My parents also blessed me with an insatiable curiousity about the natural world, including birding, rockhounding and general travel.

Now single, and with no children, I find myself well suited to the business travel schedule that my job demands, and I use this travel to enhance my own personal experiences of other countries and cultures.

I stumbled upon the orchid forum while surfing the web and have found myself learning more and more about these wonderful, mysterious and evocative plants every day.

Contributions to this publication: *Brassolaeliocattleya Goldenzelle x Blc. Oh Susannah 'Lakeview'* pg. 81, *Phragmipedium Penn's Creek Cascade* pg. 76, *Doritis pulcherrima chumporensis* pg. 75, *Paphiopedilum Hillsview HV-895* pg. 24, *Psychopsis Kahili 'Big'* pg. 11, *Rumrillara Sugar Baby* pg. 42, *Paphiopedilum Oberhausen's Diament* pg. 52, *Phragmipedium Giganteum 'My Janus'* pg. 70, *Neofinetia falcata pg. 62, and Brassolaeliocattleya (Lc. Love Knot 'H & R' x Brassolaelia Morning Glory 'H & R')* pg. 83, *Brassolaeliocattleya Rugleys Mill 'Mendenhall'* (rear cover).

ORCHID GROWING MISTAKES AND HOW TO AVOID THEM

It's a common scenario: you enjoy growing houseplants; you saw an orchid or a picture of one somewhere and you decided to try one out even though you heard they were "hard." You brought the plant home, gave it all of your tender loving care, and the orchid died anyway. You decide you're never going to try growing another one of "those things" again.

Alas! You've deprived yourself of experiencing one of life's truly rewarding pleasures: watching an orchid you've nurtured along finally burst into bloom! Below are two of the most common mistakes new orchid growers make, listed in order of frequency: overwatering, and not giving your plant enough light. If you've committed one or both of these "orchid *faux pas,"* you're not alone. These mistakes are easy to make and just as easy to avoid once you realize what you're doing wrong. So don't give up! Try, try again!

Overwatering:

If there's a single most common cause of orchid death at the hands of new growers, overwatering takes the prize. And why not? If you've tried growing an orchid before and it failed on you, you've more than likely succumbed to one of the following lines of reasoning:

1. Premise (A): In old-timey tropical jungle movies, the heroine is overcome by steam and wet heat and she often faints. Premise (B): Orchids are obviously found in the dense, swampy undergrowth of tropical jungles. Therefore, (C): Orchids must thrive in environments where heroic women get overcome by steam and wet heat and faint often. Corollary (D): I must heat and water my orchid to the degree that either I or my significant other faints when we enter the room.

2. Premise (A): Every live green thing I've ever seen growing well was planted in wet dirt. Premise (B): The orchid I just bought is planted in some kind of dry "wood chunks." Therefore, (C): These "wood chunks" are obviously just some cheapo type packing material. Corollary (D): The orchid I just bought would grow ten times better if I planted it in wet dirt.

Acting on either one of these lines of reasoning is lethal to orchids. Act on them both, and you might as well just throw the plant away now. Here's why: an orchid's roots are covered by a spongy material that stores water [**velamen**]. (Remember that an orchid's roots need air to grow properly.) Any environment around the plant--sodden bark, swampy mud--that doesn't allow the spongy material access to some air will quickly rot the roots that the spongy material is protecting. An orchid whose roots are rotting away will begin to wilt and shrivel because it no longer has any means of drawing in moisture. *It will look as if it's drying out.*

The new orchid grower, watching her plant dry out and shrivel before her very eyes, *will water the plant even more*, compounding the problem further, killing any roots that were left. Death of the plant quickly follows.

How to avoid overwatering:

Orchids commonly found for sale grow in the tropics, but not in the dark, steamy undergrowth of swampy jungles. They don't like the heat: a temperature over 90-95 F is asking for trouble. They grow where strong, diffuse light and the movement of cooler air at night is plentiful, and providing both is essential to growing them successfully. Never pot your orchid in potting soil. Use orchid bark or another type of potting mix designed especially for orchids. Never allow your orchid's pot to sit in a tray filled with water. If you find your growing medium is consistently wet and your orchid is looking dried out, repot in fresh medium as soon as possible, and cut your watering frequency at least in half to encourage new root growth. Resist the urge to dive for the watering can every time you pass your plant, and you'll be on the road to orchid-growing success!

Not Enough Light:

Next to overwatering, insufficient light falling on their orchids causes new growers the most grief, and light requirement is often the most overlooked factor when considering an orchid plant's needs. If their plants are beginning to fail, most people new to orchids will change the amount and frequency of their watering, fertilizing, heating--just about everything else--before they attempt to change their light levels, and that's no surprise: most homes, especially older ones, aren't the brightest-lit things in the world and most people already grow their indoor plants around the brightest windows they've got. Light levels feel about as permanent and unchangeable as mothers-in-law: you pretty much have to take what you get. If your orchid is blooming and you'd like to use it to brighten a darker space in your home, by all means, do so. A week or two in an area too dim to grow in won't hurt your plant at all. But a week or two is it! Don't leave your plant there! An orchid left to grow beside that droopy potted palm in the darkest corner of the house will begin to show signs of illness: thin, dark green, new growth, sagging leaves, even brownish-black crown rot if water was allowed to stand in the "hollow" where your plant's new leaves are sprouting from.

Remember, to thrive, orchids commonly found for sale need light and moving air. (There are actually some subterranean orchid species that need almost complete darkness, but we won't go into those here...) But how much light is enough? How much is too much? How do you know how much you've actually got?

To grow well, most orchids need *at least* as much light during the growing season as is found under the shade of a large tree in direct sun, with *absolutely no* direct sun hitting your orchid plant. To bloom well and heavily, Cattleyas and Vandas need as much light as is found out in the open on a cloudy, gloomy day. If that's too broad a definition, light level requirements for each of the major orchid genera expressed in *footcandles* can be found by visiting the following URL http://www.rv-orchidworks.com/cultivate/care.html (1 footcandle is the amount of light received by a surface lit by one candle one foot away.)

Too much light is usually the culprit when orchid leaves turn a bright, whitish yellow, (or black and burnt if exposed to direct sun) but for beginners, too much light is hardly ever the problem.

So how much light do you have coming in through that window? Since the perception of brightness is a subjective matter that varies with age--even gender--from person to person, the only way to really tell is to measure it, using a light meter. Meters that display brightness levels in footcandles, lux, and lumens can be bought at specialty stores, but meters like these are usually expensive, especially if you're just trying out your first orchid and don't want to invest a whole lot of money right at the beginning. If you have an older, manual camera with a built-in light meter, you can use that to measure your light levels.

Here's how:

Set the camera's film speed to ASA 200 and its shutter speed to 1/125 of a second. Aim the camera at a white sheet of paper placed where your orchid is growing. Get close enough so that the meter records only the light reflected from the paper: the paper must fill the viewfinder. Focus on the paper and adjust the lens *aperture* until a correct exposure shows on the camera's light meter. Once the exposure is correct, look down at the aperture setting on the lens. The F-stop reading will convert approximately into footcandles as follows:

F-stop	Footcandles
2.8	32
4.0	64
5.6	125
8.0	250
11	500

16	1,000
22	2,000

The vast majority of orchids grown commercially for sale require between 800 and 3000 footcandles of light to thrive and bloom. Compare these requirements to the *50,000* footcandles received by a plant in full sun, and you'll realize why orchids burn in direct sunlight. Compare the requirements to the 30 - 80 footcandles found in the typical living room and it's easy to see why most beginning orchid growers don't give their plants enough light. If your orchid is receiving the amount of light it needs, bravo! That's one hurdle you've already overcome! If your growing area is too dim, you can supplement your natural light with artificial. Fluorescent fixtures and bulbs can be bought very inexpensively at any major home maintenance outlet, and your orchids will reward you with year after year of blooms and lush growth for some time a little bit of money well spent. So don't forget about the light!

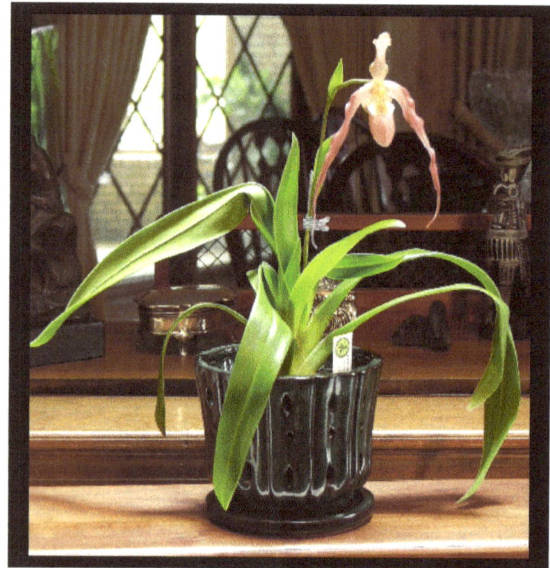

Phragmipedium Belle Hougue Point

(Phrag. Eric Young x Phrag. caudatum)

BLOOM TIME FOR ORCHIDS

It is hard to say what an orchid will do in every home since bloom time will always depend on the conditions in which you keep your orchid. These times are therefore estimates:

Phalaenopsis Orchid spikes- with their blooms' sepals and petals resembling a butterfly or moth in flight—will typically last from 6 to 12 weeks, sometimes even longer. Because the spike often does not mature all at once, it is very common for the first flowers at the spike's base to begin to wither even while new buds are still forming at the tip. Once the plant's flowers have all opened and finally dropped, you can cut the remaining spike back to within an inch of where it emerges from the "stalk" of the plant. Phalaenopsis will re-bloom on the same spike if the spike is cut farther up, 3 or so "joints" up from the base, by growing a branching spike out from the main one. This practice, however, should only be performed once before cutting the spike all the way back, since the blooms on these "artificially" created branches are typically not as large as the ones on the original inflorescence.

Cattleya Orchids, the plants most commonly associated with orchids because their huge, ruffled blooms are most often used in corsages, last only a few weeks, but the show is splendid. Once the flowers drop, the short spike and associated sheath from which the buds emerged can be cut back to the leaf axil. is receiving *too little* light. In either case, adjust the plant's location accordingly.

The blooms of **Ladyslipper Orchids**, the Paphiopedilums with their central pouches, typically remain in bloom for a good four to six weeks, sometimes longer, depending on the genus. If the plant is a multi-floral and sequential bloomer, flowers will develop at the tip of the same spike again and again, sometimes for months on end. These spikes should not be cut back until the entire spike itself has browned and died, at which point it should be cut all the way down to where it has emerged from the center of the growth. Old growths and growths which have already bloomed will never bloom again: only the new growths that will emerge from the base of the old will produce more flowers.

Dendrobium orchids also produce flowers that can last a good eight to ten weeks, sometimes more, and mature plants with multiple canes and flower spikes are real eye-catchers when in full bloom. Again, wait until all of the flowers have dropped from a spike before cutting it all the way back to where it emerged from the cane.

The warm growing **Oncidiinae alliance** such as Oncidiums and Brassias, along with their intergeneric cousins, produce blooms from the base of their pseudobulbs that can last between six to eight weeks, sometimes even longer. Mature plants often have growths which develop at different times, so when one growth is through blooming, another may just be sending up a flower spike. Keep an eye out for new spikes emerging on new growths, as these plants can provide a gorgeous show that lasts all throughout the growing season. Cut spikes all the way back once flowers have all dropped.

There are, of course, many genera of orchids which don't fall under any of the above categories, and some of those plants have blooms that last only a few days, so that blooming shouldn't be missed!

Here are some tips to keep your orchid blooming for as long as possible:

*Use a blossom booster fertilizer on your plants as soon as you notice a spike or sheath first begin to develop, and continue using it until the spike's last flower has fully opened. If your plant has multiple new growths which may spike, use the blossom booster throughout the growing season, until all of the growths' spikes have produced.

*Be careful when watering or misting not to wet the orchids' flowers. Wet flowers reduce their lifespan and can contribute to Botritis, a fungus that leaves black spots on the petals and sepals.

*Finally, don't keep your flowering orchid under a heating or air conditioning vent: this dry air will wilt orchid blooms much sooner than air with about 40 – 60% humidity in it.

ORCHID VIRUSES

DON'T CATCH THAT BUG!

Among all of the diseases that can affect orchid plants, viruses are probably the most feared.

Bacteria and fungi will do their damage—many of them are lethal—but, if caught early enough and measures taken to eliminate their effects, can be brought under control. Once virus has infected a plant however, it's as good as gone: there is no practical cure for viruses once they've invaded a plant's tissues. What's worse, infected plants that have been weakened by virus will often show signs of secondary bacterial and fungal infections that mask the viral presence, making the identification of a virus problem difficult if not impossible. There is currently no way to positively identify the presence of virus in orchids without special testing, but infected plants do show some tell-tale signs which should at least alert the grower that testing may be necessary.

So what are these signs? How do you differentiate between a fungus or bacterial infection, and a viral one?

Fungus and bacterial infections are usually characterized by black or brown spots, often soft, watery, and mushy looking, that can appear on any part of the plant. These spread quickly but, if caught before the infection reaches the plant's crown or rhizome, can be eliminated before the plant dies. Other fungal infections appear as spreading, chestnut-brown stains on the leaves, and still others, usually species of Cercospora, cause-varying degrees of leaf spotting that appear as tiny dots peppering leaves in a haze. The usual remedy for these is to cut away the affected portions using a sterilized knife or razor blade, then to apply an appropriate disease control to the entire plant. Many growers use cinnamon powder as an effective, natural fungicide, and common Listerine works very well against disease-causing bacteria.

But viruses are a different story. The three most common viruses that affect orchids are ORSV (Odontoglosum Ringspot Virus) , TMV (Tobacco Mosaic Virus), and CYMMV (Cymbidium Mosaic Virus), and they debilitate the plant by disrupting normal growth and causing malformation of plant structures. There is no practical cure. Symptoms that appear include chlorosis (the breakdown of chlorophyll that causes yellow and light brown patches) in diamond-shaped, spiraled, or mosaic-like patterns, elongated yellow spots that grow longitudinally along a leaf's veins, the distortion and curling of leaves and flower spikes, and, classically, color-break in the blooms. (Color-breaks are streaks and patches of darker or lighter color that "break" the flower's normal color-flow.)

Virus can be mechanically transmitted from an infected plant to a non-infected plant by any tool or procedure that exposes or comes into contact with the plant's sap. These include knives, pruning shears, plant stakes, wire ties, even used pots--that have not been properly sanitized before re-use. Plants rubbing together in a breeze which induces the leaf edge of one to cut into the other can transmit virus. You can transmit virus yourself by running your fingers along the length of a plant's leaves or exposing it to rough handling, and that risk is multiplied by orders of magnitude if you're a smoker or have handled tobacco just before contact.

Chewing and piercing insects can also transmit virus: scale, mealybugs, grasshoppers, and aphids are all suspected carriers, so growers whose collections are plagued by these pests run a far greater risk of viral contamination. And because viruses are so tiny, they can enter through wounds that may be completely invisible to the naked eye.

At this time, the best defense against viral attacks is good cultural habits. And while many of these practices may seem fussy, finicky, and outright paranoid to the new orchid grower, their value will be quickly appreciated once an expensive plant is lost due to virus and the loss could have been avoided.

Always sanitize / sterilize any implements you use on your orchids, before and between each orchid you work with. Knives, blades, and shears can be flamed using a soldering torch or, after wiping off any organic debris, soaked in a 10% bleach solution for five minutes. Wooden or bamboo stakes cannot be effectively sterilized due to their porosity, so should never be reused or transferred from plant to plant. Plastic pots, if reused, should be scrubbed clean and then soaked in bleach solution. Clay pots, again, because they are porous, cannot be effectively sterilized by soaking, but can be reused if heated in an oven during a "self-cleaning" cycle or baked for an hour at 500 F. Old bark medium should never be reused on another orchid plant. (Instead, mix it into the soil of your vegetable or flower garden. Your vegetables and flowers will love you for it.) Wash your hands with soap and hot water before and between each orchid you work with. If you choose to use latex gloves, be sure to change them for fresh ones before handling a new plant. The work surface you use for repotting should ideally be made of nonporous material you can easily wipe down with disinfectant before and after each repot. But if a non-porous surface isn't available, put down sheets of newspaper to do your repotting on, and discard them after each plant that you do.

If an orchid of yours has tested positive for virus, dispose of it as soon as possible, preferably by burning. If burning is illegal in your area, wrap the plant in a plastic bag, tie it, and throw it out. There is no cure, and keeping the plant around for sentimental reasons will only dramatically raise the risk that your other orchids will become infected as well. Please don't give the plant away to some unsuspecting soul or leave it out on the sidewalk for someone to pick up. Virused orchid plants are useless to everybody!

Viruses are a very real and persevering threat to orchid growers, and the risks are greater if you're careless or sloppy in your growing technique. But if you keep your growing environment clean, buy plants only from reputable dealers, and remain fastidious in your orchids' maintenance, your plants will stand a much better chance of staying virus-free and delighting you with beautiful blooms year after year.

HOME REPAIR FOR YOUR ORCHID

Here's the scenario: you take great pride in your orchid plants, and have started to build up a sizeable collection. You've situated them perfectly according to their needs, some in cool shade, others in warm sun, and you've developed the knack of knowing just when each needs a drink of water, a dose of fertilizer, or a change of position for the season.

Then, one morning, in the midst of making the rounds and checking on each of your charges, you notice a wet, brown spot on a leaf here, or a dark streak in the crown of one of your Phalaenopsis there, or, you've just come home from a two week vacation and the neighbor in charge of "taking care of things" has decided to make life easy: you find half your plants submerged knee-deep in trayfulls of water. A quick unpotting reveals that root rot has begun to set in, and—horrors!—aphids have decided to infest your favorite Oncidium.

Many home orchid growers shun commercial pesticides and fungicides for good reason: there may be children or pets in the house, and the fumes from some chemicals can often be overpowering and dangerous indoors. What to do? Are your sick plants doomed for the compost pile?

Do not fear! We asked the members of our OrchidTalk forums what, if any, home remedies were available for orchid plants which had fallen victim to an ill wind, and we received many excellent responses. As it turns out, you can fix up your ailing orchid plants in no time at all using various items commonly found around the house.

For insects: Scale and aphids are common miscreants on orchids, and if you catch them before they multiply into full-blown infestations, a cotton swab dipped in plain rubbing alcohol takes care of them. If you haven't caught them in time and need a spray, you have several choices.

*Murphy's Oil Soap, diluted as per manufacturer's instructions. Spray liberally, making sure to hit the undersides of the leaves as well as the tops.

*1 cup *regular* 409 cleaner (not the "degreasing" formula!), 1 cup rubbing alcohol, 6 cups water. Mix, and spray away.

*If you enjoy cooking, try this: in a blender, puree: 6 jalapeno or habanero peppers, 1 garlic pod (not clove—the entire pod), and 4 cups water. Pour into a saucepan and bring to a boil. Allow to cool. Add 1-tablespoon mild dishwashing liquid and one additional cup of water. Mix well, but do not shake. Pour into a handheld sprayer, and go get 'em!

*Mites can be discouraged by placing a sprig of eucalyptus on top of your potting medium.

*For fungus and bacteria: Rots commonly make their appearance on orchid leaves, often showing up as brown spots or blotches that grow in size as time goes on. These need to be dealt with quickly. Using a sterilized, single-edged razor blade or other sharp, sterilized implement, cut away the affected area by cutting into the healthy plant tissue surrounding it.

Then, try the following:

*Cinnamon, dusted liberally around the cut. Cinnamon will not only dry away any fungal infections, it has bactericidal properties as well. Be careful not to apply cinnamon to sensitive orchid roots, as its drying effect can often kill them.

*Listerine, used full strength as a spray, works wonders for bacterial infections, as does Neosporin ointment, applied directly to the affected area.

* Household bleach. Be *very careful* with this: chlorine is extremely toxic to, and can kill, orchid plants. Mix *no stronger* than one teaspoon per gallon of water and spray the plant completely for a highly effective bactericide, fungicide, and algaecide. Twelve to twenty four hours later, flush the plant and its pot with clear water! Do not forget this step!

*Hydrogen peroxide, applied full-strength to leaves or poured directly into a plant's "crown" or growing center, effectively kills the fungus responsible for crown rot.

*For root rot: Using sterilized scissors or shears, prune away any dead, dark brown and "mushy" roots. Dip the remaining roots into a bowl filled with 2 parts hydrogen peroxide, 1 part water. Let stand for 30 minutes. Transfer the plant to a bowl filled with the fertilizer solution you normally use. Let stand for 30 minutes. Soak a wadded up paper towel with water. Place the plant and wet paper towel into a Ziploc bag, being careful not to let the paper towel come into contact with the plant. Seal the bag, and place in a deeply shaded, out of the way spot for up to six weeks. The rot will have been eliminated, and new roots should begin to form.

If you don't like using poisonous plant chemicals on your orchids, you can still keep them healthy and cared for using commonly available household products, even when the inevitable pest or disease strikes from out of the blue. So never despair!

River Valley Orchidworks' OrchidTalk forums serve as an excellent source of grower information for orchid hobbyists of all levels, experts and novices alike. Registration is free, and the community couldn't be friendlier. If you have questions about your orchid plants, I urge you to register on OrchidTalk and post!

ENVIRONMENT FOR ORCHIDS

Situating and Regular Maintenance:

Three main factors influence how well or poorly your orchid plant will fare in its new home: water, fertilizer, and light. Like any other plant you grow, the closer you can simulate an orchid's natural environment, the healthier your plant will be, and you'll get rewarded with striking blooms year after year. Does this mean that orchids can't grow in your home unless you turn your living space into a tropical jungle? Not at all. Warm and temperate-growing orchids do very well indoors, as long as you provide them with the following basic requirements.

Light: Light is perhaps the most often overlooked factor in orchid-growing by beginners. Light determines whether your plant will bloom, the strength and vitality of any new growth the plant produces, and the quality and size of its leaves. In order of decreasing intensity, Vandas, Cattleyas, Dendrobiums, Phragmipediums and Oncidiums all require relatively strong light to thrive and bloom. Cattleyas and Vandas need the most, Oncidiums the least. If your plant falls under one of these genera, place it by a southern facing window that you can cover with sheers, if necessary, when the sun comes through. Under no circumstances should you expose your orchid plant to direct sun! Burning will come quickly and hard, causing black splotches to appear on the leaves and seriously damaging your plant. If your orchid's leaves feel hot to the touch, burn is imminent. Move it *immediately* to another location and spray the leaves with water to cool them down. If your plant is a Phalaenopsis or Paphiopedilum, less light is necessary so a window with an eastern exposure or a location beneath a skylight will do just fine. Again, no direct sun. Many home growers without suitable window space have supplemented natural light with artificial light, and they've achieved very great results. Warm fluorescent tubes are fine and inexpensive to start with, but as you become more involved with your orchid growing, if you can't get enough natural light, you may want to think about buying specialized metal halide fixtures and lamps that shine at the correct wavelengths. A general rule of thumb is, if your orchid's leaves are turning yellowish overall, but still have a firm and healthy texture, your plant is more than likely receiving *too much* light. If on the other hand, the leaves are turning a dark, dark green, feel flimsy, and can't seem to hold themselves upright, your plant is receiving *too little* light. In either case, adjust the plant's location accordingly.

Water: How often you should water is determined by the amount of light your plant receives, the temperature and humidity of the room, and the season of the year. Cattleyas, Dendrobiums, Oncidiums, Phalaenopsis, and Vandas produce aerial roots, meaning they grow naturally by clinging high up to the bark of trees with their roots exposed to the air. The roots of these orchids should be allowed to dry slightly between waterings. Paphiopedilums and Phragmipediums, the "slipper" orchids, are *terrestrials*: they grow in the moist humus of leaves and organic matter on the forest floor. They produce no aerial roots and the potting medium of these plants should never be allowed to completely dry out.

Experience, finally, will be your guide. But to start, poke a finger down about an inch or two into the growing medium. If it feels dry, go ahead and water. If it feels damp, leave it alone. *If you can't tell, LEAVE IT ALONE.*

Watering once a week for a plant kept indoors is usually a good place to begin developing a regimen. If you run air-conditioning, a light morning misting with a spray bottle will keep your plant's leaves from becoming desiccated. Get a feeling for your orchid's "wet weight" by lifting the pot the day after you decide to water. Get a feeling for its "dry weight" a week later, before you water. You'll soon be able to tell if your plant is thirsty just by lifting the pot. If you place your orchid in a tray to protect the surface of a table against moisture, be sure to fill the tray with gravel first! This will give your plant a little extra humidity as the water in the tray evaporates. Under no circumstances should you allow the bottom of your orchid's pot to sit submerged in a trayfull of water! Doing so is the "lazy man's" watering method and will eventually kill your plant by rotting away its roots. In the same vein, resist the urge to repot your orchid in potting soil. The root systems of all orchids need air to grow strong and thrive; potting soil compacts around the roots, preventing them from getting the air they need.

Fertilizer: The often-mentioned "rule" for when and how much to fertilize orchid plants is this: "Fertilize weekly, weakly." Any good brand of general purpose, water-soluble fertilizer will work just fine. Avoid "High Nitrogen" fertilizers that encourage green growth at the expense of flowering. Mix the fertilizer according to package directions, but mix it at one-third to one-half strength. You can use this solution every time you water in the spring and summer. About once a month or so, hold back on the fertilizer and drench your orchid's pot with plain water. This will help remove any buildup of fertilizer salts inside the pot, which, if allowed to accumulate, can burn your orchid's roots.

A little hint: Whether they're perched high in the treetops or clinging tightly to the side of a cliff, orchids rely on **air movement** for their survival. Air movement alerts pollinating insects that an orchid flower is open by bringing them its fragrance, and air movement scatters powdery orchid seed to other tree limbs when a seedpod has burst. By placing a small oscillating fan near your growing area, you'll be simulating the breezes that orchids depend on and have grown used to, and you'll be discouraging the insect pests, fungi, and crown rot that might otherwise plague your new pride and joy. Again, you're not trying to simulate a hurricane. Place the fan far enough away so that a piece of paper or ribbon in your growing area just begins to flutter when the wave of air hits it. You'll soon be well on your way to becoming a seasoned orchid grower!

Finally, in the end, make sure you let yourself *enjoy* caring for your plant! Orchid growing shouldn't be a source of stress.

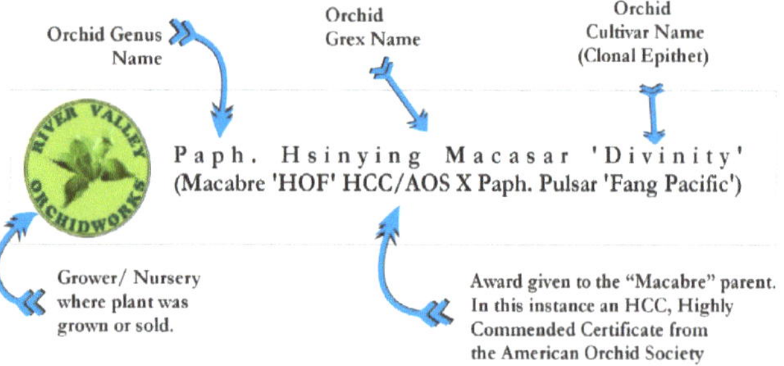

Above is an example of a typical label found in Orchid plants' pot.

ORCHID NOMENCLATURE

WHAT IS IN A NAME?

A guide to understanding how your orchid got its name.

In the orchid world, your orchid's name means everything. Fortunes can be made when a plant with a certain name receives an award, and, without its name, your orchid's value can be seriously diminished.

Unless your orchid plant is one that has been mass-produced for quick sale, it will have retained in its pot the grower's label that sets forth the plant's identification. This "dog tag" is vital, but how do you read it?
Let's look at an orchid's ID tag. Each part conveys a piece of information that lets you pick out not only your plant's name, but its heritage and, if it's awarded, the award it received.

A fully written-out label will look something like this, and the order is important:

Paph. Hsinying Macasar 'Divinity' (Macabre 'HOF' HCC/AOS X Paph. Pulsar 'Fang Pacific')

The first word, "**Paph.**", is the abbreviation for your plant's *genus name*, in this case, **Paphiopedilum**. This tells you that your plant is part of the ladyslipper group. There are hundreds and hundreds of orchid *genera* (the plural of the word *genus*).

Following the plant's genus name is the plant's *grex name*--in this case, **Hsinying Macasar**. Here, the first letters of this name are capitalized, letting you know that this particular plant is a hybrid, a cross that has been artificially produced and does not occur naturally in the wild. If the first letter of the grex name had been in lowercase, as in **lowii**, this would have identified the plant as a naturally occurring, wild species. To recap, lowercase first letter in the grex means species. Uppercase first letter in the grex means hybrid.

Next comes the cultivar name or *clonal epithet*: '**Divinity**'. This name uniquely identifies the plant's genetic makeup. In other words, many hybridizers may have propagated the grex **Hsinying Macasar** by crossing the parents that produce it. But the only plants that can bear the '**Divinity**' cultivar are those which are genetically identical to the original 'Divinity' orchid when it was first named: either vegetative divisions of the original plant, or cellular clones of the original plant. The clonal epithet or cultivar name is always enclosed in single quotation marks.

In cases where the plant's parentage is not commonly known, the cross, which produced this offspring, will be listed next, in parentheses. The pod parent (the parent who carried the fruit and produced the seed) is always listed first followed by the pollinating parent, the plant whose pollen was used to make the cross. In this case, the pod parent is **Macabre** (a hybrid) '**HOF**', and this parent has received an HCC award from the American Orchid Society, hence the abbreviations **HCC** (Highly Commended Certificate) / **AOS**. Then, the pollinating parent is listed following an "**X**", meaning, "these two plants have been crossed."

Plants that have earned awards are much more desirable to own and, very often, are much higher in price as well, depending on the number produced. Recent developments in cloning have put awarded orchids (which at one time would have only been accessible to the very wealthy) into the hands of the general public at reasonable prices. But nobody will ever know what orchid you have unless your orchid's tag remains with its pot, and plants with no identification are not allowed entry into AOS sanctioned shows for judging.

So, use your orchid's label to tell you *what* it is, *who* its parents are, and *how* to grow it (different genera have different growing requirements), and, whatever you do, don't lose that name!

ORCHID GENERA ABBREVIATIONS

Below is a listing of the orchid genera and their abbreviations included in this text.

A.	Aslla:	Ansellia
B.	Bif:	Bifrenaria
	Bl:	Brassolaelia
	Blc:	Brassolaeliocattleya
	Brs:	Brassia
	Brsdm:	Brassidium
C.	C:	Cattleya
	Ctna:	Cattleytonia
	Ctsm:	Catasetum
	Coel:	Coelogyne
	Crths:	Coryanthes
	Cyc:	Cycnoches
	Cycd:	Cycnodes
	Cym:	Cymbidium
D.	Den:	Dendrobium
	Dor:	Doritis
	Dgmra:	Degarmoara
E.	Enc:	Encyclia
	Epi:	Epidendrum
L.	L. :	Laelia
	Lc. :	Laeliocattleya
M.	Masd:	Masdevallia
	Max:	Maxillaria
	Mtssa:	Miltassia
N.	Neof:	Neofinetia
O.	Odcdm:	Odontocidium
	Odtna:	Odontonia
P.	Paph:	Paphiopedilum
	Phal:	Phalaenopsis
	Phrag:	Phragmipedium
	Pot:	Potinara
	Psychp:	Psychopsis
R.	Ren:	Renanthera
	Rdcm:	Rodricidum
	Rlla:	Rumrillara
S.	Schom:	Schromburgkia
	Sc:	Sophrocattleya
	Slc:	Sophrolaeliocattleya
	Stan:	Stanhopea
	Sp:	Sunipia
T.	Trctm:	Trichocentrum
V.	V:	Vanda
	Vuyl:	Vuylstekeara

INDEX

OrchidTalk Forum
www.rv-orchidworks.com

www.ingramcontent.com/pod-product-compliance
Lightning Source LLC
LaVergne TN
LVHW070130110826
845147LV00002B/223

* 9 7 8 0 6 1 5 1 3 9 2 1 0 *